THE INDUSTRIAL REVOLUTION

OPPOSING VIEWPOINTS®

Other Books of Related Interest:

THE INDUSTRIAL REVOLUTION
OPPOSING VIEWPOINTS®

David L. Bender, *Publisher*
Bruno Leone, *Executive Editor*

William Dudley, *Series Editor*
John C. Chalberg, Ph.D., professor of history,
 Normandale Community College, *Consulting Editor*

William Dudley, *Book Editor*

AMERICAN HISTORY SERIES

Greenhaven Press, Inc.
San Diego, California

Cover photographs, clockwise from top: 1) photograph of labor demonstrators (Archive Photos); 2) photograph of a young girl at spinning machine (Library of Congress); 3) nineteenth-century illustration of ironworks (Archive Photos); 4) photograph of Andrew Carnegie (Carnegie Library)

Library of Congress Cataloging-in-Publication Data

The industrial revolution : opposing viewpoints / William Dudley, editor.
        p.   cm. — (American history series)
    Includes bibliographical references and index.
    ISBN 1-56510-707-1 (lib. : alk. paper). —
    ISBN 1-56510-706-3 (pbk. : alk. paper)
    1. Industrial revolution—United States. I. Dudley, William, 1964–   .
    HC105.I53   1998
    330.973'08—dc21   97-48274
                                                                    CIP

©1998 by Greenhaven Press, Inc., PO Box 289009,
San Diego, CA 92198-9009

Printed in the U.S.A.

"America was born of revolt, flourished in dissent, became great through experimentation."

Henry Steele Commager, American Historian

Contents

Chapter 4: Industrial Workers and the Rise of Unionism

Chapter 5: Social Effects of the Industrial Revolution

Chapter 6: Historians Debate the Role of Robber Barons in the Industrial Revolution

Foreword

Aboard the *Arbella* as it lurched across the cold, gray Atlantic, John Winthrop was as calm as the waters surrounding him were wild. With the confidence of a leader, Winthrop gathered his Puritan companions around him. It was time to offer a sermon. England lay behind them, and years of strife and persecution for their religious beliefs were over, he said. But the Puritan abandonment of England, he reminded his followers, did not mean that England was beyond redemption. Winthrop wanted his followers to remember England even as they were leaving it behind. Their goal should be to create a new England, one far removed from the authority of the Anglican church and King Charles I. In Winthrop's words, their settlement in the New World ought to be "a city upon a hill," a just society for corrupt England to emulate.

A Chance to Start Over

One June 8, 1630, John Winthrop and his company of refugees had their first glimpse of what they came to call New England. High on the surrounding hills stood a welcoming band of fir trees whose fragrance drifted to the *Arbella* on a morning breeze. To Winthrop, the "smell off the shore [was] like the smell of a garden." This new world would, in fact, often be compared to the Garden of Eden. Here, John Winthrop would have his opportunity to start life over again. So would his family and his shipmates. So would all those who came after them. These victims of conflict in old England hoped to find peace in New England.

Winthrop, for one, had experienced much conflict in his life. As a Puritan, he was opposed to Catholicism and Anglicanism, both of which, he believed, were burdened by distracting rituals and distant hierarchies. A parliamentarian by conviction, he despised Charles I, who had spurned Parliament and created a private army to do his bidding. Winthrop believed in individual responsibility and fought against the loss of religious and political freedom. A gentleman landowner, he feared the rising economic power of a merchant class that seemed to value only money. Once Winthrop stepped aboard the *Arbella*, he hoped, these conflicts would not be a part of his American future.

Yet his Puritan religion told Winthrop that human beings are fallen creatures and that perfection, whether communal or individual, is unachievable on this earth. Therefore, he faced a paradox: On the one hand, his religion demanded that he attempt to live a perfect life in an imperfect world. On the other hand, it told him that he was destined to fail.

Soon after Winthrop disembarked from the *Arbella*, he came face-to-face with this maddening dilemma. He found himself presiding not over a utopia but over a colony caught up in disputes as troubling as any he had confronted in his English past. John Winthrop, it seems, was not the only Puritan with a dream of a heaven on earth. But others in the community saw the dream differently. They wanted greater political and religious freedom than their leader was prepared to grant. Often, Winthrop was able to handle this conflict diplomatically. For example, he expanded participation in elections and allowed the voters of Massachusetts Bay greater power.

But religious conflict was another matter because it was grounded in competing visions of the Puritan utopia. In Roger Williams and Anne Hutchinson, two of his fellow colonists, John Winthrop faced rivals unprepared to accept his definition of the perfect community. To Williams, perfection demanded that he separate himself from the Puritan institutions in his community and create an even "purer" church. Winthrop, however, disagreed and exiled Williams to Rhode Island. Hutchinson presumed that she could interpret God's will without a minister. Again, Winthrop did not agree. Hutchinson was tried on charges of heresy, convicted, and banished from Massachusetts.

John Winthrop's Massachusetts colony was the first but far from the last American attempt to build a unified, peaceful community that, in the end, only provoked a discord. This glimpse at its history reveals what Winthrop confronted: the unavoidable presence of conflict in American life.

American Assumptions

From America's origins in the early seventeenth century, Americans have often held several interrelated assumptions about their country. First, people believe that to be American is to be free. Second, because Americans did not have to free themselves from feudal lords or an entrenched aristocracy, America has been seen as a perpetual haven from the troubles and disputes that are found in the Old World.

John Winthrop lived his life as though these assumptions were true. But the opposing viewpoints presented in the American History Series should reveal that for many Americans, these assumptions were and are myths. Indeed, for numerous Americans, liberty has not always been guaranteed, and disputes have been an integral, sometimes welcome part of their life.

The American landscape has been torn apart again and again by a great variety of clashes—theological, ideological, political, economic, geographical, and social. But such a landscape is not necessarily a hopelessly divided country. If the editors hope to prove anything during the course of this series, it is not that the United States has been destroyed by conflict but rather that it has been enlivened, enriched, and even strengthened by Americans who have disagreed with one another.

Thomas Jefferson was one of the least confrontational of Americans, but he boldly and irrevocably enriched American life with his individualistic views. Like John Winthrop before him, he had a notion of an American Eden. Like Winthrop, he offered a vision of a harmonious society. And like Winthrop, he not only became enmeshed in conflict but eventually presided over a people beset by it. But unlike Winthrop, Jefferson believed this Eden was not located in a specific community but in each individual American. His Declaration of Independence from Great Britain could also be read as a declaration of independence for each individual in American society.

Jefferson's Ideal

Jefferson's ideal world was composed of "yeoman farmers," each of whom was roughly equal to the others in society's eyes, each of whom was free from the restrictions of both government and fellow citizens. Throughout his life, Jefferson offered a continuing challenge to Americans: Advance individualism and equality or see the death of the American experiment. Jefferson believed that the strength of this experiment depended upon a society of autonomous individuals and a society without great gaps between rich and poor. His challenge to his fellow Americans to create—and sustain—such a society has itself produced both economic and political conflict.

A society whose guiding document is the Declaration of Independence is a society assured of the freedom to dream—and to disagree. We know that Jefferson hated conflict, both personal and political. His tendency was to avoid confrontations of any sort, to squirrel himself away and write rather than to stand up and speak his mind. It is only through his written words that we can grasp Jefferson's utopian dream of a society of independent farmers, all pursuing their private dreams and all leading lives of middling prosperity.

Jefferson, this man of wealth and intellect, lived an essentially happy private life. But his public life was much more troublesome. From the first rumblings of the American Revolution in the 1760s to the North-South skirmishes of the 1820s that ultimately produced the Civil War, Jefferson was at or near the center of American political history. The issues were almost too many—and too crucial—for one lifetime: Jefferson had to choose between sup-

11

porting or rejecting the path of revolution. During and after the ensuing war, he was at the forefront of the battle for religious liberty. After endorsing the Constitution, he opposed the economic plans of Alexander Hamilton. At the end of the century, he fought the infamous Alien and Sedition Acts, which limited civil liberties. As president, he opposed the Federalist court, conspiracies to divide the union, and calls for a new war against England. Throughout his life, Thomas Jefferson, slaveholder, pondered the conflict between American freedom and American slavery. And from retirement at his Monticello retreat, he frowned at the rising spirit of commercialism he feared was dividing Americans and destroying his dream of American harmony.

No matter the issue, however, Thomas Jefferson invariably supported the rights of the individual. Worried as he was about the excesses of commercialism, he accepted them because his main concern was to live in a society where liberty and individualism could flourish. To Jefferson, Americans had to be free to worship as they desired. They also deserved to be free from an over-reaching government. To Jefferson, Americans should also be free to possess slaves.

Harmony, an Elusive Goal

Before reading the articles in this anthology, the editors ask readers to ponder the lives of John Winthrop and Thomas Jefferson. Each held a utopian vision, one based upon the demands of community and the other on the autonomy of the individual. Each dreamed of a country of perpetual new beginnings. Each found himself thrust into a position of leadership and found that conflict could not be avoided. Harmony, whether communal or individual, was a forever elusive goal.

The opposing visions of Winthrop and Jefferson have been at the heart of many differences among Americans from many backgrounds through the whole of American history. Moreover, their visions have provoked important responses that have helped shape American society, the American character, and many an American battle.

The editors of the American History Series have done extensive research to find representative opinions on the issues included in these volumes. They have found numerous outstanding opposing viewpoints from people of all times, classes, and genders in American history. From those, they have selected commentaries that best fit the nature and flavor of the period and topic under consideration. Every attempt was made to include the most important and relevant viewpoints in each chapter. Obviously, not every notable viewpoint could be included. Therefore, a selective, annotated bibliography has been provided at the end of each book to aid readers in seeking additional information.

The editors are confident that as this series reveals past conflicts, it will help revitalize the reader's views of the American present. In that spirit, the American History Series is dedicated to the proposition that American history is more complicated, more fascinating, and more troubling than John Winthrop or Thomas Jefferson ever dared to imagine.

John C. Chalberg
Consulting Editor

Greenhaven Press anthologies primarily consist of previously published material taken from a variety of sources, including periodicals, books, scholarly journals, newspapers, government documents, and position papers from private and public organizations. These original sources are often edited for length and to ensure their accessibility for a young adult audience. The anthology editors also change the original titles of these works in order to clearly present the main thesis of each viewpoint and to explicitly indicate the opinion presented in the viewpoint. These alterations are made in consideration of both the reading and comprehension levels of a young adult audience. Every effort is made to ensure that Greenhaven Press accurately reflects the original intent of the authors included in this anthology.

Introduction

"Rapid industrialization raised the question of whether America's republican ideals could survive in a meaningful way, . . . and whether political and economic institutions needed to be reformed in response to the changes sweeping America's economy."

The term "industrial revolution" refers to the shift of an economy from one in which most of its production is agriculturally based to one based on the mechanized manufacturing of goods in large-scale enterprises. This introduction of new technologies of production generally has dramatic social ramifications, including increases in productivity and per capita incomes, the movement of people from rural to urban areas, and the substitution of machine power for human labor in many kinds of work. Some historians argue that the change of a society from an agricultural to an industrial economy is best described as a gradual evolution rather than sudden wrenching change, but most agree that the social effects brought about by industrialization are profound enough to warrant the term "revolution."

This shift has occurred in different countries at different times. Historians place the first industrial revolution as taking place in England beginning in the mid- to late 1700s, or roughly at the same time its colonies in America were in the process of declaring independence from the Crown. In the newly formed United States, signs of industrialization were evident in New England and other parts of the nation beginning in the early 1800s. Dramatic shifts, however, did not occur until after the Civil War, when an explosion of industrial development made manufacturing the dominant sector of America's economy and enabled the United States to supplant Great Britain as the world's leading industrial power.

Prior to the eighteenth century, most of the population of England, as in other countries, was engaged in farming. Less than

10 percent of the population lived in cities. The manufacturing of goods ranging from clothing to iron weapons was a slow, painstaking process of reshaping raw materials by hand or by simple human-powered machines—activities that often took place in the home.

Three important technological developments laid the foundations for the world's first industrial revolution. The development and improvement of coal-powered steam engines—notably James Watt's design of 1769—provided a source of power for manufacturing that was more powerful and convenient than human, wood, and water power. The invention of several key devices mechanized the spinning of cotton into yarn and the weaving of yarn into cloth and helped cotton textiles to become the first important commodity to be produced in mechanized factories. A third factor was the development of coal-powered furnaces that made iron out of iron ore in great quantities. Iron (and later steel) became an important element in making durable machine parts and enabling larger buildings to be built, both of which furthered industrial expansion.

These technological developments revolutionized the way things were made and the way people were employed in Britain by the late 1700s. Factories and industrial towns sprang up around the country as people moved from rural to urban communities. Manufactured goods were made in greater quantities and with greater efficiency than ever before. The nature of work itself changed. Handicrafts carried out within the family or manor were replaced by goods manufactured in factories with machines. Workers' tasks became specialized—a person would make just part of a product rather than the whole. This "division of labor" enabled workers to be more productive.

Building factories in which machines drove production and labor was specialized required enormous amounts of money, or capital. The industrial revolution thus created a new social class of people—capitalists—who owned the factory plant and other physical means of industrial production. Most capitalists did not work at their own factories; labor was performed by a rising new class of industrial workers whose livelihood depended on the wages they earned.

Early American Debates on Industry

The changes industrialization was bringing to Great Britain were evident to many American observers by the time the United States declared its independence in 1776. Before independence, the colonies had been an important part of England's industrial development. They served as a source of raw materials and agricultural products and as a market for British manufactured goods. An early controversy in American politics was whether the new nation should maintain such trade relationships with England or emulate England's industrial revolution and develop its own manufacturing sector.

Some early American leaders, most notably Alexander Hamilton, urged that manufacturing be encouraged in the United States. Hamilton and others argued that true independence from Great Britain meant not just severing political bonds, but ending dependence on British manufactured goods. Industries in America would provide domestic markets for America's agricultural products, promote employment, and make America a more powerful and self-sufficient nation. To stimulate the development of industry, Hamilton and others proposed a system of protective tariffs on manufactured imports. Tariffs would raise the cost of such items to American consumers, who would then be more likely to buy products manufactured in America instead. The protective tariff for "infant industries" became one of America's leading perennial political issues of the nineteenth century.

Hamilton's dream of an industrialized America faced several significant barriers before it could become reality. America had little surplus capital to invest in factories and little surplus labor to work them. Those with money to spend tended to prefer to invest in more familiar and less risky ventures such as land acquisition, commerce, and the slave trade. The relatively easy availability of agricultural land in America's expanding frontier drew potential industrial workers into farming.

Finally, many Americans at this time, including Thomas Jefferson, author of the Declaration of Independence and third president of the United States, believed that the survival of republican principles in the new nation was dependent on the country's remaining an agricultural nation populated by self-sufficient independent farmers. Jefferson and others believed that the industrial factory towns of England, where workers often lived in overcrowded and unsanitary conditions, were antithetical to American ideals of equality. Thomas Cooper, in a tract against the tariff written in 1823, summarized what was a common view of the textile factories in England and their effects on its society:

> The machinery of England is, in many instances, a dreadful curse to that country. . . . The works usually go night and day, one set of boys and girls go to bed, as another set get up to work. The health, the manners, the morals, are all corrupted. They work not for themselves, but for the capitalist who employs them; . . . they are machines, as much so as the spindles they superintend. . . . The whole system tends to increase the wealth of a few capitalists, at the expense of the health, life, morals, and happiness of the wretches who labor for them. . . . We want in this happy country, no increase of proud and

16

wealthy capitalists, whose fortunes have accumulated by such means. . . . It is impossible to shut our eyes to the wonderful superiority of capital invested in agriculture, over capital invested in machinery.

Fears of the social effects of the industrial revolution were expressed as late as the 1830s by Alexis de Tocqueville, a young French nobleman who visited the United States in 1831 and 1832 and wrote *Democracy in America* based on his travels. In that famous work, he reiterated the belief held by many that the continued growth of factories threatened America's generally egalitarian society by creating a new aristocracy of industrial plutocrats and a new impoverished class of dependent workers. "At the very moment at which the science of manufactures lowers the class of workmen, it raises the class of masters," he wrote.

Proponents of manufacturing were compelled to defend its social advantages as well as its economic benefits. One of the leading promoters of tariffs to support American industries in the 1800s was Senator Henry Clay of Kentucky. In an 1820 speech in Congress, he argued that factory work instilled a work ethic and proper values in America's women and children:

> Women and children . . . who would be comparatively idle if manufactures did not exist, may be profitably employed in them. This is a very great benefit. I witnessed the advantage resulting from the employment of this description of our population in a visit which I lately made to the Waltham manufactory, near Boston. There, some hundreds of girls and boys were occupied in separate apartments. The greatest order, neatness, and apparent comfort reigned throughout the whole establishment. The daughters of respectable farmers . . . were usefully employed.

Clay goes on to argue that the new cotton textile factory he visited in Massachusetts prevented the social vices of begging and idleness that were evident at the nation's Capitol building.

> Suppose that establishment to be destroyed, what would become of all the persons who are there engaged so beneficially to themselves, and so usefully to the state? Can it be doubted that, if the crowd of little mendicant boys and girls who infest this edifice and assail us every day at its very thresholds, as we come in and go out, begging for a cent, were employed in some manufacturing establishment, it would be better for them and the city? Those who object to the manufacturing system should recollect that constant occupation is the best security for innocence and virtue, and that idleness is the parent of vice and crime.

American Industrialism
in the Early Nineteenth Century

By 1815, despite the efforts of Hamilton, Clay, and others to promote industry, America remained a nation whose people lived and worked predominantly on farms. Even in the Northeast, where most incipient American industries were located, barely 10 percent of the population lived in "urban" communities of twenty-five hundred people or more, and the proportion was even smaller in other parts of the country. Economic historian Robert L. Heilbroner estimates that only fifteen thousand people were employed in the iron or textile industries (two mainstays of Britain's industrial revolution), and perhaps 4 percent of America's population was engaged in manufacturing altogether— "manufacturing" being defined to include small-scale handicrafts, flour mills, and other enterprises.

Between 1815 and the Civil War, the industrial revolution took root in the United States, and the foundations were laid for the explosion of American industrial development in the decades to follow. The main industries were textiles, clothing, furniture, and shipbuilding. Mechanized cotton textile factories were constructed in the New England region. American inventors became recognized for their design of various mechanical and labor-saving devices. Coal deposits were discovered and developed, and the smelting and production of American iron increased; by the 1850s, American iron was competitive with British iron in the international market. A national transportation network was begun, consisting of roads, canals, and railroads. What came to be called the "American system" of manufacturing was also developed during this time by small-arms factories and other industries in the United States. This system involved the use of machines to make precisely measured interchangeable parts, enabling goods to be mass-produced. Yet despite this industrial growth, agriculture remained America's leading economic activity; in 1860 four out of five Americans still lived in rural areas.

The bulk of America's industrial enterprises were found in the Northeast; fewer factories were built in the South and on the western frontier. In the South, a society developed that was based on plantation agriculture. Relying on black slave labor, southern plantations raised tobacco and especially cotton as export cash crops. The South also became a main source of political opposition to government policies supporting industry, such as tariffs. Leaders of the region objected to paying higher prices for manufactured imports and also to government policies supporting economic development that would increase the wealth and population of the northern states.

The Civil War in many respects was a springboard for a new level of industrial development in America. Shorn of its southern representatives that had blocked previous legislation, Congress in the 1860s enacted a series of legislative measures that encouraged industrialization and economic development, including new protective tariffs, banking reforms, and support for a transcontinental railroad. The demands of the Civil War for uniforms, weapons, munitions, and supplies also stimulated the growth of large-scale industries in the North, including ready-made clothing, machine tools, farm machinery production, and food canning. Many of the famous industrialists of the post–Civil War period achieved their first business successes in filling wartime demands.

America's Second Industrial Revolution

Following the Civil War, America witnessed a new explosion of industry. In 1860, manufacturing accounted for just one-third of all U.S. production, and America still imported more manufactured goods than it exported. The value of manufactured products in America was roughly equal to the value of its agricultural output. Thirty years later, the value of manufactured goods was almost four times that of agriculture. The value of goods produced by American industry increased almost tenfold between 1870 and 1916 as industry replaced agriculture as the leading income source for Americans. America's industrial growth in the decades following the Civil War was so rapid and extensive that business historian Alfred D. Chandler Jr. has called this period of American history the Second Industrial Revolution.

Two technological developments helped stimulate this phenomenal growth of American industry. The first was the completion of national transportation and communications networks. Canals, roads, steamships, and railroads made possible the national marketing and distribution of products, while the telegraph and telephone aided in the communication necessary for large corporations to function. The construction of a nationwide railroad network (the nation's total track mileage grew from 35,000 in 1865 to 193,000 in 1890) was itself a boon to industrialization and to America's economic growth. The railroads' demands for materials stimulated the coal, iron, and steel industries, and by transporting consumer and industrial goods to national markets they assisted other industries as well.

The second major technological development was the use of electricity as a source of power, which became increasingly widespread beginning in the 1880s. It provided a more versatile and flexible source of power in place of steam and water power for industry. Electric lights and electric streetcars and trolleys changed the way American cities looked and functioned and hastened the process of urbanization. Electricity also revolutionized manufacturing processes in the chemical and metallurgical industries.

Capital and labor were both required to take advantage of these technological developments. Capital for the American industrial boom came from European investors, a new class of American industrialists, the stock market, and American investment banks. Labor came from European immigrants as well as from American rural populations, where improvements in machinery had reduced the labor necessary to run farms and had enabled many people to move to the city—a process that created a new challenge in urban planning, sanitation, and municipal services.

The confluence of available capital, labor, and technology enabled several new industries to be developed or greatly expanded. Among the industries that contributed to America's growth during this time were steel and other metals, oil, chemicals, light and heavy machinery, as well as packaged food, drug, and tobacco. Large firms—including Standard Oil, American Tobacco, National Biscuit, United Fruit, United States Steel, and General Electric—produced and sold their products nationwide and replaced the thousands of small producers who sold to local markets. Companies formed pools, trusts, and other cooperative ventures to manage competition among themselves. By the turn of the century these large corporations dominated American industry and economic life. The size and influence of private corporations in many cases dwarfed that of local, state, and federal governments.

Although factories and industrial activities existed nationwide, the industrial revolution remained predominantly centered in America's northeastern region. Following the Civil War and Reconstruction, some southern politicians and journalists, preaching the existence of a "New South," attempted to promote manufacturing in the region; they succeeded to some extent in attracting textile factories with the promise of minimal taxes and low labor costs. Between 1880 and 1900, 120 cotton mills were built in North Carolina alone, often in villages and rural areas. These cotton mills took advantage of a large and cheap labor pool consisting of white backcountry farm families. However, by 1900, the entire cotton mill output of the South was roughly half that of the production of mills within a thirty-mile radius of Providence, Rhode Island. Industrialization of the region severely lagged behind other parts of the country until after the turn of the century.

Questions About Industrialization

Industrialization transformed the United States from a nation consisting primarily of farmers to one in which more and more of its people lived in cities, worked in factories, and were consumers of mass-produced goods. By 1916 nearly half of America's population was residing in urban areas. The old Jeffersonian dream of a nation of small independent farmers was dead—even America's farmers were becoming dependent on farm machinery and the railroads to produce and market their crops. Rapid industrialization raised the question of whether America's republican ideals could survive in a meaningful way, whether industrial growth contributed positively or negatively to America's society, and whether political and economic institutions needed to be reformed in response to the changes sweeping America's economy.

Some observers held that the riches the industrial revolution created—the new labor-saving devices, consumer goods, skyscraper buildings, declining prices in industrial products, and the opportunities afforded workers and capitalists—were all marks of positive progress and evidence that American society was evolving in the right direction. America's growing population, increases in average life expectancy, and a general trend toward lower working hours were all cited as evidence of how the industrial revolution was contributing positively to American life. In *The Triumph of Democracy*, Andrew Carnegie, a self-made multimillionaire through his American steel business, wrote that the vast and increasing wealth generated by America's industries was proof of the success of the American experiment in government and society. Carnegie attested, "The United States . . . has already reached the foremost rank among nations, and is destined soon to out-distance all others in the race." He argued that this development was "largely attributable to . . . [America's] manufacturing industries."

Others were not as sanguine about the social benefits of America's industrial explosion. Some critics, such as reformer and writer Henry George, focused on the fact that not all Americans were profiting equally from industrialization—that, paradoxically, progress in technology and industry had made poverty and inequality worse than before. Machines had enabled industries to replace skilled craftsmen with poorly paid unskilled workers; large corporations and select individuals had attained fabulous wealth while the population of impoverished workers seemed to be increasing. "The march of invention has clothed mankind with powers of which a century ago the boldest imagination could not have dreamed," George wrote in *Progress and Poverty*. "But in factories where labor-saving machinery has reached its most wonderful development, little children are at work; wherever the new forces [of industry] are anything like fully utilized, large classes are maintained by charity or live on the verge of recourse to it; amid the greatest accumulations of wealth, men die of starvation. . . . The promised land flies before us like a mirage." Other critics questioned the public morality and tactics of the major industrialists, the corruption that seemed to go hand in hand with the making of large industrial fortunes, and the laissez-faire ideology that preached that government should not tamper with "economic laws" that governed wages, prices, and business practices.

The viewpoints in this volume provide a sampling of arguments focusing on the industrialization of America and the effects it had on society. Most deal with the period after the Civil War, when industry was attaining a dominant place in American life. Although they examine a variety of issues, most of these views attempt to ascertain whether American—and human—ideals could be preserved in the face of such a massive transformation of society.

CHAPTER 1

Should the United States Become a Manufacturing Nation?

Chapter Preface

The thirteen British colonies that later became the United States were founded prior to the industrial revolution, which had its beginnings in England in the 1700s. While mass industry was being born in Great Britain, its colonies in America were prospering through agriculture and trade. Favored with abundant land and timber resources, American colonists traded timber and agricultural products such as tobacco and indigo to Great Britain, from which they obtained manufactured goods. With very few exceptions, such as ship building, American manufacturing was limited to small-scale operations like town flour mills and blacksmiths. The American shoe industry, for example, consisted of shoemakers who crafted their products by hand one pair at a time, producing in New England perhaps 80,000 pairs annually, or about one pair of shoes for every forty people.

After the colonies declared and won their independence in the American Revolution, a central question facing the leaders of the new nation was whether the United States should continue to concentrate its economic energies on agriculture and commerce, or whether it should instead make a special effort to develop its own manufacturing sector. Interestingly, the leading proponents of opposing views on this question both served in the cabinet of George Washington, America's first president, and are both recognized as being among America's most influential founders.

Alexander Hamilton, secretary of the treasury from 1789 to 1795, desired for the United States to break from its dependency on Great Britain for manufactured goods. He viewed industry as an important element in the dynamic and diverse economy he envisioned for America. The establishment of factories, he argued, would make the country more self-sufficient in wartime and would create a domestic market for the products of American farms. Responding to those who claimed that American labor costs were too high to engage in profitable manufacturing, he argued that the labor of women and those of "tender years" could be utilized. Hamilton submitted various proposals to Congress, most notably his *Report on Manufactures* in 1791, that advocated government actions to promote the development of industry in the United States, including protective tariffs and government subsidies of particular industries.

In making his proposals, Hamilton had to contend with a pre-

24

vailing climate of public opinion that considered industrialization something to be avoided if at all possible. Thomas Jefferson, Washington's secretary of state, was the leading ideological opponent of Hamilton's ideas. Part of Jefferson's objections stemmed from the influence of the physiocratic school of economics, founded by French economist François Quesnay in 1750. Physiocrats held that agriculturally productive land was the only true source of wealth and that manufacturing, which changed only the form of things, did not add to the enrichment of the nation. Perhaps more importantly, Jefferson believed that the only way for the American society to survive in its republican form was to populate it with self-sufficient farmers who owned their own property and thus were subservient to no one. Great Britain's experience with the industrial revolution, Jefferson concluded, had revealed that manufacturing had a corrupting influence on society. It created a new urban class of factory workers that he described as "debased by ignorance, indigence, and oppression"— and thus certainly unable to perform the necessary duties of republican citizenship. Because of the wide abundance of land on America's expanding frontier, Jefferson and others believed that the logical course for Americans to pursue was farming. The United States could supply its wants for manufactured goods by continued trade with England if necessary.

Elements of both Hamilton's and Jefferson's ideas on manufacturing were to remain influential in American thought over the next century. The following pair of viewpoints presents the opinions of Hamilton and Jefferson on industry and the future of the United States.

VIEWPOINT 1

"While we have land to labor then, let us never wish to see our citizens occupied at a workbench."

The United States Should Remain an Agricultural Nation

Thomas Jefferson (1743–1826)

Thomas Jefferson—author of the Declaration of Independence and president of the United States from 1801 to 1809—was perhaps the most famous of the nation's early leaders who believed that the United States should remain a predominantly agricultural nation and should avoid the path of industrialization taken by England. The relative merits of manufacturing and agriculture were among the issues that put him at odds with his political rival Alexander Hamilton, who strongly supported the growth of a national industrial and manufacturing base in the United States.

Jefferson's views on agriculture and industry were complex and evolved over time. Jefferson was a lifelong promoter of science and invention, and at one point he attempted to supplement the agricultural income he received from his Monticello plantation by manufacturing and selling nails. But while he was an enthusiastic supporter of such home-based manufacturing projects, he was suspicious of large factories and what he saw as their attendant evils—especially the concentration of people into cities, which he believed would jeopardize America's republican society. Later in life, Jefferson modified his stance and argued that some manufacturing was a necessity in America for defense and other practical reasons.

The following viewpoint is in two parts. Part I is from *Notes on the State of Virginia*, Jefferson's only full-length book. Written in

From Thomas Jefferson, *Notes on Virginia*, Memorial Edition (Washington, DC: Jefferson Memorial Association, 1905).

response to a French diplomat's questions about Virginia, it was published privately in 1785 in Paris, France, where Jefferson served as U.S. ambassador from 1785 to 1789. The first American edition came out in 1788. The selection is taken from Jefferson's response to a query about Virginia's "state of manufactures, commerce, [and] interior and exterior trade." Jefferson concisely expresses his preference for agriculture over manufacturing and argues that America's vast areas of land create ideal conditions for farming. In Part II, excerpted from a 1785 letter to lawyer and diplomat John Jay, Jefferson maintains that the United States has enough land to employ most of its people in agriculture. If such is not the case in the future, Jefferson contends, people should be employed in the seagoing trade rather than as "artificers" or manufacturers, even though it may mean risking war with other nations over freedom of navigation.

I

We never had an interior trade of any importance. Our exterior commerce has suffered very much from the beginning of the present contest. During this time we have manufactured within our families the most necessary articles of clothing. Those of cotton will bear some comparison with the same kinds of manufacture in Europe; but those of wool, flax and hemp are very coarse, unsightly, and unpleasant; and such is our attachment to agriculture, and such our preference for foreign manufactures, that be it wise or unwise, our people will certainly return as soon as they can, to the raising raw materials, and exchanging them for finer manufactures than they are able to execute themselves.

The political economists of Europe have established it as a principle, that every State should endeavor to manufacture for itself; and this principle, like many others, we transfer to America, without calculating the difference of circumstance which should often produce a difference of result. In Europe the lands are either cultivated, or locked up against the cultivator. Manufacture must therefore be resorted to of necessity not of choice, to support the surplus of their people. But we have an immensity of land courting the industry of the husbandman. Is it best then that all our citizens should be employed in its improvement, or that one half should be called off from that to exercise manufactures and handicraft arts for the other? Those who labor in the earth are the chosen people of God, if ever He had a chosen people, whose breasts

He has made His peculiar deposit for substantial and genuine virtue. It is the focus in which he keeps alive that sacred fire, which otherwise might escape from the face of the earth. Corruption of morals in the mass of cultivators is a phenomenon of which no age nor nation has furnished an example. It is the mark set on those, who, not looking up to heaven, to their own soil and industry, as does the husbandman, for their subsistence, depend for it on casualties and caprice of customers. Dependence begets subservience and venality, suffocates the germ of virtue, and prepares fit tools for the designs of ambition. This, the natural progress and consequence of the arts, has sometimes perhaps been retarded by accidental circumstances; but, generally speaking, the proportion which the aggregate of the other classes of citizens bears in any State to that of its husbandmen, is the proportion of its unsound to its healthy parts, and is a good enough barometer whereby to measure its degree of corruption. While we have land to labor then, let us never wish to see our citizens occupied at a workbench, or twirling a distaff. Carpenters, masons, smiths, are wanting in husbandry; but, for the general operations of manufacture, let our workshops remain in Europe. It is better to carry provisions and materials to workmen there, than bring them to the provisions and materials, and with them their man-

In a 1786 letter, Thomas Jefferson expressed his belief that the American people "will be more virtuous, more free and more happy employed in agriculture than as carriers or manufacturers."

ners and principles. The loss by the transportation of commodities across the Atlantic will be made up in happiness and permanence of government. The mobs of great cities add just so much to the support of pure government, as sores do to the strength of the human body. It is the manners and spirit of a people which preserve a republic in vigor. A degeneracy in these is a canker which soon eats to the heart of its laws and constitution.

II

Dear Sir,—I shall sometimes ask your permission to write you letters, not official but private. The present is of this kind, and is occasioned by the question proposed in yours of June 14. "whether it would be useful to us to carry all our own productions, or none?" Were we perfectly free to decide this question, I should reason as follows. We have now lands enough to employ an infinite number of people in their cultivation. Cultivators of the earth are the most valuable citizens. They are the most vigorous, the most independant, the most virtuous, & they are tied to their country & wedded to it's liberty & interests by the most lasting bonds. As long therefore as they can find employment in this line, I would not convert them into mariners, artisans or anything else. But our citizens will find employment in this line till their numbers, & of course their productions, become too great for the demand both internal & foreign. This is not the case as yet, & probably will not be for a considerable time. As soon as it is, the surplus of hands must be turned to something else. I should then perhaps wish to turn them to the sea in preference to manufactures, because comparing the characters of the two classes I find the former the most valuable citizens. I consider the class of artificers as the panders of vice & the instruments by which the liberties of a country are generally overturned. However we are not free to decide this question on principles of theory only. Our people are decided in the opinion that it is necessary for us to take a share in the occupation of the ocean, & their established habits induce them to require that the sea be kept open to them, and that that line of policy be pursued which will render the use of that element as great as possible to them. I think it a duty in those entrusted with the administration of their affairs to conform themselves to the decided choice of their constituents: and that therefore we should in every instance preserve an equality of right to them in the transportation of commodities, in the right of fishing, & in the other uses of the sea. But what will be the consequence? Frequent wars without a doubt. Their property will be violated on the sea, & in foreign ports, their persons will be insulted, imprisoned &c. for pretended debts, contracts, crimes, contraband, &c., &c. These insults must be resented, even if we had no feelings, yet to prevent their eternal repetition, or in other words, our commerce on the ocean & in other countries must be paid for by frequent war. The justest dispositions possible in ourselves will not secure us against it. It would be necessary that all other nations were just also. Justice indeed on our part will save us from those wars which would have been produced by a contrary disposition. But to prevent those produced by the wrongs of other nations? By putting ourselves in a condition to punish them. Weakness provokes insult & injury, while a condition to punish it often prevents it. This reasoning leads to the necessity of some naval force, that being the only weapon with which we can reach an enemy.

VIEWPOINT 2

"The expediency of encouraging manufactures in the United States . . . appears at this time to be pretty generally admitted."

The United States Should Become a Manufacturing Nation

Alexander Hamilton (1755–1804)

Alexander Hamilton was appointed by President George Washington to be the nation's first secretary of the treasury in 1789; he served until 1795. Hamilton, who had been one of Washington's chief military aides during the Revolutionary War and who was one of the leading forces behind the creation and ratification of the U.S. Constitution, energetically used his position to shape America's economic policy. To this end he submitted three influential reports to Congress. The first two persuaded Congress to fund the nation's public debts at full value and to create a national bank.

The following viewpoint is excerpted from the third of Hamilton's papers, the *Report on the Subject of Manufacturers*. In the report, submitted to Congress in December 1790, Hamilton argues that the federal government should actively promote manufacturing in the new nation and enact tariffs on manufactured imports for this purpose. In justifying these proposals, Hamilton had to contend with the widespread belief that agriculture and trade should remain the mainstays of America's economy and that the government should not take action on behalf of industry.

From Alexander Hamilton, *Report on the Subject of Manufactures*, 1791.

The excerpts below are taken from the first part of Hamilton's report, in which Hamilton outlines the benefits manufacturing would offer the United States.

Although Congress did not immediately adopt Hamilton's proposals, the report remained influential for many years to come.

The expediency of encouraging manufactures in the United States, which was not long since deemed very questionable, appears at this time to be pretty generally admitted. The embarrassments which have obstructed the progress of our external trade, have led to serious reflections on the necessity of enlarging the sphere of our domestic commerce. The restrictive regulations, which, in foreign markets, abridge the vent of the increasing surplus of our agricultural produce, serve to beget an earnest desire, that a more extensive demand for that surplus may be created at home; and the complete success which has rewarded manufacturing enterprise, in some valuable branches, conspiring with the promising symptoms which attend some less mature essays in others, justify a hope, that the obstacles to the growth of this species of industry are less formidable than they were apprehended to be. . . .

There still are, nevertheless, respectable patrons of opinions unfriendly to the encouragement of manufactures. . . .

Agriculture and Productivity

It ought readily to be conceded that the cultivation of the earth, as the primary and most certain source of national supply; as the immediate and chief source of subsistence to man; as the principal source of those materials which constitute the nutriment of other kinds of labor; as including a state most favorable to the freedom and independence of the human mind—one, perhaps, most conducive to the multiplication of the human species; has intrinsically a strong claim to pre-eminence over every other kind of industry.

But, that it has a title to anything like an exclusive predilection, in any country, ought to be admitted with great caution; that it is even more productive than every other branch of industry, requires more evidence than has yet been given in support of the position. That its real interests, precious and important as, without the help of exaggeration, they truly are, will be advanced, rather than injured, by the due encouragement of manufactures, may, it is believed, be satisfactorily demonstrated. And it is also believed, that the expediency of such encouragement, in a general view, may be shown to be recommended by the most cogent and persuasive motives of national policy.

It has been maintained, that agriculture is not only the most productive, but the only productive, species of industry. The reality of this suggestion, in other respects, has, however, not been verified by any accurate detail of facts and calculations; and the general arguments which are adduced to prove it, are rather subtile and paradoxical, than solid or convincing. . . .

But without contending for the superior productiveness of manufacturing industry, it may conduce to a better judgment of the policy which ought to be pursued respecting its encouragement, to contemplate the subject under some additional aspects, tending not only to confirm the idea that this kind of industry has been improperly represented as unproductive in itself, but to evince, in addition, that the establishment and diffusion of manufactures have the effect of rendering the total mass of useful and productive labor, in a community, greater than it would otherwise be. . . .

Benefits of Manufacturing

It is now proper to proceed a step further, and to enumerate the principal circumstances from which it may be inferred that manufacturing establishments not only occasion a positive augmentation of the produce and revenue of the society, but that they contribute essentially to rendering them greater than they could possibly be, without such establishments. These circumstances are:

1. The division of labor.
2. An extension of the use of machinery.
3. Additional employment to classes of the community not ordinarily engaged in the business.
4. The promoting of emigration from foreign countries.
5. The furnishing greater scope for the diversity of talents and dispositions, which discriminate men from each other.
6. The affording a more ample and various field for enterprise.
7. The creating, in some instances, a new, and securing, in all, a more certain and steady demand for the surplus produce of the soil.

Each of these circumstances has a considerable influence upon the total mass of industrious effort in a community; together, they add to it a degree of energy and effect, which are not easily conceived. Some comments upon each of them, in the order in which they have been stated, may serve to explain their importance.

1. As to the division of labor.

It has justly been observed, that there is scarcely any thing of greater moment in the economy of a nation, than the proper division of labor. The separation of occupations, causes each to be carried to a much greater perfection, than it could possibly acquire if they were blended. This arises principally from three circumstances:

1st. The greater skill and dexterity naturally resulting from a constant and undivided application to a single object. It is evident that these properties must increase in proportion to the separation and simplification of objects, and the steadiness of the attention devoted to each; and must be less in proportion to the complication of objects, and the number among which the attention is distracted.

2d. The economy of time, by avoiding the loss of it, incident to a frequent transition from one operation to another of a different nature. This depends on various circumstances; the transition itself, the orderly disposition of the implements, machines, and materials, employed in the operation to be relinquished, the preparatory steps to the commencement of a new one, the interruption of the impulse, which the mind of a workman acquires, from being engaged in a particular operation, the distractions, hesitations, and reluctances, which attend the passage from one kind of business to another.

3d. An extension of the use of machinery. A man occupied on a single object will have it more in his power, and will be more naturally led to exert his imagination, in devising methods to facilitate and abridge labor, than if he were perplexed by a variety of independent and dissimilar operations. Besides this, the fabrication of machines, in numerous instances, becoming itself a distinct trade, the artist who follows it has all the advantages which have been enumerated, for improvement in his particular art; and, in both ways, the invention and application of machinery are extended.

And from these causes united, the mere separation of the occupation of the cultivator from that of the artificer, has the effect of augmenting the productive powers of labor, and with them, the total mass of the produce or revenue of a country. In this single view of the subject, therefore, the utility of artificers or manufacturers, towards promoting an increase of productive industry, is apparent.

2. As to an extension of the use of machinery, a point which, though partly anticipated, requires to be placed in one or two additional lights.

The employment of machinery forms an item of great importance in the general mass of national industry. It is an artificial force brought in aid of the natural force of man; and, to all the purposes of labor, is an increase of hands, an accession of strength, unencumbered too by the expense of maintaining the laborer. May it not, therefore, be fairly inferred, that those occupations which give the greatest scope to the use of this auxiliary, contribute most to the general stock of industrious effort, and, in consequence, to the general product of industry?

It shall be taken for granted, and the truth of the position referred to observation, that manufacturing pursuits are susceptible, in a greater degree, of the application of machinery, than those of agriculture. If so, all the difference is lost to a community, which, instead of manufacturing for itself, procures the fabrics requisite to its supply, from other countries. The substitution of foreign for domestic manufactures, is a transfer to foreign nations, of the advantages accruing from the employment of machinery, in the modes in which it is capable of being employed, with most utility and to the greatest extent.

America Needs Manufacturing

In 1787 the magazine American Museum *published three letters from "A Plain, but Real Friend to America" that argued that America should manufacture more of its own goods rather than import them from other countries. The following passage is excerpted from the conclusion to the second letter.*

By manufacturing ourselves, and employing our own people, we shall deliver them from the curse of idleness. We shall hold out to them a new stimulus and encouragement to industry and every useful art. We shall open an extensive field to many laudable pursuits. . . .

It is worthy of remark, that while we were dependent on Great Britain, her policy and laws restrained us as much as possible from manufacturing.—Even the great mr. [William] Pitt, in one of his famous speeches, was against permitting so much as a hob-nail to be made in the colonies. Why all this opposition to our working up those materials that God and nature have given us? Surely, because they were sensible, it was the only way to our real independence, and to render the habitable parts of our country truly valuable.— What countries are the most flourishing and most powerful in the world? Manufacturing countries. It is not hills, mountains, woods, and rivers, that constitute the true riches of a country. It is the number of industrious mechanic and manufacturing as well as agriculturing inhabitants. That a country, composed of agricultivators and shepherds, is not so valuable as one wherein a just proportion of the people attend to arts and manufactures, is known to every politician in Europe: and America will never feel her importance and dignity, until she alters her present system of trade, so ruinous to the interests, to the morals, and to the reputation of her citizens.

The cotton-mill, invented in England, within the last twenty years, is a signal illustration of the general proposition which has been just advanced. In consequence of it, all the different processes for spinning cotton, are performed by means of machines, which are put in motion by water, and attended chiefly by women and children; and by a smaller number of persons, in the whole, than are requisite in the ordinary mode of spinning. And it is an advantage of great moment, that the operations of this mill continue with convenience, during the night as well as through the day. The prodigious effect of such a machine is easily conceived. To this invention is to be attributed, essentially, the immense progress which has been so suddenly made in Great Britain, in the various fabrics of cotton.

3. As to the additional employment of classes of the community not originally engaged in the particular business.

This is not among the least valuable of the means, by which manufacturing institutions contribute to augment the general stock of industry and production. In places where these institutions prevail, besides the persons regularly engaged in them, they afford occasional and extra employment to industrious individuals and families, who are willing to devote the leisure resulting from the intermissions of their ordinary pursuits to collateral labors, as a resource for multiplying their acquisitions or their enjoyments. The husbandman himself experiences a new source of profit and support, from the increased industry of his wife and daughters, invited and stimulated by the demands of the neighboring manufactories.

Besides this advantage of occasional employment to classes having different occupations, there is another, of a nature allied to it, and of a similar tendency. This is the employment of persons who would otherwise be idle, and in many cases, a burthen on the community, either from the bias of temper, habit, infirmity of body, or some other cause, indisposing or disqualifying them for the toils of the country. It is worthy of particular remark that in general, women and children are rendered more useful, and the latter more early useful, by manufacturing establishments, than they would otherwise be. Of the number of persons employed in the cotton manufactories of Great Britain, it is computed that four-sevenths, nearly, are women and children; of whom the greatest proportion are children, and many of them of a tender age.

And thus it appears to be one of the attributes of manufactures, and one of no small consequence, to give occasion to the exertion of a greater quantity of industry, even by the same number of persons, where they happen to prevail, than would exist if there were no such establishments.

4. As to the promoting of emigration from foreign countries.

Men reluctantly quit one course of occupation and livelihood for another, unless invited to it by very apparent and proximate advantages. Many who would go from one country to another, if they had a prospect of continuing with more benefit the callings to which they have been educated, will often not be tempted to change their situation by the hope of doing better in some other way. Manufacturers who, listening to the powerful invitations of a better price for their fabrics, or their labor, of greater cheapness of provisions and raw materials, of an exemption from the chief part of the taxes, burthens, and restraints, which they endure in the old world, of greater personal independence and consequence, under the operation of a more equal government, and of what is far more precious than mere religious toleration, a perfect equality of religious privileges, would probably flock from Europe to the United States, to pursue their own trades or professions, if they were once made sensible of the advantages they would enjoy, and were inspired with an assurance of encouragement and employment, will, with difficulty, be induced to transplant themselves, with a view to becoming cultivators of land.

If it be true, then, that it is the interest of the United States to open every possible avenue to emigration from abroad, it affords a weighty argument for the encouragement of manufactures; which, for the reasons just assigned, will have the strongest tendency to multiply the inducements to it.

Here is perceived an important resource, not only for extending the population, and with it the useful and productive labor of the country, but likewise for the prosecution of manufactures, without deducting from the number of hands, which might otherwise be drawn to tillage; and even for the indemnification of agriculture, for such as might happen to be diverted from it. Many, whom manufacturing views would induce to emigrate, would, afterwards, yield to the temptations which the particular situation of this country holds out to agricultural pursuits. And while agriculture would, in other respects, derive many signal and unmingled advantages from the growth of manufactures, it is a problem whether it would gain or lose, as to the article of the number of persons employed in carrying it on.

5. As to the furnishing greater scope for the diversity of talents and dispositions, which discriminate men from each other.

This is a much more powerful mean of augmenting the fund of national industry, than may at first sight appear. It is a just observation, that minds of the strongest and most active powers for their proper objects, fall below mediocrity, and labor without effect, if confined to uncongenial pursuits. And it is thence to be inferred, that the results of human exertion may be immensely increased by diversifying its objects. When all the different kinds of industry obtain in a community, each individual can find his proper element, and can call into activity, the whole vigor of his nature. And the community is benefitted by the services of its respective members, in the manner in which each can serve it with most effect.

If there be anything in a remark often to be met with, namely, that there is, in the genius of the people of this country, a peculiar aptitude for mechanic improvements, it would operate as a forcible reason for giving opportunities to the exercise of that species of talent, by the propagation of manufactures.

6. *As to the affording a more ample and various field for enterprise.*

This also is of greater consequence in the general scale of national exertion, than might, perhaps, on a superficial view be supposed, and has effects not altogether dissimilar from those of the circumstances last noticed. To cherish and stimulate the activity of the human mind, by multiplying the objects of enterprise, is not among the least considerable of the expedients by which the wealth of a nation may be promoted. Even things in themselves not positively advantageous, sometimes become so, by their tendency to provoke exertion. Every new scene which is opened to the busy nature of man to rouse and exert itself, is the addition of a new energy to the general stock of effort.

The spirit of enterprise, useful and prolific as it is, must necessarily be contracted or expanded, in proportion to the simplicity or variety of the occupations and productions which are to be found in a society. It must be less in a nation of mere cultivators, than in a nation of cultivators and merchants; less in a nation of cultivators and merchants, than in a nation of cultivators, artificers, and merchants.

7. *As to the creating, in some instances, a new, and securing, in all, a more certain and steady demand, for the surplus produce of the soil.*

This is among the most important of the circumstances which have been indicated. It is a principal mean by which the establishment of manufactures contributes to an augmentation of the produce or revenue of a country, and has an immediate and direct relation to the prosperity of agriculture.

It is evident, that the exertions of the husbandman will be steady or fluctuating, vigorous or feeble, in proportion to the steadiness or fluctuation, adequateness or inadequateness of the markets on which he must depend, for the vent of the surplus which may be produced by his labor; and that such surplus, in the ordinary course of things, will be greater or less in the same proportion.

For the purpose of this vent, a domestic market is greatly to be preferred to a foreign one; because it is, in the nature of things, far more to be relied upon.

It is a primary object of the policy of nations, to be able to supply themselves with subsistence from their own soils; and manufacturing nations, as far as circumstances permit, endeavor to procure from the same source, the raw materials necessary for their own fabrics. This disposition, urged by the spirit of monopoly, is sometimes even carried to an injudicious extreme. It seems not always to be recollected, that nations, who have neither mines nor manufactures, can only obtain the manufactured articles of which they stand in need, by an exchange of the products of their soils; and that, if those who can best furnish them with such articles, are unwilling to give a due course to this exchange, they must, of necessity, make every possible effort to manufacture for themselves; the effect of which is, that the manufacturing nations abridge the natural advantages of their situation, through an unwillingness to permit the agricultural countries to enjoy the advantages of theirs, and sacrifice the interests of a mutually beneficial intercourse to the vain project of selling every thing and buying nothing.

But it is also a consequence of the policy which has been noted, that the foreign demand for the products of agricultural countries is, in a great degree, rather casual and occasional, than certain or constant. To what extent injurious interruptions of the demand for some of the staple commodities of the United States may have been experienced from that cause, must be referred to the judgment of those who are engaged in carrying on the commerce of the country; but, it may be safely affirmed, that such interruptions are, at times, very inconveniently felt, and that cases not unfrequently occur, in which the markets are so confined and restricted, as to render the demand very unequal to the supply.

Independently, likewise, of the artificial impediments which are created by the policy in question, there are natural causes tending to render the external demand for the surplus of agricultural nations a precarious reliance. The difference of seasons in the countries which are the consumers, make immense differences in the produce of their own soils, in different years; and consequently in the degrees of their necessity for foreign supply. Plentiful harvests with them, especially if similar ones occur at the same time in the countries which are the furnishers, occasion, of course, a glut in the markets of the latter.

The Domestic Market

Considering how fast, and how much the progress of new settlements, in the United States, must increase the surplus produce of the soil, and weighing seriously the tendency of the system which prevails amongst most of the commercial nations of Europe; whatever dependence may be placed on the force of natural circumstances to counteract the effects of an artificial policy, there appear strong reasons to regard the foreign demand for that surplus, as too uncertain a reliance, and to desire a substitute for it in an extensive domestic market.

To secure such a market there is no other expedient than to pro-

39

mote manufacturing establishments. Manufacturers, who constitute the most numerous class, after the cultivators of land, are for that reason the principal consumers of the surplus of their labor.

This idea of an extensive domestic market for the surplus produce of the soil, is of the first consequence. It is, of all things, that which most effectually conduces to a flourishing state of agriculture. If the effect of manufactories should be to detach a portion of the hands which would otherwise be engaged in tillage, it might possibly cause a smaller quantity of lands to be under cultivation; but, by their tendency to procure a more certain demand for the surplus produce of the soil, they would, at the same time, cause the lands which were in cultivation to be better improved and more productive. And while, by their influence, the condition of each individual farmer would be meliorated, the total mass of agricultural production would probably be increased. For this must evidently depend as much upon the degree of improvement, if not more, than upon the number of acres under culture.

It merits particular observation, that the multiplication of manufactories not only furnishes a market for those articles which have been accustomed to be produced in abundance in a country; but it likewise creates a demand for such as were either unknown, or produced in inconsiderable quantities. The bowels, as well as the surface of the earth, are ransacked for articles which were before neglected. Animals, plants, and minerals, acquire a utility and a value which were before unexplored.

The foregoing considerations seem sufficient to establish, as general propositions, that it is the interest of nations to diversify the industrious pursuits of the individuals who compose them. That the establishment of manufactures is calculated not only to increase the general stock of useful and productive labor, but even to improve the state of agriculture in particular; certainly to advance the interests of those who are engaged in it.

CHAPTER 2

Industrialization Before the Civil War

Chapter Preface

In 1810, Francis Cabot Lowell, a Boston merchant, traveled to Great Britain. Among the places he visited were the British factory towns of Manchester and Birmingham, where cloth was manufactured out of cotton imported from the United States. Lowell returned to Boston determined to establish textile factories in America.

In the states, however, Lowell faced several technological, financial, and social obstacles to his vision. Great Britain was determined not to export its manufacturing technology to other nations and forbade the emigration of skilled "mechanics" who could design factory machinery. Furthermore, significant amounts of capital were required to set up a mechanized factory. And workers would have to be found in a country where many people viewed factory work as undesirable and degrading.

One by one, Lowell and his associates overcame these obstacles. Financing was raised through the establishment and incorporation of the Boston Manufacturing Company and the enlistment of investments from Lowell's circle of friends and relatives in Boston. Lowell himself helped design the first factory, based on his British travel observations and with the assistance of a brilliant mechanic named Paul Moody. As for labor, Lowell recruited young unmarried women from surrounding rural areas. In 1814, in Waltham, Massachusetts, the company built America's first fully mechanized mill, in which cotton was spun into thread and then woven into cloth. The factory was a tremendous success.

Lowell died in 1817; six years later six factory buildings were completed in the new town of Lowell, Massachusetts. By 1836 the Boston Manufacturing Company and its successors had invested $6.2 million in eight companies and employed six thousand workers in mills in Waltham and Lowell.

The factories of Waltham and Lowell marked an important first step in the transformation of American manufacturing from being the province of small handicraft shops and family households to large factories with power-driven machinery and supervised employees. As such, they drew national and international attention, especially in the way workers were treated. To ensure recruits (and their families) that factory work would not be degrading or ruinous, Lowell and his partners established a system in which workers lived in clean and supervised dormitories and were provided a church, minister, and a lyceum for education in their spare time. Defenders of the "Lowell system" lauded it as an example of humane industrial progress. Critics, both within and outside the ranks of Lowell's workers, however, argued that women workers suffered under hazardous working conditions and losses of privacy and freedom. Southern advocates of black slavery even claimed that the lot of black slaves was better than that of Lowell "wage-slaves." And in 1834 eight hundred Lowell mill women went on strike to protest wage reductions. It was the largest strike in America up to that time.

The New England textile factories were but part of the industrial and economic changes that swept America in the nineteenth century prior to the Civil War. Small textile manufacturing centers were being established in New York, Philadelphia, and Paterson, New Jersey. Eli Whitney and other American inventors and manufacturers gradually developed an "American system" of manufacturing based on interchangeable parts. The building of roads, canals, and railroads created significant economic expansion in many parts of America and opened new markets for the nation's industries. However, as one of the earliest and most famous centers of American manufacturing, the factories at Lowell and Waltham are a worthwhile focus in examining industrial development in America prior to the Civil War.

VIEWPOINT 1

"They [the factory workers] were healthy in appearance . . . and had the manners and deportment of young women: not of degraded brutes of burden."

The Factories in Lowell Benefit Their Workers

Charles Dickens (1812–1870)

One of the earliest and most famous sites of the industrial revolution in America was Lowell, a Massachusetts town that became a center of textile manufacturing. The community was named after Francis Cabot Lowell, a wealthy Boston merchant who toured England from 1810 to 1812 and visited several cotton mills and factories in that country. He returned to Boston with plans for the newly invented power loom and visions of replicating and improving the British factory system in America. The Boston Manufacturing Company, which he founded and directed, built a cotton mill in Waltham, Massachusetts, in 1814 that was the first in the world to house all the mechanized steps for processing raw cotton into finished cloth. Powered by water and employing three hundred workers, it was a great economic success and inspired the building of more factories.

Expansion in Waltham soon reached the limits of its available water power. Six years after Lowell's death in 1817, his partners, reorganized under the Merrimack Manufacturing Company, bought land and built a water-powered factory in the small farming community of East Chelsford. It was the first step in creating a planned industrial community. By 1837 the town, renamed Lowell, had a population of over 17,000 people and nine separate textile manufacturing firms that employed 7,800 workers and manufactured more than one million yards of cloth per week.

The advanced technology of the factories and large capitaliza-

From Charles Dickens, *American Notes*, 1842.

tion of the firms were only part of what became known as the "Lowell system" of manufacturing. Another important component was the way the large workforce was recruited and managed. Most of the "operatives" at Lowell's factories were girls and young women from farms in the region. To attract them—and to allay fears that they would live in overcrowded slums characteristic of factory towns in England—the management at Lowell built boardinghouses in which workers would live communally and under strict supervision. Workers who ignored the ten o'clock curfews and mandatory church attendance, or who made trouble in other ways, were blacklisted from employment. Those who obeyed the rules, however, could take advantage of a library, night schools, and other educational and cultural amenities funded by their employers.

Lowell soon became an American showcase for the economic and social benefits of industrialization and as such attracted the attention of many foreign visitors and dignitaries who toured the factories. One such visitor was the famed English novelist Charles Dickens, who traveled in America in 1842 and wrote a book, *American Notes*, based on his experiences. The following viewpoint is taken from his chapter on Lowell. Dickens did not hesitate to criticize slavery and other aspects of American society and culture in *American Notes*, and much of his previous and subsequent writings and novels decried the social effects of industrialism in England. However, like many other foreign observers, Dickens was favorably impressed with Lowell, arguing that workers there were generally happy, healthy, and striving to improve themselves.

Before leaving Boston, I devoted one day to an excursion to Lowell. I assign a separate chapter to this visit; not because I am about to describe it at any great length, but because I remember it as a thing by itself, and am desirous that my readers should do the same. . . .

I was met at the station at Lowell by a gentleman intimately connected with the management of the factories there; and gladly putting myself under his guidance, drove off at once to that quarter of the town in which the works, the object of my visit, were situated. Although only just of age—for if my recollection serve me, it has been a manufacturing town barely one-and-twenty years—Lowell is a large, populous, thriving place. Those indications of its youth which first attract the eye, give it a quaintness and oddity of character which, to a visitor from the old country, is amusing enough. It was a very dirty winter's day, and nothing in the whole town looked old to me, except the mud, which in some parts was almost knee-deep, and might have been deposited there, on the subsiding of the waters after the Deluge. In one place, there was a new wooden church, which, having no steeple, and being yet unpainted, looked like an enormous packing-case without any direction upon it. In another there was a large hotel, whose walls and colonnades were so crisp, and thin, and light, that it had exactly the appearance of being built with cards. I was careful not to draw my breath as we passed, and trembled when I saw a workman come out upon the roof, lest with one thoughtless stamp of his foot he should crush the structure beneath him, and bring it rattling down. The very river that moves the machinery in the mills (for they are all worked by water power), seems to acquire a new character from the fresh buildings of bright red brick and painted wood among which it takes its course; and to be as light-headed, thoughtless, and brisk a young river, in its murmurings and tumblings, as one would desire to see. One would swear that every "Bakery," "Grocery," and "Bookbindery," and other kind of store, took its shutters down for the first time, and started in business yesterday. The golden pestles and mortars fixed as signs upon the sun-blind frames outside the Druggists', appear to have been just turned out of the United States' Mint; and when I saw a baby of some week or ten days old in a woman's arms at a street corner, I found myself unconsciously wondering where it came from: never supposing for an instant that it could have been born in such a young town as that.

There are several factories in Lowell, each of which belongs to what we should term a Company of Proprietors, but what they call in America a Corporation. I went over several of these; such as a woollen factory, a carpet factory, and a cotton factory: examined them in every part; and saw them in their ordinary working aspect, with no preparation of any kind, or departure from their ordinary every-day proceedings. I may add that I am well acquainted with our manufacturing towns in England, and have visited many mills in Manchester and elsewhere in the same manner.

The Factory Girls

I happened to arrive at the first factory just as the dinner hour was over, and the girls were returning to their work; indeed the stairs of the mill were thronged with them as I ascended. They were all well dressed, but not to my thinking above their condition; for I like to see the humbler class of society careful of their dress and appearance, and even, if they please, decorated with such little trinkets as come within the compass of their means. . . .

These girls, as I have said, were all well dressed: and that phrase necessarily includes extreme cleanliness. They had serviceable bonnets, good warm cloaks, and shawls; and were not above clogs and patterns. Moreover, there were places in the mill in which they could deposit these things without injury; and there were conveniences for washing. They were healthy in appearance, many of them remarkably so, and had the manners and deportment of young women: not of degraded brutes of burden. If I had seen in one of those mills (but I did not, though I looked for something of this kind with a sharp eye), the most lisping, mincing, affected, and ridiculous young creature that my imagination could suggest, I should have thought of the careless, moping, slatternly, degraded, dull reverse (I *have* seen that), and should have been still well pleased to look upon her.

A view of Lowell, Massachusetts, at about the time of Charles Dickens's visit.

The rooms in which they worked, were as well ordered as themselves. In the windows of some, there were green plants, which were trained to shade the glass; in all, there was as much fresh air, cleanliness, and comfort, as the nature of the occupation would possibly admit of. Out of so large a number of females, many of whom were only then just verging upon womanhood, it may be reasonably supposed that some were delicate and fragile in appearance: no doubt there were. But I solemnly declare, that from all the crowd I saw in the different factories that day, I cannot recall or separate one young face that gave me a painful impression; not one young girl whom, assuming it to be matter of necessity that she should gain her daily bread by the labour of her hands, I would have removed from those works if I had had the power.

They reside in various boarding-houses near at hand. The owners of the mills are particularly careful to allow no persons to enter upon the possession of these houses, whose characters have not undergone the most searching and thorough inquiry. Any complaint that is made against them, by the boarders, or by any one else, is fully investigated; and if good ground of complaint be shown to exist against them, they are removed, and their occupation is handed over to some more deserving person. There are a few children employed in these factories, but not many. The laws of the State forbid their working more than nine months in the year, and require that they be educated during the other three. For this purpose there are schools in Lowell; and there are churches and chapels of various persuasions, in which the young women may observe that form of worship in which they have been educated.

At some distance from the factories, and on the highest and pleasantest ground in the neighbourhood, stands their hospital, or boarding-house for the sick: it is the best house in those parts, and was built by an eminent merchant for his own residence. . . . [I]t is not parcelled out into wards, but is divided into convenient chambers, each of which has all the comforts of a very comfortable home. The principal medical attendant resides under the same roof; and were the patients members of his own family, they could not be better cared for, or attended with greater gentleness and consideration. The weekly charge in this establishment for each female patient is three dollars, or twelve shillings English; but no girl employed by any of the corporations is ever excluded for want of the means of payment. That they do not very often want the means, may be gathered from the fact, that in July 1841 no fewer than nine hundred and seventy-eight of these girls were depositors in the Lowell Savings Bank: the amount of whose joint savings was estimated at one hundred thousand dollars, or twenty thousand English pounds.

Three Startling Facts

I am now going to state three facts, which will startle a large class of readers on this side of the Atlantic, very much.

Firstly, there is a joint-stock piano in a great many of the boarding-houses. Secondly, nearly all these young ladies subscribe to circulating libraries. Thirdly, they have got up among themselves a periodical called THE LOWELL OFFERING, "A repository of original articles, written exclusively by females actively employed in the mills,"—which is duly printed, published, and sold; and whereof I brought away from Lowell four hundred good solid pages, which I have read from beginning to end.

The large class of readers, startled by these facts, will exclaim, with one voice, "How very preposterous!" On my deferentially

48

inquiring why, they will answer, "These things are above their station." In reply to that objection, I would beg to ask what their station is.

It is their station to work. And they *do* work. They labour in these mills, upon an average, twelve hours a day, which is unquestionably work, and pretty tight work too. Perhaps it is above their station to indulge in such amusements, on any terms. Are we quite sure that we in England have not formed our ideas of the "station" of working people, from accustoming ourselves to the contemplation of that class as they are, and not as they might be? I think that if we examine our own feelings, we shall find that the pianos, and the circulating libraries, and even the Lowell Offering, startle us by their novelty, and not by their bearing upon any abstract question of right or wrong.

For myself, I know no station in which, the occupation of today cheerfully done and the occupation of to-morrow cheerfully looked to, any one of these pursuits is not most humanizing and laudable. I know no station which is rendered more endurable to the person in it, or more safe to the person out of it, by having ignorance for its associate. I know no station which has a right to monopolize the means of mutual instruction, improvement, and rational entertainment; or which has ever continued to be a station very long, after seeking to do so.

Of the merits of the Lowell Offering as a literary production, I will only observe, putting entirely out of sight the fact of the articles having been written by these girls after the arduous labours of the day, that it will compare advantageously with a great many English Annuals. It is pleasant to find that many of its Tales are of the Mills and of those who work in them; that they inculcate habits of self-denial and contentment, and teach good doctrines of enlarged benevolence. A strong feeling for the beauties of nature, as displayed in the solitudes the writers have left at home, breathes through its pages like wholesome village air; and though a circulating library is a favourable school for the study of such topics, it has very scant allusion to fine clothes, fine marriages, fine houses, or fine life. Some persons might object to the papers being signed occasionally with rather fine names, but this is an American fashion. One of the provinces of the State Legislature of Massachusetts is to alter ugly names into pretty ones, as the children improve upon the tastes of their parents. These changes costing little or nothing, scores of Mary Annes are solemnly converted into Bevelinas every session. . . .

Lowell and British Factories

In this brief account of Lowell, and inadequate expression of the gratification it yielded me, and cannot fail to afford to any foreigner to whom the condition of such people at home is a subject of interest and anxious speculation, I have carefully abstained from drawing a comparison between these factories and those of our own land. Many of the circumstances whose strong influence has been at work for years in our manufacturing towns have not arisen here; and there is no manufacturing population in Lowell, so to speak: for these girls (often the daughters of small farmers) come from other States, remain a few years in the mills, and then go home for good.

The contrast would be a strong one, for it would be between the Good and Evil, the living light and deepest shadow. I abstain from it, because I deem it just to do so. But I only the more earnestly abjure all those whose eyes may rest on these pages, to pause and reflect upon the difference between this town and those great haunts of desperate misery: to call to mind, if they can in the midst of party strife and squabble, the efforts that must be made to purge them of their suffering and danger: and last, and foremost, to remember how the precious Time is rushing by.

"We would call upon every operative in our city . . . to awake from the lethargy which has fallen upon them, and assert . . . their rights."

The Factories in Lowell Oppress Their Workers

"Amelia" (dates unknown)

The factories at Lowell, Massachusetts, comprised the first large-scale mechanized factory complex built in the United States. By 1855 Lowell, called the "city of spindles," had 52 mills employing 8,800 women and 4,400 men and making 2.25 million yards of cotton cloth each week. Previous American textile factories, such as the 1790 mill designed by English immigrant Samuel Slater in Rhode Island, were much smaller. They employed an average of 70 workers, most of whom were families of men, women, and young children. Lowell's factories, on the other hand, averaged several hundred workers, the majority of whom were single young women. To attract them (and reassure families that their daughters would not be "ruined" by factory work) the mill owners in Lowell provided chaperoned boardinghouses, schools, churches, lecture halls, and other amenities, including the *Lowell Offering*, a subsidized newspaper written by and for factory workers.

Many people praised the humaneness of the "Lowell system." However, not all "mill girls" were as appreciative of their situation, which generally included twelve- or thirteen-hour working days, noisy and sometimes dangerous workplaces, restrictive regulations, and periodic layoffs, wage cutbacks, and work speedups. In 1845 the Lowell Female Labor Reform Association—one of the first trade unions of industrial women in the United States—was founded by Lowell cotton mill workers. One of its

From "Amelia," "Some of the Beauties of Our Factory System—Otherwise, Lowell Slavery," *Factory Tracts*, no. 1 (Boston: Lowell Female Labor Reform Association, 1845).

first activities was the publication of "Factory Tracts"— pamphlets consisting of articles and poetry designed "to give a true position of the Factory system and its effects upon the health and happiness of the operatives." The following viewpoint is taken from an article by "Amelia" that, after having been rejected for publication by the *Lowell Offering*, appeared in the first of the tracts. Amelia presents her views on the conditions at Lowell. She criticizes the low wages and long hours of factory work, the fact that workers are bound to employers for twelve months at a time, that only workers with a "regular discharge" are able to seek employment elsewhere, and other aspects of factory life.

For the purpose of illustration, let us go with that light-hearted, joyous young girl who is about for the first time to leave the home of her childhood, that home around which clusters so many beautiful and holy associations, pleasant memories, and quiet joys; to leave, too, a mother's cheerful smile, a father's care and protection; and wend her way toward this far famed "city of spindles," this promised land of the imagination, in whose praise she has doubtless heard so much.

The First Year

Let us trace her progress during her first year's residence, and see whether she indeed realizes those golden prospects which have been held out to her. Follow her now as she enters that large gloomy looking building—she is in search of employment, and has been told that she might here obtain an eligible situation. She is sadly wearied with her journey, and withal somewhat annoyed by the noise, confusion, and strange faces all around her. So, after a brief conversation with the overseer, she concludes to accept the first situation which offers; and reserving to herself a sufficient portion of time in which to obtain the necessary rest after her unwonted exertions, and the gratification of a stranger's curiosity regarding the place in which she is now to make her future home, she retires to her boarding-house, to arrange matters as much to her mind as may be.

The intervening time passes rapidly away, and she soon finds herself once more within the confines of that close noisy apartment, and is forthwith installed in her new situation—first, however, premising that she has been sent to the Counting-room, and receives therefrom a Regulation paper, containing the rules by which she must be governed while in their employ; and lo! here is the beginning of mischief; for in addition to the tyrannous and oppressive rules which meet her astonished eyes, she finds herself compelled to remain for the space of twelve months in the very place she then occupies, however reasonable and just cause of complaint might be hers, or however strong the wish for dismission; thus, in fact, constituting herself a slave, a very slave to the caprices of him for whom she labors. Several incidents coming to the knowledge of the writer, might be somewhat interesting in this connection, as tending to show the prejudicial influence exerted upon the interests of the operative by this unjust requisition. The first is of a lady who has been engaged as an operative for a number of years, and recently entered a weaving room on the Massachusetts Corporation; the overseers having assured her previous to her entrance, that she should realize the sum of $2.25 per week, exclusive of board; which she finding it impossible to do, appealed to the Counting-room for a line enabling her to engage elsewhere but it was peremptorily refused.

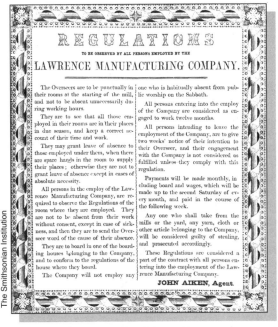

REGULATIONS

TO BE OBSERVED BY ALL PERSONS EMPLOYED BY THE

LAWRENCE MANUFACTURING COMPANY.

The Overseers are to be punctually in their rooms at the starting of the mill, and not to be absent unnecessarily during working hours.

They are to see that all those employed in their rooms are in their places in due season, and keep a correct account of their time and work.

They may grant leave of absence to those employed under them, when there are spare hands in the room to supply their places; otherwise they are not to grant leave of absence except in cases of absolute necessity.

All persons in the employ of the Lawrence Manufacturing Company, are required to observe the Regulations of the room where they are employed. They are not to be absent from their work without consent, except in case of sickness, and then they are to send the Overseer word of the cause of their absence.

They are to board in one of the boarding houses belonging to the Company, and to conform to the regulations of the house where they board.

The Company will not employ any

one who is habitually absent from public worship on the Sabbath.

All persons entering into the employ of the Company are considered as engaged to work twelve months.

All persons intending to leave the employment of the Company, are to give two weeks' notice of their intention to their Overseer, and their engagement with the Company is not considered as fulfilled unless they comply with this regulation.

Payments will be made monthly, including board and wages, which will be made up to the second Saturday of every month, and paid in the course of the following week.

Any one who shall take from the mills or the yard, any yarn, cloth or other article belonging to the Company, will be considered guilty of stealing, and prosecuted accordingly.

These Regulations are considered a part of the contract with all persons entering into the employment of the Lawrence Manufacturing Company.

JOHN AIKEN, Agent

Employee regulations were among the source of complaints for "Amelia" and other factory workers.

The next is of a more general bearing, concerning quite a number of individuals employed on the Lawrence Corporation, where the owners have recently erected and put in motion a new mill, at the same time stopping one of the old, in which said persons were employed. Now as they did not voluntarily leave their situations, but were discharged therefrom on account of suspension of operations by the company; they had an undoubted right to choose their own place of labor; and as the work in the new mill is vastly more laborious, and the wages less than can be obtained in many parts of the city, they signified their wish to go elsewhere, but are insolently told that they shall labor there or not at all; and will not be released until their year has expired, when if they can *possibly* find *no* further excuse for delay, they *may* deign to bestow upon them what is in common parlance termed, a "regular discharge;" thus enabling them to pass from one prison house to another. Concerning this precious document, it is only necessary to say, that it very precisely reminds one of that which the dealers in human flesh at the South are wont to give and receive as the transfer of one piece of property from one owner to another. Now, reader, what think you? is not this the height of the beautiful and are not we operatives an ungrateful set of creatures that we do not properly appreciate, and be highly thankful for such unparalleled generosity on the part of our employers?

Long Hours

But to return to our toiling Maiden,—the next beautiful feature which she discovers in this *glorious* system is, the long number of hours which she is obliged to spend in the above named close, unwholesome apartment. It is not enough, that like the poor peasant of Ireland, or the Russian serf who labors from sun to sun, but during one half of the year, she must still continue to toil on, long after Nature's lamp has ceased to lend its aid—nor will even this suffice to satisfy the grasping avarice of her employer; for she is also through the winter months required to rise, partake of her morning meal, and be at her station in the mill, while the sun is yet sleeping behind the eastern hills; thus working on an average, at least twelve hours and three fourths per day, exclusive of the time allotted for her hasty meals, which is in winter simply one half hour at noon,— in the spring is allowed the same at morn, and during the summer is added 15 minutes to the half hour at noon. Then too, when she is at last released from her wearisome day's toil, still may she not depart in peace. No! her footsteps must be dogged to see that they do not stray beyond the corporation limits, and she *must,* whether she will or no, be subjected to the manifold inconveniences of a large crowded boarding-house, where too, the price paid for her accommodation is so utterly insignificant, that it will not ensure to her the common comforts of life; she is obliged to sleep in a small comfortless, half ventilated apartment containing some half a dozen occupants each; but no matter, *she is an operative*—it is all well enough for her; there is no "abuse" about it; no, indeed; so think our employers,—but do we think so? time will show. Here, too, comes up a case which strikingly illustrates the petty tyranny of the employer. A little girl, some 12 or 13 years of age, the daughter of a poor widow, dependent on her daily toil for a livelihood, worked on one of the Corporations, boarding with her mother; who dying left her to the care of an aunt, residing but a few steps from the Corporation—but the poor little creature all unqualified as she was, to provide for her own wants, was *compelled* to leave her home and the motherly care bestowed upon her, and enter one of these same large crowded boarding-houses. We do but give the facts in this case and they need no comment for every one *must* see the utter heartlessness which prompted such conduct toward a mere child.

A Real Picture

Reader will you pronounce this a mere fancy sketch, written for the sake of effect? It is not so. It is a real picture of "Factory life;" nor is it one half so bad as might truthfully and justly have been drawn. But it has been asked, and doubtless will be again, why, if these evils are so aggravating, have they been so long and so peacefully borne? Ah! and why have they? It is a question well

The "Beauties of Factory Life"

A worker named Juliana complained in a June 12, 1846, letter to the newspaper Voice of Industry *about unrealistically pleasant depictions of factory life presented in books such as one written by minister Henry A. Miles* (Lowell, As It Was, and As It Is, *published in 1846).*

Those who write so effusively about the "Beauties of Factory Life," tell us that we are indeed happy creatures, and how truly grateful and humbly submissive we should be. Can it be that any of us are so stupified as not to realize the exalted station and truly delightful influences which we enjoy? If so, let them take a glance at pages 195 and 196 of Rev. H. Miles' book, and they will surely awake to gratitude and be content. Pianos, teachers of music, evening schools, lectures, libraries and all these sorts of advantages are, says he, enjoyed by the operatives. (Query—when do they find time for all or any of these? When exhausted nature demands repose?) Very pretty picture that to write about; but we who work in the factory know the sober reality to be quite another thing altogether.

After all, it is easier to write a book than it is to *do* right. It is easier to smooth over and plaster up a deep festering rotten system, which is sapping the life-blood of our nation, widening and deepening the yawning gulf which will ere long swallow up the laboring classes in dependent servitude and serfdom, like that of Europe, than it is to probe to the very bottom of this death-spreading monster.

worthy of our consideration, and we would call upon every operative in *our* city, aye, throughout the length and breadth of the land, to awake from the lethargy which has fallen upon them, and assert and maintain their rights. We call upon you for action—*united and immediate action*. But, says one, let us wait till we are stronger. In the language of one of old, we ask, when shall we be stronger? Will it be the next week, or the next year? Will it be when we are reduced to the service conditions of the poor operatives of England? for verily we shall be and that right soon, if matters be suffered to remain as they are. Says another, how shall we act? we are but one amongst a thousand, what shall we do that our influence may be felt in this vast multitude? We answer there is in this city an Association called the Female Labor Reform Association, having for its professed object, the amelioration of the condition of the operative. Enrolled upon its records are the names of five hundred members—come then, and add thereto five hundred or rather five thousand more, and in the strength of our united influence we will soon show these *drivelling* cotton lords, this mushroom aristocracy of New England, who so arrogantly aspire to lord it over God's heritage, that our rights cannot be trampled upon with impunity; that we will no longer submit to that arbitrary power which has for the last ten years been so abundantly exercised over us.

One word ere we close, to the hardy independent yeomanry and mechanics, among the Granite Hills of New Hampshire, the woody forests of Maine, the cloud capped mountains of Vermont, and the busy, bustling towns of the old Bay State—ye! who have daughters and sisters toiling in these sickly prison-houses which are scattered far and wide over each of these States, we appeal to you for aid in this matter. Do you ask how that aid can be administered? We answer through the Ballot Box. Yes! if you have one spark of sympathy for our condition, carry it there, and see to it that you send to preside in the Councils of each Commonwealth, men who have hearts as well as heads, souls as well as bodies; men who will watch zealously over the interests of the laborer in every department; who will protect him by the strong arm of the law from the encroachments of arbitrary power; who will see that he is not deprived of those rights and privileges which God and Nature have bestowed upon him—yes,

> From every rolling river,
>   From mountain, vale and plain,
> We call on you to deliver
>   Us, from the tyrant's chain:

And shall we call in vain? We trust not. More anon.

Viewpoint 3

"If the slave has never been a free man, we think, . . . his sufferings are less than those of the free laborer at wages."

Industrial Workers Are Worse Off than Black Slaves

Orestes A. Brownson (1803–1876)

The development of the factory system of wage labor in early nineteenth-century America, especially in New England, coincided with the rise of the movement to abolish slavery. Both critics and defenders of slavery compared the wage system to the slavery system of labor; both systems were contrasted with the American ideal of a nation of self-employed farmers and artisans. Some argued that the system of slavery in the South was actually more humane and just than the wage labor system of the North.

The following viewpoint is by Orestes A. Brownson, a New England writer and religious leader and one-time associate of Ralph Waldo Emerson and Henry David Thoreau. At the time the viewpoint was written, Brownson was a Unitarian minister and an activist in the Democratic Party. In the essay, which is taken from an 1840 issue of the *Boston Quarterly Review*, a journal Brownson founded in 1838, he asserts that wage laborers, such as the women who work in the textile factories in Lowell, Massachusetts, experience greater hardship than black slaves. Although he condemns slavery, he argues that slaves are at least provided food and shelter by their masters and are spared the constant worry of starvation due to unemployment or low wages. Contrary to the impressions provided by "distinguished visitors"

From Orestes A. Brownson, "The Laboring Classes," *Boston Quarterly Review*, July 1840.

to Lowell and other factories, he maintains, the factory system of labor causes most workers to "wear out their health, spirits, and morals." Unlike fifty years ago, he writes, workers no longer have the option of moving to new lands and becoming farmers. He contends that owners of factories who decry slavery in the South are hypocrites who are exploiting the labor of others.

In regard to labor two systems obtain; one that of slave labor, the other that of free labor. Of the two, the first is, in our judgment, except so far as the feelings are concerned, decidedly the least oppressive. If the slave has never been a free man, we think, as a general rule, his sufferings are less than those of the free laborer at wages. As to actual freedom one has just about as much as the other. The laborer at wages has all the disadvantages of freedom and none of its blessings, while the slave, if denied the blessings, is freed from the disadvantages. We are no advocates of slavery, we are as heartily opposed to it as any modern abolitionist can be; but we say frankly that, if there must always be a laboring population distinct from proprietors and employers, we regard the slave system as decidedly preferable to the system at wages. It is no pleasant thing to go days without food, to lie idle for weeks, seeking work and finding none, to rise in the morning with a wife and children you love, and know not where to procure them a breakfast, and to see constantly before you no brighter prospect than the almshouse. Yet these are no unfrequent incidents in the lives of our laboring population. Even in seasons of general prosperity, when there was only the ordinary cry of "hard times," we have seen hundreds of people in a not very populous village, in a wealthy portion of our common country, suffering for the want of the necessaries of life, willing to work, and yet finding no work to do. Many and many is the application of a poor man for work, merely for his food, we have seen rejected. These things are little thought of, for the applicants are poor; they fill no conspicuous place in society, and they have no biographers. But their wrongs are chronicled in heaven. It is said there is no want in this country. There may be less than in some other countries. But death by actual starvation in this country is, we apprehend, no uncommon occurrence. The sufferings of a quiet, unassuming, but useful class of females in our cities, in general sempstresses, too proud to get or to apply to the almshouse, are not easily told. They are industrious; they do all that they can find to do; but yet the little there is for them to do, and the miserable pittance they receive for it, is hardly sufficient to keep soul and body together. And yet there is a man who employs them to make shirts, trousers, &c., and grows rich on their labors. He is one of our respectable citizens, perhaps is praised in the newspapers for his liberal donations to some charitable institution. He passes among us as a pattern of morality, and is honored as a worthy Christian. And why should he not be, since our *Christian* community is made up of such as he, and since our clergy would not dare question his piety, lest they should incur the reproach of infidelity, and lose their standing, and their salaries? Nay, since our clergy are raised up, educated, fashioned, and sustained by such as he? Not a few of our churches rest on Mammon for their foundation. The basement is a trader's shop.

Factory Workers

We pass through our manufacturing villages, most of them appear neat and flourishing. The operatives are well dressed, and we are told, well paid. They are said to be healthy, contented, and happy. This is the fair side of the picture; the side exhibited to distinguished visitors. There is a dark side, moral as well as physical. Of the common operatives, few, if any, by their wages, acquire a competence. A few of what Carlyle terms not inaptly the *body-servants* are well paid, and now and then an agent or an overseer rides in his coach. But the great mass wear out their health, spirits, and morals, without becoming one whit better off than when they commenced labor. The bills of mortality in these factory villages are not striking, we admit, for the poor girls when they can toil no longer go home to die. The average life, working life we mean, of the girls that come to [work in the factories at] Lowell, for instance, from Maine, New Hampshire, and Vermont, we have been assured, is only about three years. What becomes of them then? Few of them ever marry; fewer still ever return to their native places with reputations unimpaired. "She has worked in a Factory," is almost enough to damn to infamy the most worthy and virtuous girl. We know no sadder sight on earth than one of our factory villages presents, when the bell at break of day, or at the hour of breakfast, or dinner, calls out its hundreds or thousands of operatives. We stand and look at these hard working men and women hurrying in all directions, and ask ourselves, where go the proceeds of their labors? The man who employs them, and for whom they are toiling as so many slaves, is one of our city nabobs, revelling in luxury; or he is a member of our legislature, enacting laws to put money in his own pocket; or he is a member of Congress, contending for a high Tariff to tax the poor for the benefit of the rich; or in these times he is shedding crocodile tears over the deplorable condition of the poor laborer, while he docks his wages twenty-five per cent. . . . And this man too would fain pass for a Christian and a republican. He shouts for liberty, stickles for equality, and is horrified at a Southern planter who keeps slaves.

One thing is certain; that of the amount actually produced by the operative, he retains a less proportion than it costs the master to feed, clothe, and lodge his slave. Wages is a cunning device of the devil, for the benefit of tender consciences, who would retain all the advantages of the slave system, without the expense, trouble, and odium of being slave-holders.

Slavery Is More Humane

George Fitzhugh, a Virginia lawyer, was one of the most outspoken defenders of slavery. He argued that slaves were better off than workers in New England, England, and France. The following passage is taken from an 1851 pamphlet that was reprinted in his 1854 book Sociology for the South.

Slavery is too costly, too humane and merciful an institution for France, England or New England. The free competition of labor and capital in those countries where labor is redundant, is certain to bring the wages of labor down to the minimum amount that will support human life. The employers of free laborers, like the riders of hired horses, try to get the most possible work out of them, for the least hire. They boast of the low rates at which they procure labor, and still hold up their heads in society uncensured and unreproved. No slaveholder was ever so brutal as to boast of the low wages he paid his slaves, to pride himself on feeding and clothing them badly—neglecting the young, the aged, the sick and infirm; such a man would be hooted from society as a monster. Society hardly tolerates inhumanity to horses, much less to slaves. But disguise the process a little, and it is a popular virtue to oppress free white poor people. Get the labor of the able-bodied husband as cheap as you can, and leave his wife, children and aged parents to starve, and you are the beau ideal of a man in England and New England. Public opinion, as well as natural feeling, requires a man to pay his slave high wages; the same public opinion commends your cleverness in paying low wages to free laborers, and nature and conscience oppose no obstacles to the screwing process.

Messrs. Thome and Kimball, in their account of emancipation of the West Indies, [James A. Thome and J. Horace Kimball, *Emancipation in the West Indies* (New York: American Anti-Slavery Society, 1838)] establish the fact that the employer may have the same amount of labor done, twenty-five percent, cheaper than the master. What does this fact prove, if not that wages is a more successful method of taxing labor than slavery? We really believe our Northern system of labor is more oppressive, and even more mischievous to morals, than the Southern. We, however, war against both. We have no toleration for either system. We would see the slave a man, but a free man, not a mere operative at wages. This he would not be were he now emancipated. Could the abolitionists effect all they propose, they would do the slave no service. Should emancipation work as well as they say, still it would do the slave no good. He would be a slave still, although with the title and cares of a freeman. If then we had no constitutional objections to abolitionism, we could not, for the reason here implied, be abolitionists.

The slave system, however, in name and form, is gradually disappearing from Christendom. It will not subsist much longer. But its place is taken by the system of labor at wages, and this system, we hold, is no improvement upon the one it supplants. Nevertheless the system of wages will triumph. It is the system which in name sounds honester than slavery, and in substance is more profitable to the master. It yields the wages of iniquity, without its opprobrium. It will therefore supplant slavery, and be sustained—for a time.

Now, what is the prospect of those who fall under the operation of this system? We ask, is there a reasonable chance that any considerable portion of the present generation of laborers, shall ever become owners of a sufficient portion of the funds of production, to be able to sustain themselves by laboring on their own capital, that is, as independent laborers? We need not ask this question, for everybody knows there is not. Well, is the condition of a laborer at wages the best that the great mass of the working people ought to be able to aspire to? Is it a condition,—nay can it be made a condition,—with which a man should be satisfied; in which he should be contented to live and die?

Worsening Conditions

In our own country this condition has existed under its most favorable aspects, and has been made as good as it can be. It has reached all the excellence of which it is susceptible. It is now not improving but growing worse. The actual condition of the workingman to-day, viewed in all its bearings, is not so good as it was fifty years ago. If we have not been altogether misinformed, fifty years ago, health and industrious habits, constituted no mean stock in trade, and with them almost any man might aspire to competence and independence. But it is so no longer. The wilderness has receded, and already the new lands are beyond the reach of the mere laborer, and the employer has him at his mercy. If the present relation subsist, we see nothing better for him in reserve than what he now possesses, but something altogether worse.

We are not ignorant of the fact that men born poor become wealthy, and that men born to wealth become poor; but this fact does not necessarily diminish the numbers of the poor, nor augment the numbers of the rich. The relative numbers of the two classes remain, or may remain, the same. But be this as it may; one fact is certain, no man born poor has ever, by his wages, as a simple operative, risen to the class of the wealthy. Rich he may have become, but it has not been by his own manual labor. He has in some way contrived to tax for his benefit the labor of others. He may have accumulated a few dollars which he has placed at usury, or invested in trade; or he may, as a master workman, obtain a premium on his journeymen; or he may have from a clerk passed to a partner, or from a workman to an overseer. The simple market wages for ordinary labor, has never been adequate to raise him from poverty to wealth. This fact is decisive of the whole controversy, and proves that the system of wages must be supplanted by some other system, or else one half of the human race must forever be the virtual slaves of the other.

VIEWPOINT 4

"It is in the power of every young girl who comes here to work . . . to acquire every accomplishment, and get as good an education as any lady in the country. Have the slaves that privilege?"

Industrial Workers Are Not Worse Off than Black Slaves

Clementine Averill (dates unknown)

Many defenders of the South argued that its agricultural society was superior to the industrial economy evolving in the northern states—and, more specifically, that slaves in the South were better off than factory workers who worked for wages in places like Lowell, Massachusetts. In 1850 Jeremiah Clemens, a senator from Alabama, asked a series of questions concerning the state of factory workers and asserted that the "Southern slaves are better off than the Northern operatives." Clementine Averill, a "factory-girl" from Lowell, Massachusetts, wrote a reply letter to Clemens that was published in the New York *Tribune* and is reprinted here. Answering his questions one by one, she describes the conditions of her employment in favorable terms and argues that there is no real comparison between her situation and that of chattel slaves.

LETTER FROM A FACTORY-GIRL TO SENATOR CLEMENS
Communicated for *The Weekly Tribune*.

Lowell, March 6, 1850.

From Clementine Averill, "Letter from a Factory-Girl to Senator Clemens," Lowell *Weekly Tribune*, March 6, 1850.

Mr. Clemens,—Sir, in some of the late papers I have read several questions which you asked concerning the New England operatives. They have been well answered perhaps, but enough has not yet been said, and I deem it proper that the operatives should answer for themselves.

Pay and Conditions of Work

1st, You wish to know what pay we have. I will speak only for the girls, and think I am stating it very low when I say that we average two dollars a week beside our board. Hundreds of girls in these mills clear from three to five dollars a week, while others, who have not been here long, and are not used to the work, make less than two dollars. If my wages are ever reduced lower than that, I shall seek employment elsewhere.

2nd, Children are never taken from their parents and put into the mill. What an idea! No person has a right to take a child from its parents, whether they be black or white, bond or free, unless there is danger of the child's suffering harm by remaining with its parents. Girls come here from the country of their own free will, because they can earn more money, and because they wish to see and know more of the world.

3d, One manufacturer will employ laborers dismissed by another if they bring a regular discharge and have given two weeks' notice previous to leaving.

4th, We never work more than twelve and a half hours a day; the majority would not be willing to work less, if their earnings were less, as they only intend working a few years, and they wish to make all they can while here, for they have only one object in view.

5th, When operatives are sick they select their own physician, and usually have money enough laid by to supply all their wants. If they are sick long, and have not money enough, those who have give to them freely; for let me tell you, there is warmhearted charity here, as well as hard work and economy.

6th, I have inquired, but have not ascertained that one person ever went from a factory to a poor-house in this city.

7th, Any person can see us, who wishes to, by calling for us at the counting-room, or after hours of labor by calling at our boarding-places.

8th, The factory girls generally marry, and their husbands are expected to care for them when old. There are some, however, who do not marry, but such often have hundreds and thousands of dollars at interest; if you do not believe it, come and examine the bank-books and railroad stocks for yourself.

9th, We have as much and as good food as we want. We usually have warm biscuit, or nice toast and pie, with good bread and butter, coffee and tea, for breakfast; for dinner, meat and potatoes, with vegetables, tomatoes and pickles, pudding or pie, with bread, butter, coffee and tea; for supper we have nice bread or warm biscuit, with some kind of sauce, cake, pie, and tea. But these questions seem to relate merely to our animal wants. We have all that is necessary for the health and comfort of the body, if that is all; and the richest person needs no more. But is the body all? Have we no minds to improve, no hearts to purify? Truly, to provide for our physical wants is our first great duty, in order that our mental faculties may be fully developed. If we had no higher nature than the animal, life would not be worth possessing; but we have Godlike faculties to cultivate and expand, without limit and without end. What is the object of our existence, if it is not to glorify God? and how shall we glorify him but by striving to be like him, aiming at the perfection of our whole nature, and aiding all within our influence in their ownward progress to perfection? Do you think we would come here and toil early and late with no other object in view than the gratification of mere animal propensities? No, we would not try to live; and this is

---

Slaves Lack Liberty

The following excerpt is taken from an August 5, 1847, article in the National Anti-Slavery Standard *refuting the assertion that industrial wage earners are worse off than black slaves.*

Even in England, the condition of the poorest people is far preferable to that of the American slaves, for they are recognized as men having rights—men to be cared for, and legislated for—men who hope for a chance to be legislators themselves, and who will, by and by, have the chance. The American slave is entirely a different being, and though he may have enough to eat and to wear, and a place to lay his bones upon after a day's otherwise unrequited toil, yet he is not a *man*, but a *chattel*. This is all the difference in the world. . . .

There is no condition, here in New England, at least, which bears the least resemblance to the condition of the Southern chattels— nothing which deserves the name of White Slavery. There are a thousand disabilities which the poor labour under, and to find a speedy remedy for these should be the wish of every man, and not only the wish, but the *effort*. A consideration of evil to the negroes should blind no one to the hardships of his neighbours; and it is not likely to. But it should be recollected that the extinction of chattel slavery—the ownership of man by another man—is to precede other reforms. . . . A man must own *himself* before he can own anything else—soil, or house, or furniture, or railroad stock; and the abolition of Slavery will be the only way to bring about a general reform in the condition of man throughout the world.

wherein consists the insult, both in your questions and in your remarks in the Senate; as though to provide for the body was all we had to live for, as though we had no immortal minds to train for usefulness and a glorious existence.

Comparisons with Slavery

Let us see whether the "Southern slaves are better off than the Northern operatives." As I have said, we have all that is necessary for health and comfort. Do the slaves have more? It is in the power of every young girl who comes here to work, if she has good health and no one but herself to provide for, to acquire every accomplishment, and get as good an education as any lady in the country. Have the slaves that privilege? By giving two weeks' notice we can leave when we please, visit our friends, attend any school, or travel for pleasure or information. Some of us have visited the White Mountains, Niagara Falls, and the city of Washington; have talked with the President, and visited the tomb of him who was greatest and best. Would that our present rulers had a portion of the same spirit which animated him; then would misrule and oppression cease, and the gathering storm pass harmless by. Can the slaves leave when they please, and go where they please? Are they allowed to attend school, or travel for pleasure, and sit at the same table with any gentlemen or lady? Some of the operatives of this city have been teachers in institutions of learning in your own State. Why do your people send here for teachers if your slaves are better off than they? Shame on the man who would stand up in the Senate of the United States, and say that the slaves at the South are better off than the operatives of New England; such a man is not fit for any office in a free country. Are we torn from our friends and kindred, sold and driven about like cattle, chained and whipped, and not allowed to speak one word in self-defense? We can appeal to the laws for redress, while the slaves cannot. . . . And now, Mr. Clemens, I would most earnestly invite you, Mr. Foote, [Henry Stuart Foote, U.S. Senator from Mississippi] and all other Southern men who want to know anything about us, to come and see us. We will treat you with all the politeness in our power. I should be pleased to see you at my boarding-place, No. 61 Kirk Street, Boott Corporation. In closing, I must say that I pity not only the slave, but the slave-owner. I pity him for his want of principle, for his hardness of heart and wrong education. May God, in his infinite mercy, convince all pro-slavery men of the great sin of holding their fellow-men in bondage! May he turn their hearts from cruelty and oppression to the love of himself and all mankind! Please excuse me for omitting the "Hon." before your name. I cannot apply titles where they are not deserved.

Clementine Averill

CHAPTER 3

Wealth, Poverty, and Industrialization in the Gilded Age

Chapter Preface

Prior to the Civil War, a national meatpacking industry did not exist. People who did not live on farms obtained meat from local butchers. Transporting either meat or live animals from the producing areas in the Midwest to the consumer markets in America's eastern cities proved too difficult or costly to profitably undertake.

In the 1870s, a New England cattle buyer named Gustavus Swift recognized that America's improving railroad network and the invention of the refrigerated boxcar created an opportunity to sell meat to national rather than local markets. Within a few years his plants in Chicago were slaughtering, processing, and shipping millions of pounds of meat and meat by-products annually and marketing them through a national network of agents. By centralizing his operations and buying and selling meat on a massive scale, Swift was able to lower costs for consumers while amassing a fortune for himself and his company.

The story of Swift and the meatpacking industry can serve as a microcosm for the changes sweeping America's economy after the Civil War. The explosion of industrial development, the rise of new technologies, the railroad's ability to transport goods long distances, and the replacement of local businesses with large-scale enterprises that sold mass-produced goods to a national market created both individual fortunes and corporate enterprises of unprecedented size. The concentrations of wealth and power among these select individuals and companies were both lauded and criticized.

Many people praised the entrepreneurs of this time as paragons of thrift, hard work, and business ingenuity whose wealth was a natural reward for their efforts. Large corporations, they argued, were necessary to organize, pay for, and implement complex and expensive industrial operations such as steel manufacturing. Adapting British biologist Charles Darwin's theory of natural selection to economics, many business leaders held that their material successes were a natural outcome of business competition in which the winners would grow and prosper, the losers would disappear, and society in general would benefit. As the son of John D. Rockefeller, whose Standard Oil Company controlled more than 90 percent of the growing petroleum industry by 1880, asserted,

68

The growth of a large business is merely the survival of the fittest. . . . The American Beauty Rose can be produced only by sacrificing the early buds which grow around it. This is not an evil tendency in business. It is merely the working out of a law of nature and a law of God.

By the same token, Americans who were poor were regarded as lacking the willpower and ingenuity to pull themselves up. "There is not a poor person in the United States who was not made poor by his own shortcomings," attested Russell Conwell, a minister who became rich for his "Acres of Diamonds" lectures in which he celebrated the attainment of wealth as a Christian duty.

However, not all Americans celebrated the concentrations of wealth that were an integral part of America's post–Civil War industrial revolution. Social critics such as Henry George and Edward Bellamy criticized the poverty and inequality found in American society even as new industries created great wealth for a few. They argued that political and economic reforms should rectify this fault. Others deemed the rise of large corporations, largely unregulated and in many cases dwarfing the size of governments, as being harmful to the public good. Journalist Henry Demarest Lloyd, for instance, in his 1894 book *Wealth Against Commonwealth*, accused Rockefeller's Standard Oil Company of unfairly monopolizing the petroleum industry. Lloyd and others contended that industries in which competition had been destroyed by corporate consolidation or monopoly should be brought under government regulation or ownership to ensure that the American public would not be abused.

America's post–Civil War industrial revolution placed the issues of wealth and poverty at the forefront of American life. The following viewpoints present some differing opinions on the effects of large-scale industrialization.

VIEWPOINT 1

"Beneath all political problems lies the social problem of the distribution of wealth."

Concentrations of Wealth Harm America

Henry George (1839–1897)

Henry George was a social reformer whose prolific writings on social and economic conditions, especially his 1879 book *Progress and Poverty*, were widely read. George's prescription of a "single tax" on property to replace all other taxes was never enacted by the states or by Congress, but he remained an influential critic of America until his death.

The following viewpoint is taken from George's 1883 book *Social Problems*. George asserts that advances in technology and industrialization have helped to transform American society from a relatively egalitarian one into one in which a fortunate few amass immense wealth while large numbers of workers and their families remain poor and powerless. George criticizes concentrations of wealth for two main reasons. First, he argues that wealthy individuals such as railroad magnates Henry Villard and Jay Gould are able to influence government decision making, thereby threatening America's democratic system of government. Second, he contends that personal fortunes are being made through methods of "spoliation"—including stock speculation, tariff laws, and monopolies—that exploit others and do not benefit society as a whole. George rejects arguments that economic inequalities reflect personal attributes of intelligence or laziness, asserting that they are instead the products of social conditions that could be corrected with the proper reforms.

From Henry George, *Social Problems* (New York, 1883).

There is in all the past nothing to compare with the rapid changes now going on in the civilized world. It seems as though in the European race, and in the nineteenth century, man was just beginning to live—just grasping his tools and becoming conscious of his powers. The snail's pace of crawling ages has suddenly become the headlong rush of the locomotive, speeding faster and faster. This rapid progress is primarily in industrial methods and material powers. But industrial changes imply social changes and necessitate political changes. Progressive societies outgrow institutions as children outgrow clothes. Social progress always requires greater intelligence in the management of public affairs; but this the more as progress is rapid and change quicker. . . .

Wealth and Civilization

A civilization which tends to concentrate wealth and power in the hands of a fortunate few, and to make of others mere human machines, must inevitably evolve anarchy and bring destruction. But a civilization is possible in which the poorest could have all the comforts and conveniences now enjoyed by the rich; in which prisons and almshouses would be needless, and charitable societies unthought of. Such a civilization waits only for the social intelligence that will adapt means to ends. Powers that might give plenty to all are already in our hands. Though there is poverty and want, there is, yet, seeming embarrassment from the very excess of wealth-producing forces. "Give us but a market," say manufacturers, "and we will supply goods without end!" "Give us but work!" cry idle men.

The evils that begin to appear spring from the fact that the application of intelligence to social affairs has not kept pace with the application of intelligence to individual needs and material ends. Natural science strides forward, but political science lags. With all our progress in the arts which produce wealth, we have made no progress in securing its equitable distribution. Knowledge has vastly increased; industry and commerce have been revolutionized; but whether free trade or protection is best for a nation we are not yet agreed. We have brought machinery to a pitch of perfection that, fifty years ago, could not have been imagined; but, in the presence of political corruption, we seem as helpless as idiots. The East River bridge is a crowning triumph of mechanical skill; but to get it built a leading citizen of Brooklyn had to carry to New York sixty thousand dollars in a carpet-bag to bribe New York aldermen. The human soul that thought out the great bridge is prisoned in a crazed and broken body that lies bedfast, and could watch it grow only by peering through a telescope. Nevertheless, the weight of the immense mass is estimated and adjusted for every inch. But the skill of the engineer could not prevent condemned wire being smuggled into the cable.

The progress of civilization requires that more and more intelligence be devoted to social affairs, and this not the intelligence of the few, but that of the many. We cannot safely leave politics to politicians, or political economy to college professors. The people themselves must think, because the people alone can act.

In a "journal of civilization" a professed teacher declares the saving word for society to be that each shall mind his own business. This is the gospel of selfishness, soothing as soft flutes to those who, having fared well themselves, think everybody should be satisfied. But the salvation of society, the hope for the free, full development of humanity, is in the gospel of brotherhood—the gospel of Christ. Social progress makes the well-being of all more and more the business of each; it binds all closer and closer together in bonds from which none can escape. He who observes the law and the proprieties, and cares for his family, yet takes no interest in the general weal, and gives no thought to those who are trodden under foot, save now and then to bestow alms, is not a true Christian. Nor is he a good citizen. The duty of the citizen is more and harder than this. . . .

There is a suggestive fact that must impress any one who thinks over the history of past eras and preceding civilizations. The great, wealthy and powerful nations have always lost their freedom; it is only in small, poor and isolated communities that Liberty has been maintained. So true is this that the poets have always sung that Liberty loves the rocks and the mountains; that she shrinks from wealth and power and splendor, from the crowded city and the busy mart. . . .

The mere growth of society involves danger of the gradual conversion of government into something independent of and beyond the people, and the gradual seizure of its powers by a ruling class—though not necessarily a class marked off by personal titles and a hereditary status, for, as history shows, personal titles and hereditary status do not accompany the concentration of power, but follow it. The same methods which, in a little town where each knows his neighbor and matters of common interest are under the common eye, enable the citizens freely to govern themselves, may, in a great city, as we have in many cases seen, enable an organized ring of plunderers to gain and hold the government. So, too, as we see in Congress, and even in our State legislatures, the growth of the country and the greater number of interests make the proportion of the votes of a representative, of which his constituents know or care to know, less and less. And so, too, the executive and judicial departments tend constantly to pass beyond the scrutiny of the people.

But to the changes produced by growth are, with us, added the changes brought about by improved industrial methods. The tendency of steam and of machinery is to the division of labor, to the concentration of wealth and power. Workmen are becoming massed by hundreds and thousands in the employ of single individuals and firms; small storekeepers and merchants are becoming the clerks and salesmen of great business houses; we have already corporations whose revenues and pay rolls belittle those of the greatest States. And with this concentration grows the facility of combination among these great business interests. How readily the railroad companies, the coal operators, the steel producers, even the match manufacturers, combine, either to regulate prices or to use the powers of government! The tendency in all branches of industry is to the formation of rings against which the individual is helpless, and which exert their power upon government whenever their interests may thus be served.

The Corruption of Government

It is not merely positively, but negatively, that great aggregations of wealth, whether individual or corporate, tend to corrupt government and take it out of the control of the masses of the people. "Nothing is more timorous than a million dollars—except two million dollars." Great wealth always supports the party in power, no matter how corrupt it may be. It never exerts itself for reform, for it instinctively fears change. It never struggles against misgovernment. When threatened by the holders of political power it does not agitate, nor appeal to the people; it buys them off. It is in this way, no less than by its direct interference, that aggregated wealth corrupts government, and helps to make politics a trade. Our organized lobbies, both legislative and Congressional, rely as much upon the fears as upon the hopes of moneyed interests. When "business" is dull, their resource is to get up a bill which some moneyed interest will pay them to beat. So, too, these large moneyed interests will subscribe to political funds, on the principle of keeping on the right side of those in power, just as the railroad companies deadhead [transport for free] President [Chester A.] Arthur when he goes to Florida to fish.

The more corrupt a government the easier wealth can use it. Where legislation is to be bought, the rich make the laws; where justice is to be purchased, the rich have the ear of the courts. And if, for this reason, great wealth does not absolutely prefer corrupt government to pure government, it becomes none the less a corrupting influence. A community composed of very rich and very poor falls an easy prey to whoever can seize power. The very poor have not spirit and intelligence enough to resist; the very rich have too much at stake.

The rise in the United States of monstrous fortunes, the aggregation of enormous wealth in the hands of corporations, necessarily implies the loss by the people of governmental control. Democratic forms may be maintained, but there can be as much tyranny and misgovernment under democratic forms as any other—in fact, they lend themselves most readily to tyranny and misgovernment. Forms count for little. The Romans expelled

---

Extremes of Wealth and Poverty

James Weaver, a former Civil War general and the Populist Party candidate for president in 1892, contrasted the lives of the very rich and the very poor in his 1892 pamphlet A Call to Action.

In the year 1884, as we are told by Ward McAllister in his book entitled *Society as I Found It,* a wealthy gentleman gave a banquet at Delmonico's at which the moderate number of seventy-two guests, ladies and gentlemen, were entertained. . . . The table was constructed with a miniature lake in the center thirty feet in length, enclosed by a network of golden wire which reached to the ceiling, forming a great cage. Four immense swans were secured from one of the parks and placed in this lake. High banks of flowers of every hue surrounded the lake and covered the entire table, leaving barely enough room for the plates and wine glasses. . . .

And then the feast! All the dishes which ingenuity could invent or the history of past extravagance suggest were spread before the guests. The oldest and costliest wines known to the trade flowed like the water that leaped down the cascades in the banqueting hall. . . .

In the year 1890, young Astor, a scion of the celebrated family which has so long been prominent in New York financial circles, was married. Both the groom and the bride represented millions of wealth and the wedding was an imposing and gorgeous affair. Twenty-five thousand dollars were expended on the day's ceremony. The presents were valued at $2 million, and the couple and their attendants and a number of friends immediately departed on an expensive yachting cruise which was to cost them $10,000 a month to maintain. . . .

About the time these princely entertainments were given, and in the same year with some of them, one of the metropolitan journals caused a careful canvass to be made of the unemployed of that city. The number was found to be *150,000 persons who were daily unsuccessfully seeking work within the city limits of New York.* Another 150,000 earn less than 60 cents per day. Thousands of these are poor girls who work from eleven to sixteen hours per day. In the year 1890, over 23,000 families, numbering about 100,000 people, were forcibly evicted in New York City owing to their inability to pay rent; and one-tenth of all who died in that city during the year were buried in the Potters Field.

their kings, and continued to abhor the very name of king. But under the name of Caesars and Imperators, that at first meant no more than our "Boss," they crouched before tyrants more absolute than kings. We have already, under the popular name of "bosses," developed political Caesars in municipalities and states. If this development continues, in time there will come a national boss. We are young; but we are growing. The day may arrive when the "Boss of America" will be to the modern world what Caesar was to the Roman world. This, at least, is certain: Democratic government in more than name can exist only where wealth is distributed with something like equality—where the great mass of citizens are personally free and independent, neither fettered by their poverty nor made subject by their wealth. There is, after all, some sense in a property qualification. The man who is dependent on a master for his living is not a free man. To give the suffrage to slaves is only to give votes to their owners. That universal suffrage may add to, instead of decreasing, the political power of wealth we see when mill-owners and mine operators vote their hands. The freedom to earn, without fear or favor, a comfortable living, ought to go with the freedom to vote. Thus alone can a sound basis for republican institutions be secured. How can a man be said to have a country where he has no right to a square inch of soil; where he has nothing but his hands, and, urged by starvation, must bid against his fellows for the privilege of using them? When it comes to voting tramps, some principle has been carried to a ridiculous and dangerous extreme. I have known elections to be decided by the carting of paupers from the almshouse to the polls. But such decisions can scarcely be in the interest of good government.

Beneath all political problems lies the social problem of the distribution of wealth. This our people do not generally recognize, and they listen to quacks who propose to cure the symptoms without touching the disease. "Let us elect good men to office," say the quacks. Yes; let us catch little birds by sprinkling salt on their tails!

It behooves us to look facts in the face. The experiment of popular government in the United States is clearly a failure. Not that it is a failure everywhere and in everything. An experiment of this kind does not have to be fully worked out to be proved a failure. But speaking generally of the whole country, from the Atlantic to the Pacific, and from the Lakes to the Gulf, our government by the people has in large degree become, is in larger degree becoming, government by the strong and unscrupulous.

The people, of course, continue to vote; but the people are losing their power. Money and organization tell more and more in elections. In some sections bribery has become chronic, and numbers of voters expect regularly to sell their votes. In some sections large employers regularly bulldoze their hands into voting as *they* wish. In municipal, State and Federal politics the power of the "machine" is increasing. In many places it has become so strong that the ordinary citizen has no more influence in the government under which he lives than he would have in China. He is, in reality, not one of the governing classes, but one of the governed. He occasionally, in disgust, votes for "the other man," or "the other party;" but, generally, to find that he has effected only a change of masters, or secured the same masters under different names. And he is beginning to accept the situation, and to leave politics to politicians, as something with which an honest, self-respecting man cannot afford meddle. . . .

As for the great railroad managers, they may well say, "The people be d—d!" When they want the power of the people they buy the people's masters. The map of the United States is colored to show States and Territories. A map of real political powers would ignore State lines. Here would be a big patch representing the domains of Vanderbilt; there Jay Gould's dominions would be brightly marked. In another place would be set off the empire of Stanford and Huntington; in another the newer empire of Henry Villard. The States and parts of States that own the sway of the Pennsylvania Central would be distinguished from those ruled by the Baltimore and Ohio; and so on. In our National Senate, sovereign members of the Union are supposed to be represented; but what are more truly represented are railroad kings and great moneyed interests, though occasionally a mine jobber from Nevada or Colorado, not inimical to the ruling powers, is suffered to buy himself a seat for glory. And the Bench as well as the Senate is being filled with corporation henchmen. A railroad king makes his attorney a judge of last resort, as the great lord used to make his chaplain a bishop. . . .

The people are largely conscious of all this, and there is among the masses much dissatisfaction. But there is a lack of that intelligent interest necessary to adapt political organization to changing conditions. The popular idea of reform seems to be merely a change of men or a change of parties, not a change of system. Political children, we attribute to bad men or wicked parties what really springs from deep general causes. . . .

Can Anyone Be Rich?

The comfortable theory that it is in the nature of things that some should be poor and some should be rich, and that the gross and constantly increasing inequalities in the distribution of wealth imply no fault in our institutions, pervades our literature, and is taught in the press, in the church, in school and in college.

This is a free country, we are told—every man has a vote and every man has a chance. The laborer's son may become President; poor boys of to-day will be millionaires thirty or forty years from now, and the millionaire's grandchildren will probably be poor. What more can be asked? If a man has energy, industry, prudence and foresight, he may win his way to great wealth. If he has not the ability to do this he must not complain of those who have. If some enjoy much and do little, it is because they, or their parents, possessed superior qualities which enabled them to "acquire property" or "make money." If others must work hard and get little, it is because they have not yet got their start, because they are ignorant, shiftless, unwilling to practise that economy necessary for the first accumulation of capital; or because their fathers were wanting in these respects. The inequalities in condition result from the inequalities of human nature, from the difference in the powers and capacities of different men. If one has to toil ten or twelve hours a day for a few hundred dollars a year, while another, doing little or no hard work, gets an income of many thousands, it is because all that the former contributes to the augmentation of the common stock of wealth is little more than the mere force of his muscles. He can expect little more than the animal, because he brings into play little more than animal powers. He is but a private in the ranks of the great army of industry, who has but to stand still or march, as he is bid. The other is the organizer, the general, who guides and wields the whole great machine, who must think, plan and provide; and his larger income is only commensurate with the far higher and rarer powers which he exercises, and the far greater importance of the function he fulfils. Shall not education have its reward, and skill its payment? What incentive would there be to the toil needed to learn to do anything well were great prizes not to be gained by those who learn to excel? It would not merely be gross injustice to refuse a Raphael or a Rubens more than a house-painter, but it would prevent the development of great painters. To destroy inequalities in condition would be to destroy the incentive to progress. To quarrel with them is to quarrel with the laws of nature. We might as well rail against the length of the days or the phases of the moon; complain that there are valleys and mountains; zones of tropical heat and regions of eternal ice. And were we by violent measures to divide wealth equally, we should accomplish nothing but harm; in a little while there would be inequalities as great as before.

This, in substance, is the teaching which we constantly hear. It is accepted by some because it is flattering to their vanity, in accordance with their interests or pleasing to their hope; by others, because it is dinned into their ears. Like all false theories that ob-

Andrew Carnegie's Wealth

Andrew Carnegie, one of America's leading nineteenth-century industrialists, wrote a famous 1889 article in which he defended the accumulation of wealth, but argued the rich had the responsibility to dispose of their wealth responsibly. Hugh Price Hughes, a British clergyman, argued in an 1890 review of Carnegie's article that the accumulation of wealth itself was immoral.

In a really Christian country—that is to say, in a community reconstructed upon a Christian basis—a millionaire would be an economic impossibility. Jesus Christ distinctly prohibited the accumulation of wealth. . . . No one now argues that millionaires are needed to carry out great public works like the Bridgewater Canal, because modern joint-stock enterprise, and the ever-increasing activity of the State, make us entirely independent of millionaires, and, indeed, capable of enterprises which no millionaire could attempt. They have now no beneficent *raison d'être*. They are the unnatural product of artificial social regulations. . . . Millionaires at one end of the scale involve paupers at the other end, and even so excellent a man as Mr. Carnegie is too dear at that price. Whatever may be thought of Mr. Henry George's doctrines and deductions, no one can deny that his facts are indisputable, and that Mr. Carnegie's 'progress' is accompanied by the growing 'poverty' of his less fortunate fellow-countrymen. I say 'less fortunate' because I am sure Mr. Carnegie is much too sensible a man to suppose for a moment that his vast fortune represents a proportionate superiority over the rest of his fellow citizens, or even over those who combined to create his fortune. . . .

In no sense whatever is a Pennsylvania millionaire ironmaster a natural, and therefore an inevitable, product. There is a total fallacy at the very foundation of Mr. Carnegie's argument. He assumes that millionaires are necessary results of modern industrial enterprise, and that consequently the only question ethical writers can discuss is the best way of enabling these unfortunate persons to get honestly and beneficently rid of their superfluous wealth. But there is a much more important prior question—how to save them from the calamity of finding themselves the possessors of a huge fortune which is full of most perilous temptation, both to themselves and to their children.

tain wide acceptance, it contains much truth. But it is truth isolated from other truth or alloyed with falsehood.

To try to pump out a ship with a hole in her hull would be hopeless; but that is not to say that leaks may not be stopped and ships pumped dry. It is undeniable that, under present conditions, inequalities in fortune would tend to reassert themselves even if arbitrarily leveled for a moment; but that does not prove that the conditions from which this tendency to inequality springs may not be altered. Nor because there are differences in human qualities and powers does it follow that existing inequalities of fortune are thus accounted for. I have seen very fast compositors and very slow compositors, but the fastest I ever saw could not set twice as much type as the slowest, and I doubt if in other trades the variations are greater. Between normal men the difference of a sixth or seventh is a great difference in height—the tallest giant ever known was scarcely more than four times as tall as the smallest dwarf ever known, and I doubt if any good observer will say that the mental differences of men are greater than the physical differences. Yet we already have men hundreds of millions of times richer than other men.

That he who produces should have, that he who saves should enjoy, is consistent with human reason and with the natural order. But existing inequalities of wealth cannot be justified on this ground. As a matter of fact, how many great fortunes can be truthfully said to have been fairly earned? How many of them represent wealth produced by their possessors or those from whom their present possessors derived them? Did there not go to the formation of all of them something more than superior industry and skill? Such qualities may give the first start, but when fortunes begin to roll up into millions there will always be found some element of monopoly, some appropriation of wealth produced by others. Often there is a total absence of superior industry, skill or self-denial, and merely better luck or greater unscrupulousness.

An acquaintance of mine died in San Francisco recently, leaving $4,000,000, which will go to heirs to be looked up in England. I have known many men more industrious, more skilful, more temperate than he—men who did not or who will not leave a cent. This man did not get his wealth by his industry, skill or temperance. He no more produced it than did those lucky relations in England who may now do nothing for the rest of their lives. He became rich by getting hold of a piece of land in the early days, which, as San Francisco grew, became very valuable. His wealth represented not what he had earned, but what the monopoly of this bit of the earth's surface enabled him to appropriate of the earnings of others.

A man died in Pittsburgh, the other day, leaving $3,000,000. He may or may not have been particularly industrious, skilful and economical, but it was not by virtue of these qualities that he got so rich. It was because he went to Washington and helped lobby through a bill which, by way of "protecting American workmen against the pauper labor of Europe," gave him the advantage of a sixty-per-cent. tariff. To the day of his death he was a stanch protectionist, and said free trade would ruin our "infant industries."

Evidently the $3,000,000 which he was enabled to lay by from his own little cherub of an "infant industry" did not represent what he had added to production. It was the advantage given him by the tariff that enabled him to scoop it up from other people's earnings.

Great Fortunes

This element of monopoly, of appropriation and spoliation will, when we come to analyze them, be found largely to account for all great fortunes. . . .

Take the great Gould fortune. Mr. Gould might have got his first little start by superior industry and superior self-denial. But it is not that which has made him the master of a hundred millions. It was by wrecking railroads, buying judges, corrupting legislatures, getting up rings and pools and combinations to raise or depress stock values and transportation rates.

So, likewise, of the great fortunes which the Pacific railroads have created. They have been made by lobbying through profligate donations of lands, bonds and subsidies, by the operations of Crédit Mobilier and Contract and Finance Companies, by monopolizing and gouging. And so of fortunes made by such combinations as the Standard Oil Company, the Bessemer Steel Ring, the Whisky Tax Ring, the Lucifer Match Ring, and the various rings for the "protection of the American workman from the pauper labor of Europe.". . .

Through all great fortunes, and, in fact, through nearly all acquisitions that in these days can fairly be termed fortunes, these elements of monopoly, of spoliation, of gambling run. The head of one of the largest manufacturing firms in the United States said to me recently, "It is not on our ordinary business that we make our money; it is where we can get a monopoly." And this, I think, is generally true.

The Evils of Monopolists

Consider the important part in building up fortunes which the increase of land values has had, and is having, in the United States. This is, of course, monopoly, pure and simple. When land increases in value it does not mean that its owner has added to the general wealth. The owner may never have seen the land or done aught to improve it. He may, and often does, live in a distant city or in another country. Increase of land values simply means that the owners, by virtue of their appropriation of something that existed before man was, have the power of taking a larger share of the wealth produced by other people's labor. Consider how much the monopolies created and the advantages given to the unscrupulous by the tariff and by our system of internal taxation—how much the railroad (a business in its nature a monopoly), telegraph, gas, water and other similar monopolies, have done to concentrate wealth; how special rates, pools, combinations, corners, stock-watering and stock-gambling, the destructive use of wealth in driving off or buying off opposition which the public must finally pay for, and many other things which these will suggest, have operated to build up large fortunes, and it will at least appear that the unequal distribution of wealth is due in great measure to sheer spoliation; that the reason why those who work hard get so little, while so many who work little get so much, is, in very large measure, that the earnings of the one class are, in one way or another, filched away from them to swell the incomes of the other.

That individuals are constantly making their way from the ranks of those who get less than their earnings to the ranks of those who get more than their earnings, no more proves this state of things right than the fact that merchant sailors were constantly becoming pirates and participating in the profits of piracy, would prove that piracy was right and that no effort should be made to suppress it.

I am not denouncing the rich, nor seeking, by speaking of these things, to excite envy and hatred; but if we would get a clear understanding of social problems, we must recognize the fact that it is due to monopolies which we permit and create, to advantages which we give one man over another, to methods of extortion sanctioned by law and by public opinion, that some men are enabled to get so enormously rich while others remain so miserably poor. If we look around us and note the elements of monopoly, extortion and spoliation which go to the building up of all, or nearly all, fortunes, we see on the one hand how disingenuous are those who preach to us that there is nothing wrong in social relations and that the inequalities in the distribution of wealth spring from the inequalities of human nature; and on the other hand, we see how wild are those who talk as though capital were a public enemy, and propose plans for arbitrarily restricting the acquisition of wealth. Capital is a good; the capitalist is a helper, if he is not also a monopolist. We can safely let any one get as rich as he can if he will not despoil others in doing so.

The Ideal Social State

There are deep wrongs in the present constitution of society, but they are not wrongs inherent in the constitution of man nor in those social laws which are as truly the laws of the Creator as are the laws of the physical universe. They are wrongs resulting from bad adjustments which it is within our power to amend. The ideal social state is not that in which each gets an equal amount of wealth, but in which each gets in proportion to his contribution to the general stock. And in such a social state there would not be less incentive to exertion than now; there would be far more incentive. Men will be more industrious and more moral, better workmen and better citizens, if each takes his earnings and carries them home to his family, than where they put their earnings in a "pot" and gamble for them until some have far more than they could have earned, and others have little or nothing.

VIEWPOINT 2

"Not evil, but good, has come to the race from the accumulation of wealth by those who have had the ability and energy to produce it."

Concentrations of Wealth Help America

Andrew Carnegie (1835–1919)

Andrew Carnegie was in some respects a personification of the industrial revolution in America and the wealth it created, both for the nation and for individual industrialists. A Scottish immigrant who rose from poverty to become a successful investor and railway executive, Carnegie entered the fledgling steel industry while in his thirties. Exploiting the Bessemer process and other new technologies, using careful and coordinated accounting practices, and keeping tight control over wages and salaries, Carnegie was able to attain domination of the steel industry in the United States while dropping the price of steel from over $100 a ton in 1873 to less than $20 a ton by the 1890s. In addition to steel mills, Carnegie owned coal fields, iron ore mines, and shipping companies. The steel his enterprises made helped construct America's railroads, machines, bridges, and buildings, made America's steel industry number one in the world, and amassed Carnegie a fortune estimated at one point to be more than $400 million.

Some criticized the rise of wealthy individuals such as Carnegie as a harmful effect of the industrial revolution. In the following viewpoint, which is excerpted from an article that first appeared in the June 1889 issue of the *North American Review*, Carnegie defends the creation of concentrations of wealth as an inevitable and necessary part of industrial progress. He also contends that

From Andrew Carnegie, "Wealth," *North American Review*, June 1889.

affluent people should responsibly contribute their fortune to worthy social causes. Before he died, Carnegie himself gave away much of his fortune to various philanthropies, including public libraries, research foundations, and organizations such as the Carnegie Endowment for International Peace.

The problem of our age is the proper administration of wealth, that the ties of brotherhood may still bind together the rich and poor in harmonious relationship. The conditions of human life have not only been changed, but revolutionized, within the past few hundred years. In former days there was little difference between the dwelling, dress, food, and environment of the chief and those of his retainers. The Indians are today where civilized man then was. When visiting the Sioux, I was led to the wigwam of the chief. It was like the others in external appearance, and even within the difference was trifling between it and those of the poorest of his braves. The contrast between the palace of the millionaire and the cottage of the laborer with us today measures the change which has come with civilization. This change, however, is not to be deplored, but welcomed as highly beneficial. It is well, nay, essential, for the progress of the race that the houses of some should be homes for all that is highest and best in literature and the arts, and for all the refinements of civilization, rather than that none should be so. Much better this great irregularity than universal squalor. Without wealth there can be no Maecenas [a generous patron of the arts]. The "good old times" were not good old times. Neither master nor servant was as well situated then as today. A relapse to old conditions would be disastrous to both—not the least so to him who serves—and would sweep away civilization with it. But whether the change be for good or ill, it is upon us, beyond our power to alter, and, therefore, to be accepted and made the best of. It is a waste of time to criticize the inevitable.

It is easy to see how the change has come. One illustration will serve for almost every phase of the cause. In the manufacture of products we have the whole story. It applies to all combinations of human industry, as stimulated and enlarged by the inventions of this scientific age. Formerly, articles were manufactured at the domestic hearth, or in small shops which formed part of the household. The master and his apprentices worked side by side, the latter living with the master, and therefore subject to the same conditions. When these apprentices rose to be masters, there was little or no change in their mode of life, and they, in turn, educated succeeding apprentices in the same routine. There was, substantially, social equality, and even political equality, for those engaged in industrial pursuits had then little or no voice in the State.

The inevitable result of such a mode of manufacture was crude articles at high prices. Today the world obtains commodities of excellent quality at prices which even the preceding generation would have deemed incredible. In the commercial world similar causes have produced similar results, and the race is benefited thereby. The poor enjoy what the rich could not before afford. What were the luxuries have become the necessaries of life. The laborer has now more comforts than the farmer had a few generations ago. The farmer has more luxuries than the landlord had, and is more richly clad and better housed. The landlord has books and pictures rarer and appointments more artistic than the king could then obtain.

The price we pay for this salutary change is, no doubt, great. We assemble thousands of operatives in the factory, and in the mine, of whom the employer can know little or nothing, and to whom he is little better than a myth. All intercourse between them is at an end. Rigid castes are formed, and, as usual, mutual ignorance breeds mutual distrust. Each caste is without sympathy with the other, and ready to credit anything disparaging in regard to it. Under the law of competition, the employer of thousands is forced into the strictest economies, among which the rates paid to labor figure prominently, and often there is friction between the employer and the employed, between capital and labor, between rich and poor. Human society loses homogeneity.

Concentrations of Wealth Are Essential

The price which society pays for the law of competition, like the price it pays for cheap comforts and luxuries, is also great; but the advantages of this law are also greater still than its cost—for it is to this law that we owe our wonderful material development, which brings improved conditions in its train. But, whether the law be benign or not, we must say of it, as we say of the change in the conditions of men to which we have referred: It is here; we cannot evade it; no substitutes for it have been found; and while the law may be sometimes hard for the individual, it is best for the race, because it insures the survival of the fittest in every department. We accept and welcome, therefore, as conditions to which we must accommodate ourselves, great inequality of environment; the concentration of business, industrial and commercial, in the hands of a few; and the law of competition between these, as being not only beneficial, but essential to the future progress of the race. Having accepted these, it follows that there must be great scope for the exercise of special ability in the merchant and in the manufacturer who has to conduct affairs upon a great scale. That this talent for organization and management is rare among men is proved by the fact that it invariably secures enormous rewards for its possessor, no matter where or under what laws or conditions. The experienced in affairs always rate the MAN whose services can be obtained as a partner as not only the first consideration, but such as render the question of his capital scarcely worth considering: for able men soon create capital; in the hands of those without the special talent required, capital soon takes wings. Such men become interested in firms or corporations using millions; and, estimating only simple interest to be made upon the capital invested, it is inevitable that their income must exceed their expenditure and that they must, therefore, accumulate wealth. Nor is there any middle ground which such men can occupy, because the great manufacturing or commercial concern which does not earn at least interest upon its capital soon becomes bankrupt. It must either go forward or fall behind; to stand still is impossible. It is a condition essential to its successful operation that it should be thus far profitable, and even that, in addition to interest on capital, it should make profit. It is a law, as certain as any of the others named, that men possessed of this peculiar talent for affairs, under the free play of economic forces must, of necessity, soon be in receipt of more revenue than can be judiciously expended upon themselves, and this law is as beneficial for the race as the others.

Attacks on Civilization

Objections to the foundations upon which society is based are not in order, because the condition of the race is better with these than it has been with any other which has been tried. Of the effect of any new substitutes proposed we cannot be sure. The Socialist or Anarchist who seeks to overturn present conditions is to be regarded as attacking the foundation upon which civilization itself rests, for civilization took its start from the day when the capable, industrious workman said to his incompetent and lazy fellow, "If thou dost not sow, thou shalt not reap," and thus ended primitive Communism by separating the drones from the bees. One who studies this subject will soon be brought face to face with the conclusion that upon the sacredness of property civilization itself depends—the right of the laborer to his hundred dollars in the savings-bank, and equally the legal right of the millionaire to his millions. Every man must be allowed "to sit under his own vine and fig-tree, with none to make afraid," if human society is to advance, or even to remain so far advanced as it is. To those who propose to substitute Communism for this intense Individualism, the answer therefore is: The race has tried that. All progress from that barbarous day to the present time has resulted from its displacement. Not evil, but good, has come to the race from the accumulation of wealth by those who have had the ability and energy to produce it. But even if we admit for a moment that it might be better for the race to discard its present foundation, Individualism—that it is a nobler ideal that man should labor, not for himself alone, but in and for a brotherhood of his fellows, and share with them all in common, realizing [Emanuel] Swedenborg's idea of heaven, where, as he says, the angels derive their happiness, not from laboring for self, but for each other—even admit all this, and a sufficient answer is, This is not evolution, but revolution. It necessitates the changing of human nature itself—a work of eons, even if it were good to change it, which we cannot know.

Andrew Carnegie rose from poverty to become one of the world's richest men. In 1901 he sold his steel company interest to the United States Steel Corporation, a corporate entity created by Wall Street financier J. Pierpont Morgan, for $250 million.

It is not practicable in our day or in our age. Even if desirable theoretically, it belongs to another and long-succeeding sociological stratum. Our duty is with what is practicable now—with the next step possible in our day and generation. It is criminal to waste our energies in endeavoring to uproot, when all we can profitably accomplish is to bend the universal tree of humanity a little in the direction most favorable to the production of good fruit under existing circumstances. We might as well urge the destruction of the highest existing type of man because he failed to reach our ideal as to favor the destruction of Individualism, Private Property, the Law of Accumulation of Wealth, and the Law of Competition; for these are the highest result of human experience, the soil in which society, so far, has produced the best fruit. Unequally or unjustly, perhaps, as these laws sometimes operate, and imperfect as they appear to the Idealist, they are, nevertheless, like the highest type of man, the best and most valuable of all that humanity has yet accomplished.

We start, then, with a condition of affairs under which the best interests of the race are promoted, but which inevitably gives wealth to the few. Thus far, accepting conditions as they exist, the situation can be surveyed and pronounced good. The question then arises—and if the foregoing be correct, it is the only question with which we have to deal—What is the proper mode of administering wealth after the laws upon which civilization is founded have thrown it into the hands of the few? And it is of this great question that I believe I offer the true solution. It will be understood that fortunes are here spoken of, not moderate sums saved by many years of effort, the returns from which are required for the comfortable maintenance and education of families. This is not wealth, but only competence, which it should be the aim of all to acquire, and which it is for the best interests of society should be acquired.

Disposing of Surplus Wealth

There are but three modes in which surplus wealth can be disposed of. It can be left to the families of the decedents; or it can be bequeathed for public purposes; or, finally, it can be administered by its possessors during their lives. Under the first and second modes most of the wealth of the world that has reached the few has hitherto been applied. Let us in turn consider each of these modes. The first is the most injudicious. In monarchical countries, the estates and the greatest portion of the wealth are left to the first son, that the vanity of the parent may be gratified by the thought that his name and title are to descend unimpaired to succeeding generations. The condition of this class in Europe today teaches the failure of such hopes or ambitions. The successors have become impoverished through their follies, or from the fall in the value of land. Even in Great Britain the strict law of entail has been found inadequate to maintain an hereditary class. Its soil is rapidly passing into the hands of the stranger. Under republican institutions the division of property among the children is much fairer; but the question which forces itself upon thoughtful men in all lands is, Why should men leave great fortunes to their children? If this is done from affection, is it not misguided affection? Observation teaches that, generally speaking, it is not well for the children that they should be so burdened. Neither is it well for the State. Beyond providing for the wife and daughters moderate sources of income, and very moderate allowances indeed, if any, for the sons, men may well hesitate; for it is no longer questionable that great sums bequeathed often work more for the injury than for the good of the recipients. Wise men will soon conclude that, for the best interests of the members of their families, and of the State, such bequests are an improper use of their means. . . .

As to the second mode, that of leaving wealth at death for public uses, it may be said that this is only a means for the disposal of wealth, provided a man is content to wait until he is dead before he becomes of much good in the world. Knowledge of the results of legacies bequeathed is not calculated to inspire the brightest hopes of much posthumous good being accomplished by them. The cases are not few in which the real object sought by the testator is not attained, nor are they few in which his real wishes are thwarted. In many cases the bequests are so used as to become only monuments of his folly. It is well to remember that it requires the exercise of not less ability than that which acquired it, to use wealth so as to be really beneficial to the community. Besides this, it may fairly be said that no man is to be extolled for doing what he cannot help doing, nor is he to be thanked by the community to which he only leaves wealth at death. Men who leave vast sums in this way may fairly be thought men who would not have left it at all had they been able to take it with them. The memories of such cannot be held in grateful remembrance, for there is no grace in their gifts. It is not to be wondered at that such bequests seem so generally to lack the blessing. . . .

There remains, then, only one mode of using great fortunes; but in this we have the true antidote for the temporary unequal distribution of wealth, the reconciliation of the rich and the poor—a reign of harmony, another ideal, differing, indeed, from that of the Communist in requiring only the further evolution of existing conditions, not the total overthrow of our civilization. It is founded upon the present most intense Individualism, and the race is prepared to put it in practice by degrees whenever it pleases. Under its sway we shall have an ideal State, in which the surplus wealth of the few will become, in the best sense, the property of the many, because administered for the common good; and this wealth, passing through the hands of the few, can be made a much more potent force for the elevation of our race than if distributed in small sums to the people themselves. Even the poorest can be made to see this, and to agree that great sums gathered by some of their fellow-citizens and spent for public purposes, from which the masses reap the principal benefit, are more valuable to them than if scattered among themselves in trifling amounts through the course of many years.

If we consider the results which flow from the Cooper Institute [an adult education institute founded by industrialist and philanthropist Peter Cooper], for instance, to the best portion of the race in New York not possessed of means, and compare these with those which would have ensued for the good of the masses from an equal sum distributed by Mr. Cooper in his lifetime in the form of wages, which is the highest form of distribution, being for work done and not for charity, we can form some estimate of the possibilities for the improvement of the race which lie embedded in the present law of the accumulation of wealth. Much of this sum, if distributed in small quantities among the people, would have been wasted in the indulgence of appetite, some of it in excess, and it may be doubted whether even the part put to the best use, that of adding to the comforts of the home, would have yielded results for the race, as a race, at all comparable to those which are flowing and are to flow from the Cooper Institute from generation to generation. Let the advocate of violent or radical change ponder well this thought. . . .

The Duty of the Man of Wealth

This, then, is held to be the duty of the man of wealth: To set an example of modest, unostentatious living, shunning display or extravagance; to provide moderately for the legitimate wants of those dependent upon him; and, after doing so, to consider all surplus revenues which come to him simply as trust funds, which he is called upon to administer, and strictly bound as a matter of duty to administer in the manner which, in his judgment, is best calculated to produce the most beneficial results for the community—the man of wealth thus becoming the mere trustee and agent for his poorer brethren, bringing to their service his superior wisdom, experience, and ability to administer, doing for them better than they would or could do for themselves. . . .

In bestowing charity, the main consideration should be to help those who will help themselves; to provide part of the means by which those who desire to improve may do so; to give those who desire to rise the aids by which they may rise; to assist, but rarely or never to do all. Neither the individual nor the race is improved by almsgiving. Those worthy of assistance, except in rare cases, seldom require assistance. The really valuable men of the race never do, except in case of accident or sudden change. Every one has, of course, cases of individuals brought to his own knowledge where temporary assistance can do genuine good, and these he will not overlook. But the amount which can be wisely given by the individual for individuals is necessarily limited by his lack of knowledge of the circumstances connected with each. He is the only true reformer who is as careful and as anxious not to aid the unworthy as he is to aid the worthy, and, perhaps, even more so, for in almsgiving more injury is probably done by rewarding vice than by relieving virtue.

The rich man is thus almost restricted to following the examples of Peter Cooper, Enoch Pratt of Baltimore, . . . and others, who know that the best means of benefiting the community is to place within its reach the ladders upon which the aspiring can rise—free libraries, parks, and means of recreation, by which men are helped in body and mind; works of art, certain to give pleasure and improve the public taste; and public institutions of various kinds, which will improve the general condition of the people; in this manner returning their surplus wealth to the mass of their fellows in the forms best calculated to do them lasting good.

Thus is the problem of rich and poor to be solved. The laws of accumulation will be left free, the laws of distribution free. Individualism will continue, but the millionaire will be but a trustee for the poor, intrusted for a season with a great part of the increased wealth of the community, for administering it for the community far better than it could or would have done for itself. The best minds will thus have reached a stage in the development of the race in which it is clearly seen that there is no mode of disposing of surplus wealth creditable to thoughtful and earnest men into whose hands it flows, save by using it year by year for the general good. This day already dawns. Men may die without incurring the pity of their fellows, still sharers in great business enterprises from which their capital cannot be or has not been withdrawn, and which is left chiefly at death for public uses; yet the day is not far distant when the man who dies leaving behind him millions of available wealth, which was free for him to administer during life, will pass away "unwept, unhonored, and unsung," no matter to what uses he leaves the dross which he cannot take with him. Of such as these the public verdict will then be "The man who dies thus rich dies disgraced."

Such, in my opinion, is the true gospel concerning wealth, obedience to which is destined some day to solve the problem of the rich and the poor, and to bring "Peace on earth, among men good will."

VIEWPOINT 3

"We Socialists propose that society in its collective capacity shall produce, not for profit, but in abundance to satisfy human wants."

Industrialization Has Created the Need for Radical Social Reform

Eugene V. Debs (1855–1926)

Eugene V. Debs was a labor organizer who ran for president five times between 1900 and 1920 as the nominee of the Socialist Party. The following viewpoint is taken from a May 23, 1908, speech he made in Girard, Kansas, upon receiving the party's nomination for president in that year's election.

Born and raised in the small town of Terre Haute, Indiana, Debs became a railway worker and secretary of the local lodge of the Brotherhood of Locomotive Firemen. He rose to become national secretary and treasurer of the organization, but by 1893 he had come to believe that the craft unionism it represented held workers back by dividing them into separate groups. He left the brotherhood to organize the American Railway Union—an industrial union that welcomed all classes of railway workers. Membership in the ARU soared after a successful strike against the Great Northern Railroad in 1893. However, the ARU's 1894 strike against the Pullman Company of Chicago was broken after the company received assistance from the federal government; Chicago was occupied by federal troops and Debs was sentenced to prison by a federal judge for disobeying a court injunction against strikes. The Pullman experience led Debs to conclude that trade unions alone could not improve the state of America's

From Eugene V. Debs, speech given in Girard, Kansas, May 23, 1908.

workers and that socialism was the answer to the problems of the nation's poor and working classes.

In his 1908 speech, Debs argues that changes in industry over the past fifty years have taken away the economic independence of working Americans by making their livelihood dependent on a wealthy few who control the machinery and capital, creating masses of demoralized and impoverished people in America's cities. He asserts that the only way for most Americans to realize the benefits of industrialism for themselves is to place the factories and other properties under public ownership and control.

The Socialist Party was only one of several organizations that called for radical change in America's economy and society during this period. Others included the Populist Party, which peaked in the 1890s, and the Industrial Workers of the World (IWW), founded in 1905. Debs achieved his best showing in a presidential election in 1912, when he received 6 percent of the vote.

My friends, I am opposed to the system of society in which we live today, not because I lack the natural equipment to do for myself, but because I am not satisfied to make myself comfortable knowing that there are thousands upon thousands of my fellow men who suffer for the barest necessities of life. We were taught under the old ethic that man's business upon this earth was to look out for himself. That was the ethic of the jungle; the ethic of the wild beast. Take care of yourself, no matter what may become of your fellow man. Thousands of years ago the question was asked: "Am I my brother's keeper?" That question has never yet been answered in a way that is satisfactory to civilized society.

Yes, I am my brother's keeper. I am under a moral obligation to him that is inspired, not by any maudlin sentimentality, but by the higher duty I owe to myself. What would you think of me if I were capable of seating myself at a table and gorging myself with food and saw about me the children of my fellow beings starving to death?

Allow me to say to you, my fellow men, that nature has spread a great table bounteously for all of the children of men. There is room for all and there is a plate and a place and food for all, and any system of society that denies a single one the right and the opportunity to freely help himself to nature's bounties is an unjust and iniquitous system that ought to be abolished in the interest of a higher humanity and a civilization worthy of the name. . . .

I am in revolt against capitalism (and that doesn't mean to say, my friends, that I am hating you—not the slightest). I am opposed to capitalism because I love my fellow men, and if I am opposing you for what I believe to be your good, and though you spat upon me with contempt I should still oppose you to the extent of my power.

I don't hate the workingman because he has turned against me. I know the poor fellow is too ignorant to understand his self-interest, and I know that as a rule the workingman is the friend of his enemy and the enemy of his friend. He votes for men who represent a system in which labor is simply merchandise; in which the man who works the hardest and longest has the least to show for it.

If there is a man on this earth who is entitled to all the comforts and luxuries of this life in abundance it is the man whose labor produces them. If he is not, who is? Does he get them in the present system? . . .

A Right to Work

According to the most reliable reports at our command, as I speak here this afternoon there are at least four millions of workingmen daily searching for employment. Have you ever found yourself in that unspeakably sad predicament? Have you ever had to go up the street, begging for work, in a great city thronged with humanity—and, by the way, my friends, people are never quite so strange to each other as when they are forced into artificial, crowded and stifled relationship.

I would rather be friendless out on the American desert than to be friendless in New York or Chicago. Have you ever walked up one side of the street and come back on the other side, while your wife, Mary, was waiting at home with three or four children for you to report that you had found work? Quite fortunately for me I had an experience of similar nature quite early in my life. Quite fortunately because, had I not known from my own experience just what it is to have to beg for work, just what it is to be shown the door as if I were a very offensive intruder, had I not known what it is to suffer for the want of food, had I not seen every door closed and barred in my face, had I not found myself friendless and alone in the city as a boy looking for work, and in vain, perhaps I would not be here this afternoon. I might have grown up, as some others have who have been, as they regard themselves, fortunate. I might have waved aside my fellowmen and said, "Do as I have done. If you are without work it is your own fault. Look at me; I am self-made. No man is under the necessity of looking for work if he is willing to work."

Nothing is more humiliating than to have to beg for work, and a system in which any man has to beg for work stands condemned.

No man can defend it. Now the rights of one are as sacred as the rights of a million. Suppose you happen to be the one who has no work. This republic is a failure so far as you are concerned. Every man has the inalienable right to work.

A Revolution in Industry

Now, there has been a revolution in industry during the last fifty years, but the trouble with most people is that they haven't kept pace with it. They don't know anything about it and they are especially innocent in regard to it in the small western cities and states, where the same old conditions of a century ago still largely prevail. Your grandfather could help himself anywhere. All he needed was some cheap, simple primitive tools and he could then apply his labor to the resources of nature with his individual tools and produce what he needed. That era in our history produced our greatest men. Lincoln himself sprang from this primitive state of society. People have said, "Why, he had no chance. See how great he became." Yes, but Lincoln had for his comrades great, green-plumed forest monarchs. He could put his arms about them and hear their heart-throbs, as they whispered; "Go on, Abe, a great destiny awaits you." He was in partnership with nature. He associated with birds and bees and flowers, and he was in the fields and heard the rippling music of the laughing brooks and streams. Nature took him to her bosom and nourished him, and from his unpolluted heart there sprang his noble aspirations.

Had Lincoln been born in a sweatshop he would never have been heard of.

How is it with the babe that is born in Mott street, or in the lower Bowery, or in the east side of New York City? That is where thousands, tens of thousands and hundreds of thousands of babes are born who are to constitute our future generations.

I have seen children ten years of age in New York City who had never seen a live chicken. The babes there don't know what it is to put their tiny feet on a blade of grass. It is the most densely populated spot on earth.

You have seen your bee-hive—just fancy a human bee-hive of which yours is the miniature and you have the industrial hive under capitalism. If you have never seen this condition you are excusable for not being a Socialist. Come to New York, Chicago, San Francisco with me; remain with me just twenty-four hours, and then look into my face as I shall look into yours when I ask: "What about Socialism now?" These children by hundreds and thousands are born in sub-cellars, where a whole grown family is crowded together in one room, where modesty between the sexes is absolutely impossible. They are surrounded by filth and vermin. From their birth they see nothing but immorality and vice and crime. They are tainted in the cradle. They are inoculated by their surroundings and they are doomed from the beginning. This system takes their lives just as certainly as if a dagger were thrust into their quivering little hearts, and let me say to you that it were better for many thousands of them if they had never seen the light.

Socialist Party Platform

The 1912 Socialist Party platform included the following passages on industrialism, capitalism, and the plight of American workers.

The Socialist party declares that the capitalist system has outgrown its historical function, and has become utterly incapable of meeting the problems now confronting society. We denounce this outgrown system as incompetent and corrupt and the source of unspeakable misery and suffering to the whole working class.

Under this system the industrial equipment of the nation has passed into the absolute control of a plutocracy which exacts an annual tribute of hundreds of millions of dollars from the producers. Unafraid of any organized resistance, it stretches out its greedy hands over the still undeveloped resources of the nation—the land, the mines, the forests and the water powers of every State of the Union.

In spite of the multiplication of labor-saving machines and improved methods in industry which cheapen the cost of production, the share of the producers grows ever less, and the prices of all the necessities of life steadily increase. The boasted prosperity of this nation is for the owning class alone. To the rest it means only greater hardship and misery. The high cost of living is felt in every home. Millions of wage-workers have seen the purchasing power of their wages decrease until life has become a desperate battle for mere existence.

Now I submit, my friends, that such a condition as this is indefensible in the twentieth century. . . .

Nature's storehouse is full to the surface of the earth. All of the raw materials are deposited here in abundance. We have the most marvelous machinery the world has ever known. Man has long since become master of the natural forces and made them work for him. Now he has but to touch a button and the wheels begin to spin and the machinery to whirr, and wealth is produced on every hand in increasing abundance.

Why should any man, woman or child suffer for food, clothing or shelter? Why? The question cannot be answered. Don't tell me that some men are too lazy to work. Suppose they are too lazy to work, what do you think of a social system that produces men too lazy to work? If a man is too lazy to work don't treat him with contempt. Don't look down upon him with scorn as if you were a superior being. If there is a man who is too lazy to work there is something the matter with him. He wasn't born right or he was perverted in this system. You could not, if you tried, keep a normal man inactive, and if you did he would go stark mad. Go to any penitentiary and you will find the men there begging for the privilege of doing work.

Can you tell me why there wasn't a tramp in the United States in 1860? In that day, if some one had said "tramp," no one would have known what was meant by it. If human nature is innately depraved and men would rather ride on brake-beams and sleep in holes and caves instead of comfortable beds, if they would do that from pure choice and from natural depravity, why were they not built that way fifty years ago? Fifty years ago capitalism was in its earlier stages. Fifty years ago work was still mainly done by hand, and every boy could learn a trade and every boy could master the tools and go to work. That is why there were no tramps. In fifty years that simple tool has become a mammoth machine. It gets larger and larger all the time. It has crowded the hand tool out of production. With the machine came the capitalist.

Machines and Capitalism

There were no capitalists, nor was there such a thing as capital before the beginning of the present system. Capitalists came with machinery. Up to the time that machinery supplanted the hand tool the little employer was himself a workingman. No matter what the shop or factory, you would find the employer working side by side with his men. He was a superior workman who got more orders than he could fill and employed others to help him, but he had to pay them the equivalent of what they produced because if he did not they would pack up their tools and go into business for themselves.

Now, the individual tool has become the mammoth machine. It has multiplied production by hundreds. The old tool was individually owned and used. The modern tool, in the form of a great machine, is social in every conception of it. Look at one of these giant machines. Come to the Appeal Office and look at the press in operation. Here the progressive conception of the ages is crystallized. What individual shall put his hand on this social agency and say, "This is mine! He who would apply labor here must first pay tribute to me."

The hand tool has been very largely supplanted by this machine. Not many tools arc left. You arc still producing in a very small way here in Girard, but your production is flickering out gradually. It is but a question of time until it will expire entirely.

In spite of all that can be said or done to the contrary production is organizing upon a larger and larger scale and becoming entirely co-operative. This has crowded out the smaller competitor and gradually opened the way for a new social order.

Your material interest and mine in the society of the future will be the same. Instead of having to fight each other like animals, as we do today, and seeking to glorify the brute struggle for existence—of which every civilized human being ought to be ashamed—instead of this, our material interests are going to be mutual. We are going to jointly own these mammoth machines, and we are going to operate them as joint partners and we are going to divide all the products among ourselves.

We are not going to send our surplus to the Goulds and Vanderbilts of New York. We are not going to pile up a billion of dollars in John D. Rockefeller's hands—a vast pyramid from the height of which he can look down with scorn and contempt upon the "common herd." John D. Rockefeller's great fortune is built upon your ignorance. When you know enough to know what your interest is you will support the great party that is organized upon the principle of collective ownership of the means of life. This party will sweep into power upon the issue of emancipation just as republicanism swept into power upon the abolition question half a century ago. . . .

The Socialist Movement

There will be a change one of these days. The world is just beginning to awaken, and is soon to sing its first anthem of freedom. All the signs of the times are cheering. Twenty-five years ago there was but a handful of Socialists; today there are a half million. When the polls are closed next fall you will be astounded. The Socialist movement is in alliance with the forces of progress. We are today where the abolitionists were in 1858. They had a million and a quarter of votes. There was dissension in the whig, republican and free soil parties, but the time had come for a great change, and the republican party was formed in spite of the bickerings and contentions of men. Lincoln made the great speech in that year that gave him the nomination and afterward made him President of the United States.

If you had said to the people in 1858, "In two years from now the republican party is going to sweep the country and seat the president," you would have been laughed to scorn. The socialist party stands today where the republican party stood fifty years ago. It is in alliance with the forces of evolution, the one party that has a clear-cut, overmastering, overshadowing issue; the party that stands for the people, and the only party that stands for all the people. In this system we have one set who are called capitalists, and another set who are called workers; and they are at war with each other.

Now, we Socialists propose that society in its collective capacity shall produce, not for profit, but in abundance to satisfy human wants; that every man shall have the inalienable right to work, and receive the full equivalent of all he produces; that every man may stand fearlessly erect in the pride and majesty of his own manhood.

Every man and every woman will then be economically free. They can, without let or hindrance, apply their labor, with the best machinery that can be devised, to all the natural resources, do the work of society and produce for all; and then receive in exchange a certificate of value equivalent to that of their production. Then society will improve its institutions in proportion to the progress of invention. Whether in the city or on the farm, all things productive will be carried forward on a gigantic scale. All industry will be completely organized. Society for the first time will have a scientific foundation. Every man, by being economically free, will have some time for himself. He can then take a full and perfect breath. He can enjoy life with his wife and children, because then he will have a home.

We are not going to destroy private property. We are going to establish private property—all the private property necessary to house man, keep him in comfort and satisfy his wants. Eighty per cent of the people of the United States have no property today. A few have got it all. They have dispossessed the people, and when we get into power we will dispossess them. We will reduce the workday and give every man a chance. We will go to the parks, and we will have music, because we will have time to play music and desire to hear it. . . .

I am not a prophet. I can no more penetrate the future than you can. I do study the forces that underlie society and the trend of evolution. I can tell by what we have passed through about what we will have in the future; and I know that capitalism can be abolished and the people put in possession. Now, when we have taken possession, and we jointly own the means of production, we will no longer have to fight each other to live; our interests, instead of being competitive, will be co-operative. We will work side by side. Your interest will be mine and mine will be yours. That is the economic condition from which will spring the humane social relation of the future.

When we are in partnership and have stopped clutching each other's throats, when we have stopped enslaving each other, we will stand together, hands clasped, and be friends. We will be comrades, we will be brothers, and we will begin the march to the grandest civilization the human race has ever known.

VIEWPOINT 4

"It is the greatest folly of which a man can be capable, to sit down with a slate and pencil to plan out a new social world."

Radical Social Reform Is Unworkable and Unnecessary

William Graham Sumner (1840–1910)

During the late nineteenth century, when the United States was in the throes of industrialization and economic change, various organizations, movements, and political parties—including the Socialist Party—were founded in order to bring about radical political, social, and economic reforms in America. Activists argued that reforms were necessary to address what they believed to be pressing social problems, including growing extremes of wealth and poverty and corruption in government. However, not all people agreed that radical reform was needed. The following viewpoint is by William Graham Sumner, a professor of social and political science at Yale University from 1872 to 1909. A prolific writer and lecturer on social issues, he was noted for his spirited criticism of the ideas of social reformers such as Eugene V. Debs.

Sumner was among a group of thinkers who applied the ideas of British naturalist Charles Darwin to explain economic and social inequality in human societies. Darwin had developed the theory that biological species continually evolved through natural selection; "Social Darwinists" argued that the evolution of human societies was an analogous struggle of the "survival of the fittest." The transformation from agricultural to industrial societies and the resulting social disruptions—including economic inequal-

From William Graham Sumner, "The Absurd Effort to Make the World Over," *Forum*, March 1894.

ity—were, according to Social Darwinists, the natural result of free competition and differences in human abilities. Sumner and others contended that all attempts to alleviate the problems of the weak and poor or to bring about social equality would weaken the competitive pressures that created wealth and drove human progress. Humanity faced two alternatives, Sumner once wrote: "liberty, inequality, survival of the fittest" or "liberty, equality, survival of the unfittest." In the following excerpt from an 1894 article in *Forum* magazine, Sumner criticizes arguments for radical social reform in America and argues that attempts at "reconstructing the industrial system on the principles of democracy" are fatally misguided and would have harmful unintended consequences.

It will not probably be denied that the burden of proof is on those who affirm that our social condition is utterly diseased and in need of radical regeneration. My task at present, therefore, is entirely negative and critical: to examine the allegations of fact and the doctrines which are put forward to prove the correctness of the diagnosis and to warrant the use of the remedies proposed.

The propositions put forward by social reformers nowadays are chiefly of two kinds. There are assertions in historical form, chiefly in regard to the comparison of existing with earlier social states, which are plainly based on defective historical knowledge, or at most on current stock historical dicta which are uncritical and incorrect. Writers very often assert that something never existed before because they do not know that it ever existed before, or that something is worse than ever before because they are not possessed of detailed information about what has existed before. The other class of propositions consists of dogmatic statements which, whether true or not, are unverifiable. This class of propositions is the pest and bane of current economic and social discussion. Upon a more or less superficial view of some phenomenon a suggestion arises which is embodied in a philosophical proposition and promulgated as a truth. From the form and nature of such propositions they can always be brought under the head of "ethics." This word at least gives them an air of elevated sentiment and purpose, which is the only warrant they possess. It is impossible to test or verify them by any investigation or logical process whatsoever. It is therefore very difficult for anyone who feels a high responsibility for historical statements, and who absolutely rejects any statement which is unverifiable, to find a common platform for discussion or to join issue satisfactorily in taking the negative.

When anyone asserts that the class of skilled and unskilled manual laborers of the United States is worse off now in respect to diet, clothing, lodgings, furniture, fuel, and lights; in respect to the age at which they can marry; the number of children they can provide for; the start in life which they can give to their children, and their chances of accumulating capital, than they ever have been at any former time, he makes a reckless assertion for which no facts have been offered in proof. Upon an appeal to facts, the contrary of this assertion would be clearly established. It suffices, therefore, to challenge those who are responsible for the assertion to make it good.

Industrial Organization

If it is said that the employed class are under much more stringent discipline than they were thirty years ago or earlier, it is true. It is not true that there has been any qualitative change in this respect within thirty years, but it is true that a movement which began at the first settlement of the country has been advancing with constant acceleration and has become a noticeable feature within our time. This movement is the advance in the industrial organization. The first settlement was made by agriculturists, and for a long time there was scarcely any organization. There were scattered farmers, each working for himself, and some small towns with only rudimentary commerce and handicrafts. As the country has filled up, the arts and professions have been differentiated and the industrial organization has been advancing. This fact and its significance has hardly been noticed at all; but the stage of the industrial organization existing at any time, and the rate of advance in its development, are the absolutely controlling social facts. Nine-tenths of the socialistic and semi-socialistic, and sentimental or ethical, suggestions by which we are overwhelmed come from failure to understand the phenomena of the industrial organization and its expansion. It controls us all because we are all in it. It creates the conditions of our existence, sets the limits of our social activity, regulates the bonds of our social relations, determines our conceptions of good and evil, suggests our life-philosophy, molds our inherited political institutions, and reforms the oldest and toughest customs, like marriage and property. I repeat that the turmoil of heterogeneous and antagonistic social whims and speculations in which we live is due to the failure to understand what the industrial organization is and its all-pervading control over human life, while the traditions of our school of philosophy lead us always to approach the industrial organization, not from the side of objective study, but from that of philosophical doctrine. Hence it is that we find that the method of measuring what we see happening by what are called ethical standards, and of proposing to attack the phenomena by methods thence deduced, is so popular.

The advance of a new country from the very simplest social coordination up to the highest organization is a most interesting and instructive chance to study the development of the organization. It has of course been attended all the way along by stricter subordination and higher discipline. All organization implies restriction of liberty. The gain of power is won by narrowing individual range. The methods of business in colonial days were loose and slack to an inconceivable degree. The movement of industry has been all the time toward promptitude, punctuality, and reliability. It has been attended all the way by lamentations about the good old times; about the decline of small industries; about the lost spirit of comradeship between employer and employee; about the narrowing of the interests of the workman; about his conversion into a machine or into a "ware," and about industrial war. These lamentations have all had reference to unquestionable phenomena attendant on advancing organization. In all occupations the same movement is discernible—in the learned professions, in schools, in trade, commerce, and transportation. It is to go on faster than ever, now that the continent is filled up by the first superficial layer of population over its whole extent and the intensification of industry has begun. The great inventions both make the intension of the organization possible and make it inevitable, with all its consequences, whatever they may be. I must expect to be told here, according to the current fashions of thinking, that we ought to control the development of the organization. The first instinct of the modern man is to get a law passed to forbid or prevent what, in his wisdom, he disapproves. A thing which is inevitable, however, is one which we cannot control. We have to make up our minds to it, adjust ourselves to it, and sit down to live with it. Its inevitableness may he disputed, in which case we must reexamine it; but if our analysis is correct, when we reach what is inevitable we reach the end, and our regulations must apply to ourselves, not to the social facts.

Now the intensification of the social organization is what gives us greater social power. It is to it that we owe our increased comfort and abundance. We are none of us ready to sacrifice this. On the contrary, we want more of it. We would not return to the colonial simplicity and the colonial exiguity if we could. If not, then we must pay the price. Our life is bounded on every side by conditions. We can have this if we will agree to submit to that. In the case of industrial power and product the great condition is combination of force under discipline and strict coordination. Hence the wild language about wage-slavery and capitalistic tyranny.

In any state of society no great achievements can be produced without great force. Formerly great force was attainable only by slavery aggregating the power of great numbers of men. Roman civilization was built on this. Ours has been built on steam. It is to be built on electricity. Then we are all forced into an organization around these natural forces and adapted to the methods of their application; and although we indulge in rhetoric about political liberty, nevertheless we find ourselves bound tight in a new set of conditions, which control the modes of our existence and determine the directions in which alone economic and social liberty can go.

Captains of Industry

If it is said that there are some persons in our time who have become rapidly and in a great degree rich, it is true; if it is said that large aggregations of wealth in the control of individuals is a social danger, it is not true.

The movement of the industrial organization which has just been described has brought out a great demand for men capable of managing great enterprises. Such have been called "captains of industry." The analogy with military leaders suggested by this name is not misleading. The great leaders in the development of the industrial organization need those talents of executive and administrative skill, power to command, courage, and fortitude, which were formerly called for in military affairs and scarcely anywhere else. The industrial army is also as dependent on its captains as a military body is on its generals. One of the worst features of the existing system is that the employees have a constant risk in their employer. If he is not competent to manage the business with success, they suffer with him. Capital also is dependent on the skill of the captain of industry for the certainty and magnitude of its profits. Under these circumstances there has been a great demand for men having the requisite ability for this function. As the organization has advanced, with more impersonal bonds of coherence and wider scope of operations, the value of this functionary has rapidly increased. The possession of the requisite ability is a natural monopoly. Consequently, all the conditions have concurred to give to those who possessed this monopoly excessive and constantly advancing rates of remuneration.

Another social function of the first importance in an intense organization is the solution of those crises in the operation of it which are called the conjuncture of the market. It is through the market that the lines of relation run which preserve the system in harmonious and rhythmical operation. The conjuncture is the momentary sharper misadjustment of supply and demand which indicates that a redistribution of productive effort is called for.

The industrial organization needs to be insured against these conjunctures, which, if neglected, produce a crisis and catastrophe; and it needs that they shall be anticipated and guarded against as far as skill and foresight can do it. The rewards of this function for the bankers and capitalists who perform it are very great. The captains of industry and the capitalists who operate on the conjuncture, therefore, if they are successful, win, in these days, great fortunes in a short time. There are no earnings which are more legitimate or for which greater services are rendered to the whole industrial body. The popular notions about this matter really assume that all the wealth accumulated by these classes of persons would be here just the same if they had not existed. They are supposed to have appropriated it out of the common stock. This is so far from being true that, on the contrary, their own wealth would not be but for themselves; and besides that, millions more of wealth, many-fold greater than their own, scattered in the hands of thousands, would not exist but for them.

Within the last two years I have traveled from end to end of the German Empire several times on all kinds of trains. I reached the conviction, looking at the matter from the passenger's standpoint, that, if the Germans could find a Cornelius Vanderbilt [an American railroad tycoon] and put their railroads in his hands for twenty-five years, letting him reorganize the system and make twenty-five million dollars out of it for himself in that period, they would make an excellent bargain.

Wealth and Society

But it is repeated until it has become a commonplace which people are afraid to question, that there is some social danger in the possession of large amounts of wealth by individuals. I ask, Why? I heard a lecture two years ago by a man who holds perhaps the first chair of political economy in the world. He said, among other things, that there was great danger in our day from great accumulations; that this danger ought to be met by taxation, and he referred to the fortune of the Rothschilds and to the great fortunes made in America to prove his point. He omitted, however, to state in what the danger consisted or to specify what harm has ever been done by the Rothschild fortunes or by the great fortunes accumulated in America. It seemed to me that the assertions he was making, and the measures he was recommending, ex-cathedra, were very serious to be thrown out so recklessly. It is hardly to be expected that novelists, popular magazinists, amateur economists, and politicians will be more responsible. It would be easy, however, to show what good is done by accumulations of capital in a few hands—that is, under close and direct management, permitting prompt and accurate application; also to tell what harm is done by loose and unfounded denunciations of any social component or any social group. In the recent debates on the income tax the assumption that great accumulations of wealth are socially harmful and ought to be broken down by taxation was treated as an axiom, and we had direct proof how dangerous it is to fit out the average politician with such unverified and unverifiable dogmas as his warrant for his modes of handling the direful tool of taxation.

The Law of Wages

Many economists argued that labor was a commodity whose wages, set by supply and demand, could not be raised by law or fiat. The following passage is excerpted from a speech that economic writer A.S. Wheeler delivered to the Commercial Club of Boston on October 16, 1886.

Neither sentimental nor moral considerations can settle the rate of wages any more than they can regulate the rate of interest for money or the price of wheat or cloth. . . . The wages of those employed in the labor which enters into the production of those commodities, therefore, must be governed by this law of demand and supply. This is no matter of theory or speculation. Law rules here as in nature, a law not enacted by any legislature and depending for its execution on governmental officials, but law arising from the nature of things and which is self-executing.

Fortunate it is that such is the case. Communistic, socialistic, and all sorts of theories have been tried, often by well-meaning persons, who have been sincerely desirous of doing good to their fellowmen, but they have been failures.

Great figures are set out as to the magnitude of certain fortunes and the proportionate amount of the national wealth held by a fraction of the population, and eloquent exclamation-points are set against them. If the figures were beyond criticism, what would they prove? Where is the rich man who is oppressing anybody? If there was one, the newspapers would ring with it. The facts about the accumulation of wealth do not constitute a plutocracy, as I will show below. Wealth, in itself considered, is only power, like steam, or electricity, or knowledge. The question of its good or ill turns on the question how it will be used. To prove any harm in aggregations of wealth it must be shown that great wealth is, as a rule, in the ordinary course of social affairs, put to a mischievous use. This cannot be shown beyond the very slightest degree, if at all.

Therefore, all the allegations of general mischief, social corruption, wrong, and evil in our society must be referred back to those who make them for particulars and specifications. As they are offered to us we cannot allow them to stand, because we discern in them faulty observation of facts, or incorrect interpretation of facts, or a construction of facts according to some philosophy, or misunderstanding of phenomena and their relations, or incorrect inferences, or crooked deductions.

Assuming, however, that the charges against the existing "capitalistic"—that is, industrial—order of things are established, it is proposed to remedy the ill by reconstructing the industrial system on the principles of democracy. Once more we must untangle the snarl of half ideas and muddled facts.

Defining Democracy

Democracy is, of course, a word to conjure with. We have a democratic-republican political system, and we like it so well that we are prone to take any new step which can be recommended as "democratic" or which will round out some "principle" of democracy to a fuller fulfillment. Everything connected with this domain of political thought is crusted over with false historical traditions, cheap philosophy, and undefined terms, but it is useless to try to criticize it. The whole drift of the world for five hundred years has been toward democracy. That drift, produced by great discoveries and inventions, and by the discovery of a new continent, has raised the middle class out of the servile class. In alliance with the crown they crushed the feudal classes. They made the crown absolute in order to do it. Then they turned against the crown and, with the aid of the handicraftsmen and peasants, conquered it. Now the next conflict which must inevitably come is that between the middle capitalist class and the proletariat, as the word has come to be used. If a certain construction is put on this conflict, it may be called that between democracy and plutocracy, for it seems that industrialism must be developed into plutocracy by the conflict itself. That is the conflict which stands before civilized society to-day. All the signs of the times indicate its commencement, and it is big with fate to mankind and to civilization.

Although we cannot criticise democracy profitably, it may be said of it, with reference to our present subject, that up to this time democracy never has done anything, either in politics, social affairs, or industry, to prove its power to bless mankind. . . .

Unintended Consequences

The question, therefore, arises, if it is proposed to reorganize the social system on the principles of American democracy, whether the institutions of industrialism are to be retained. If so, all the virus of capitalism will be retained. It is forgotten, in many

107

schemes of social reformation in which it is proposed to mix what we like with what we do not like, in order to extirpate the latter, that each must undergo a reaction from the other, and that what we like may be extirpated by what we do not like. We may find that instead of democratizing capitalism we have capitalized democracy—that is, have brought in plutocracy. Plutocracy is a political system in which the ruling force is wealth. The denunciation of capital which we hear from all the reformers is the most eloquent proof that the greatest power in the world to-day is capital. They know that it is, and confess it most when they deny it most strenuously. At present the power of capital is social and industrial, and only in a small degree political. So far as capital is political, it is on account of political abuses, such as tariffs and special legislation on the one hand and legislative strikes on the other. These conditions exist in the democracy to which it is proposed to transfer the industries. What does that mean except bringing all the power of capital once for all into the political arena and precipitating the conflict of democracy and plutocracy at once? Can anyone imagine that the masterfulness, the overbearing disposition, the greed of gain, and the ruthlessness in methods, which are the faults of the master of industry at his worst, would cease when he was a functionary of the State, which had relieved him of risk and endowed him with authority? Can anyone imagine that politicians would no longer be corruptly fond of money, intriguing, and crafty when they were charged, not only with patronage and government contracts, but also with factories, stores, ships, and railroads? Could we expect anything except that, when the politician and the master of industry were joined in one, we should have the vices of both unchecked by the restraints of either? In any socialistic state there will be one set of positions which will offer chances of wealth beyond the wildest dreams of avarice; *viz.*, on the governing committees. Then there will be rich men whose wealth will indeed be a menace to social interests, and instead of industrial peace there will be such war as no one has dreamed of yet: the war between the political ins and outs—that is, between those who are on the committee and those who want to get on it.

We must not drop the subject of democracy without one word more. The Greeks already had occasion to notice a most serious distinction between two principles of democracy which lie at its roots. Plutarch says that Solon got the archonship in part by promising equality, which some understood of esteem and dignity, others of measure and number. There is one democratic principle which means that each man should be esteemed for his merit and worth, for just what he is, without regard to birth, wealth, rank, or other adventitious circumstances. The other prin-

108

ciple is that each one of us ought to be equal to all the others in what he gets and enjoys. The first principle is only partially realizable, but, so far as it goes, it is elevating and socially progressive and profitable. The second is not capable of an intelligible statement. The first is a principle of industrialization. It proceeds from and is intelligible only in a society built on the industrial virtues, free endeavor, security of property, and repression of the baser vices; that is, in a society whose industrial system is built on labor and exchange. The other is only a rule of division for robbers who have to divide plunder or monks who have to divide gifts. If, therefore, we want to democratize industry in the sense of the first principle, we need only perfect what we have now, especially on its political side. If we try to democratize it in the sense of the other principle, we corrupt politics at one stroke; we enter upon an industrial enterprise which will waste capital and bring us all to poverty, and we set loose greed and envy as ruling social passions.

The Limits of Human Reform

If this poor old world is as bad as they say, one more reflection may check the zeal of the headlong reformer. It is at any rate a tough old world. It has taken its trend and curvature and all its twists and tangles from a long course of formation. All its wry and crooked gnarls and knobs are therefore stiff and stubborn. If we puny men by our arts can do anything at all to straighten them, it will only be by modifying the tendencies of some of the forces at work, so that, after a sufficient time, their action may be changed a little and slowly the lines of movement may be modified. This effort, however, can at most be only slight, and it will take a long time. In the meantime spontaneous forces will be at work, compared with which our efforts are like those of a man trying to deflect a river, and these forces will have changed the whole problem before our interferences have time to make themselves felt. The great stream of time and earthly things will sweep on just the same in spite of us. It bears with it now all the errors and follies of the past, the wreckage of all the philosophies, the fragments of all the civilizations, the wisdom of all the abandoned ethical systems, the debris of all the institutions, and the penalties of all the mistakes. It is only in imagination that we stand by and look at and criticize it and plan to change it. Everyone of us is a child of his age and cannot get out of it. He is in the stream and is swept along with it. All his sciences and philosophy come to him out of it. Therefore the tide will not be changed by us. It will swallow up both us and our experiments. It will absorb the efforts at change and take them into itself as new but trivial components, and the great movement of tradition and work will

109

go on unchanged by our fads and schemes. The things which will change it are the great discoveries and inventions, the new reactions inside the social organism, and the changes in the earth itself on account of changes in the cosmical forces. These causes will make it just what, in fidelity to them, it ought to be. The men will be carried along with it and be made by it. The utmost they can do by their cleverness will be to note and record their course as they are carried along, which is what we do now, and is that which leads us to the vain fancy that we can make or guide the movement. That is why it is the greatest folly of which a man can be capable, to sit down with a slate and pencil to plan out a new social world.

VIEWPOINT 5

"Have you found trusts that were keen to protect the lungs and the health and the freedom of their employees? Have you found trusts that thought as much of their men as they did of their machinery?"

Industrial Trusts Are Harmful

Woodrow Wilson (1856–1924)

In 1859 in western Pennsylvania, Edwin L. Drake and William Smith drilled a hole and struck oil at a depth of sixty-nine feet—the world's first known tapping of oil at its source. Within a few years the substance, used for lighting kerosene lamps and for lubrication, had become the basis for a chaotic industry. Hundreds of oil drillers, refiners, and transporters competed for business, thereby creating drastic price fluctuations. By 1880, however, close to 90 percent of the oil business was under the control of one man—John D. Rockefeller, founder of Standard Oil Company. Rockefeller used efficient oil refining techniques, a shrewd sense for business, and aggressive tactics to drive out or merge with his competitors and consolidate the petroleum industry under his control. Among the tactics he utilized to achieve dominance in the industry were predatory pricing (selling below cost to steal business from local competitors) and secret deals with railroads. In 1882 he and his chief counsel, Samuel C.T. Dodd, created a legal arrangement in which multiple corporations could transfer their stock to a central corporation to be held "in trust." Under this arrangement, Standard Oil's board of directors in its New York City headquarters controlled the operations of forty corporations nationwide. Rockefeller had created the first and largest industrial trust.

From Woodrow Wilson, *The New Freedom* (New York: Doubleday, 1913).

During the time of Rockefeller's ascent in the oil industry, most other important segments of America's economy underwent a similar process, with the result that economic power was increasingly concentrated into fewer entities as corporations merged and trusts and other arrangements were established. The word "trust" came to refer to any large industrial combination that monopolized a certain product; people spoke of the sugar trust, the banking trust, the steel trust, and others. By 1900 almost half of all of America's manufacturing output was being produced by fewer than 2 percent of its manufacturing companies. Many critics argued that the emergence of such large industrial combinations threatened to destroy economic opportunity and take control of the American government from the people. In response to these concerns, Congress passed the Sherman Antitrust Act in 1890. Under its auspices Presidents Theodore Roosevelt and William Howard Taft initiated "trust busting" suits against several large concerns, including Standard Oil, which was forced to break up into separate companies in 1911. But many viewed these actions as insufficient responses to the problem of trusts.

The following viewpoint is by Woodrow Wilson, a former academic, college president, and New Jersey governor who ran for president in 1912. His campaign speeches were collected and published in the 1913 book *The New Freedom*, from which this viewpoint is excerpted. Wilson distinguished himself from his two main opponents, incumbent president Taft and former president Roosevelt, by emphasizing his opposition to trusts and monopolies. He argues that the national government should take action to break up trusts, eliminate social and economic privilege, and restore free business competition. He contrasts his views with those of Roosevelt, who argued that the federal government should supervise and regulate (but not break up) industrial trusts.

Wilson won the 1912 presidential election and eventually served two terms. Among his domestic achievements as president was passage of the Clayton Antitrust Act, which tightened some of the loopholes of the Sherman Antitrust Act and forbade several business practices believed to be harmful to free and open competition. He also created the Federal Trade Commission, a five-member presidentially appointed "watchdog" agency to regulate unlawful trading practices.

Since I entered politics, I have chiefly had men's views confided to me privately. Some of the biggest men in the United

States, in the field of commerce and manufacture, are afraid of somebody, are afraid of something. They know that there is a power somewhere so organized, so subtle, so watchful, so interlocked, so complete, so pervasive, that they had better not speak above their breath when they speak in condemnation of it.

They know that America is not a place of which it can be said, as it used to be, that a man may choose his own calling and pursue it just as far as his abilities enable him to pursue it; because to-day, if he enters certain fields, there are organizations which will use means against him that will prevent his building up a business which they do not want to have built up; organizations that will see to it that the ground is cut from under him and the markets shut against him. For if he begins to sell to certain retail dealers, to any retail dealers, the monopoly will refuse to sell to those dealers, and those dealers, afraid, will not buy the new man's wares.

No Longer a Land of Opportunity

And this is the country which has lifted to the admiration of the world its ideals of absolutely free opportunity, where no man is supposed to be under any limitation except the limitations of his character and of his mind; where there is supposed to be no distinction of class, no distinction of blood, no distinction of social status, but where men win or lose on their merits.

I lay it very close to my own conscience as a public man whether we can any longer stand at our doors and welcome all newcomers upon those terms. American industry is not free, as once it was free; American enterprise is not free; the man with only a little capital is finding it harder to get into the field, more and more impossible to compete with the big fellow. Why? Because the laws of this country do not prevent the strong from crushing the weak. That is the reason, and because the strong have crushed the weak the strong dominate the industry and the economic life of this country. No man can deny that the lines of endeavor have more and more narrowed and stiffened; no man who knows anything about the development of industry in this country can have failed to observe that the larger kinds of credit are more and more difficult to obtain, unless you obtain them upon the terms of uniting your efforts with those who already control the industries of the country; and nobody can fail to observe that any man who tries to set himself up in competition with any process of manufacture which has been taken under the control of large combinations of capital will presently find himself either squeezed out or obliged to sell and allow himself to be absorbed.

There is a great deal that needs reconstruction in the United States. I should like to take a census of the business men,—I mean the rank and file of the business men,—as to whether they think that business conditions in this country, or rather whether the organization of business in this country, is satisfactory or not. I know what they would say if they dared. If they could vote secretly they would vote overwhelmingly that the present organization of business was meant for the big fellows and was not meant for the little fellows; that it was meant for those who are at the top and was meant to exclude those who are at the bottom; that it was meant to shut out beginners, to prevent new entries in the race, to prevent the building up of competitive enterprises that would interfere with the monopolies which the great trusts have built up.

What this country needs above everything else is a body of laws which will look after the men who are on the make rather than the men who are already made. Because the men who are already made are not going to live indefinitely, and they are not always kind enough to leave sons as able and as honest as they are. . . .

Are Trusts Inevitable?

Gentlemen say, they have been saying for a long time, and, therefore, I assume that they believe, that trusts are inevitable. They don't say that big business is inevitable. They don't say merely that the elaboration of business upon a great co-operative scale is characteristic of our time and has come about by the natural operation of modern civilization. We would admit that. But they say that the particular kind of combinations that are now controlling our economic development came into existence naturally and were inevitable; and that, therefore, we have to accept them as unavoidable and administer our development through them. They take the analogy of the railways. The railways were clearly inevitable if we were to have transportation, but railways after they are once built stay put. You can't transfer a railroad at convenience; and you can't shut up one part of it and work another part. It is in the nature of what economists, those tedious persons, call natural monopolies; simply because the whole circumstances of their use are so stiff that you can't alter them. Such are the analogies which these gentlemen choose when they discuss the modern trust.

I admit the popularity of the theory that the trusts have come about through the natural development of business conditions in the United States, and that it is a mistake to try to oppose the processes by which they have been built up, because those processes belong to the very nature of business in our time, and that therefore the only thing we can do, and the only thing we ought to attempt to do, is to accept them as inevitable arrangements and make the best out of it that we can by regulation.

114

I answer, nevertheless, that this attitude rests upon a confusion of thought. Big business is no doubt to a large extent necessary and natural. The development of business upon a great scale, upon a great scale of cooperation, is inevitable, and, let me add, is probably desirable. But that is a very different matter from the development of trusts, because the trusts have not grown. They have been artificially created; they have been put together, not by natural processes, but by the will, the deliberate planning will, of men who were more powerful than their neighbors in the business world, and who wished to make their power secure against competition.

The trusts do not belong to the period of infant industries. They are not the products of the time, that old laborious time, when the great continent we live on was undeveloped, the young nation struggling to find itself and get upon its feet amidst older and more experienced competitors. They belong to a very recent and very sophisticated age, when men knew what they wanted and knew how to get it by the favor of the government.

How Trusts Are Made

Did you ever look into the way a trust was made? It is very natural, in one sense, in the same sense in which human greed is natural. If I haven't efficiency enough to beat my rivals, then the thing I am inclined to do is to get together with my rivals and say: "Don't let's cut each other's throats; let's combine and determine prices for ourselves; determine the output, and thereby determine the prices: and dominate and control the market." That is very natural. That has been done ever since freebooting was established. That has been done ever since power was used to establish control. The reason that the masters of combination have sought to shut out competition is that the basis of control under competition is brains and efficiency. I admit that any large corporation built up by the legitimate processes of business, by economy, by efficiency, is natural; and I am not afraid of it, no matter how big it grows. It can stay big only by doing its work more thoroughly than anybody else. And there is a point of bigness,—as every business man in this country knows, though some of them will not admit it,—where you pass the limit of efficiency and get into the region of clumsiness and unwieldiness. You can make your combine so extensive that you can't digest it into a single system; you can get so many parts that you can't assemble them as you would an effective piece of machinery. The point of efficiency is overstepped in the natural process of development oftentimes, and it has been overstepped many times in the artificial and deliberate formation of trusts.

A trust is formed in this way: a few gentlemen "promote"

it—that is to say, they get it up, being given enormous fees for their kindness, which fees are loaded on to the undertaking in the form of securities of one kind or another. The argument of the promoters is, not that every one who comes into the combination can carry on his business more efficiently than he did before; the argument is: we will assign to you as your share in the pool twice, three times, four times, or five times what you could have sold your business for to an individual competitor who would have to run it on an economic and competitive basis. We can afford to buy it at such a figure because we are shutting out competition. We can afford to make the stock of the combination half a dozen times what it naturally would be and pay dividends on it, because there will be nobody to dispute the prices we shall fix.

Talk of that as sound business? Talk of that as inevitable? It is based upon nothing except power. It is not based upon efficiency. It is no wonder that the big trusts are not prospering in proportion to such competitors as they still have in such parts of their business as competitors have access to; they are prospering freely only in those fields to which competition has no access. . . .

Industrial Absolutism

Louis D. Brandeis, a prominent lawyer who was active in social causes, worked with Woodrow Wilson in his 1912 campaign for the presidency and shared Wilson's belief that the economic power of big corporations and trusts threatened American society. The following passage is taken from testimony given by Brandeis on January 23, 1915, to the United States Commission on Industrial Relations, an investigative body created by Congress to examine the working conditions of industrial workers and the economic impact of industrial corporations.

My observation leads me to believe that while there are many contributing causes to [labor] unrest, that there is one cause which is fundamental. That is the necessary conflict—the contrast between our political liberty and our industrial absolutism. We are as free politically, perhaps, as free as it is possible for us to be. Every male has his voice and vote. . . .

On the other hand, in dealing with industrial problems the position of the ordinary worker is exactly the reverse. The individual employee has no effective voice or vote. And the main objection, as I see it, to the very large corporation is, that it makes possible—and in many cases makes inevitable—the exercise of industrial absolutism. It is not merely the case of the individual worker against employer which, even if he is a reasonably sized employer, presents a serious situation calling for the interposition of a union to protect the individual. But we have the situation of an employer so potent, so well-

Unfair Competition

I take my stand absolutely, where every progressive ought to take his stand, on the proposition that private monopoly is indefensible and intolerable. And there I will fight my battle. And I know how to fight it. Everybody who has even read the newspapers knows the means by which these men built up their power and created these monopolies. Any decently equipped lawyer can suggest to you statutes by which the whole business can be stopped. What these gentlemen do not want is this: they do not want to be compelled to meet all comers on equal terms. I am perfectly willing that they should beat any competitor by fair means; but I know the foul means they have adopted, and I know that they can be stopped by law. If they think that coming into the market upon the basis of mere efficiency, upon the mere basis of knowing how to manufacture goods better than anybody else and to sell them cheaper than anybody else, they can carry the immense amount of water that they have put into their enterprises in order to buy up rivals, then they are perfectly welcome

organized, with such concentrated forces and with such extraordinary powers of reserve and the ability to endure against strikes and other efforts of a union, that the relatively loosely organized masses of even strong unions are unable to cope with the situation. We are dealing here with a question, not of motive, but of condition. Now, the large corporation and the managers of the powerful corporation are probably in large part actuated by motives just the same as an employer of a tenth of their size. Neither of them, as a rule, wishes to have his liberty abridged; but the smaller concern usually comes to the conclusion that it is necessary that it should be, where an important union must be dealt with. But when a great financial power has developed—when there exists these powerful organizations, which can successfully summon forces from all parts of the country, which can afford to use tremendous amounts of money in any conflict to carry out what they deem to be their business principle, and can also afford to suffer large losses—you have necessarily a condition of inequality between the two contending forces. Such contests, though undertaken with the best motives and with strong conviction on the part of the corporate managers that they are seeking what is for the best interests not only of the company but of the community, lead to absolutism. The result, in the cases of these large corporations, may be to develop a benevolent absolutism, but it is an absolutism all the same; and it is that which makes the great corporation so dangerous. There develops within the State a state so powerful that the ordinary social and industrial forces existing are insufficient to cope with it.

to try it. But there must be no squeezing out of the beginner, no crippling his credit; no discrimination against retailers who buy from a rival; no threats against concerns who sell supplies to a rival; no holding back of raw material from him; no secret arrangements against him. All the fair competition you choose, but no unfair competition of any kind. And then when unfair competition is eliminated, let us see these gentlemen carry their tanks of water on their backs. All that I ask and all I shall fight for is that they shall come into the field against merit and brains everywhere. If they can beat other American brains, then they have got the best brains.

But if you want to know how far brains go, as things now are, suppose you try to match your better wares against these gentlemen, and see them undersell you before your market is any bigger than the locality and make it absolutely impossible for you to get a fast foothold. If you want to know how brains count, originate some invention which will improve the kind of machinery they are using, and then see if you can borrow enough money to manufacture it. You may be offered something for your patent by the corporation,—which will perhaps lock it up in a safe and go on using the old machinery; but you will not be allowed to manufacture. I know men who have tried it, and they could not get the money, because the great money lenders of this country are in the arrangement with the great manufacturers of this country, and they do not propose to see their control of the market interfered with by outsiders. And who are outsiders? Why, all the rest of the people of the United States are outsiders.

They are rapidly making us outsiders with respect even of the things that come from the bosom of the earth, and which belong to us in a peculiar sense. Certain monopolies in this country have gained almost complete control of the raw material, chiefly in the mines, out of which the great body of manufactures are carried on, and they now discriminate, when they will, in the sale of that raw material between those who are rivals of the monopoly and those who submit to the monopoly. We must soon come to the point where we shall say to the men who own these essentials of industry that they have got to part with these essentials by sale to all citizens of the United States with the same readiness and upon the same terms. Or else we shall tie up the resources of this country under private control in such fashion as will make our independent development absolutely impossible. . . .

I have been told by a great many men that the idea I have, that by restoring competition you can restore industrial freedom, is based upon a failure to observe the actual happenings of the last decades in this country; because, they say, it is just free competition that has made it possible for the big to crush the little. I reply, it is not free competition that has done that; it is illicit competition. It is competition of the kind that the law ought to stop, and can stop,—this crushing of the little man. . . .

Monopolies and Theodore Roosevelt

The doctrine that monopoly is inevitable and that the only course open to the people of the United States is to submit to and regulate it found a champion during the campaign of 1912 in the new party, or branch of the Republican party, founded under the leadership of Mr. [Theodore] Roosevelt. . . .

You know that Mr. Roosevelt long ago classified trusts for us as good and bad, and he said that he was afraid only of the bad ones. Now he does not desire that there should be any more bad ones, but proposes that they should all be made good by discipline, directly applied by a commission of executive appointment. All he explicitly complains of is lack of publicity and lack of fairness; not the exercise of power, for throughout that plank [of the new party platform] the power of the great corporations is accepted as the inevitable consequence of the modern organization of industry. All that it is proposed to do is to take them under control and regulation. The national administration having for sixteen years been virtually under the regulation of the trusts, it would be merely a family matter were the parts reversed and were the other members of the family to exercise the regulation. And the trusts, apparently, which might, in such circumstances, comfortably continue to administer our affairs under the mollifying influences of the federal government, would then, if you please, be the instrumentalities by which all the humanistic, benevolent program of the rest of that interesting platform would be carried out!

The third [Roosevelt's] party says that the present system of our industry and trade has come to stay. Mind you, these artificially built up things, these things that can't maintain themselves in the market without monopoly, have come to stay, and the only thing that the government can do, the only thing that the third party proposes should be done, is to set up a commission to regulate them. It accepts them. It says: "We will not undertake, it were futile to undertake, to prevent monopoly, but we will go into an arrangement by which we will make these monopolies kind to you. We will guarantee that they shall be pitiful. We will guarantee that they shall pay the right wages. We will guarantee that they shall do everything kind and public-spirited, which they have never heretofore shown the least inclination to do."

Don't you realize that that is a blind alley? You can't find your way to liberty that way. You can't find your way to social reform through the forces that have made social reform necessary. . . .

The Crucial Decision

Shall we try to get the grip of monopoly away from our lives, or shall we not? Shall we withhold our hand and say monopoly is inevitable, that all that we can do is to regulate it? Shall we say that all that we can do is to put government in competition with monopoly and try its strength against it? Shall we admit that the creature of our own hands is stronger than we are? We have been dreading all along the time when the combined power of high finance would be greater than the power of the government. Have we come to a time when the President of the United States or any man who wishes to be the President must doff his cap in the presence of this high finance, and say, "You are our inevitable master, but we will see how we can make the best of it"?

We are at the parting of the ways. We have, not one or two or three, but many, established and formidable monopolies in the United States. We have, not one or two, but many, fields of endeavor into which it is difficult, if not impossible, for the independent man to enter. We have restricted credit, we have restricted opportunity, we have controlled development, and we have come to be one of the worst ruled, one of the most completely controlled and dominated, governments in the civilized world—no longer a government by free opinion, no longer a government by conviction and the vote of the majority, but a government by the opinion and the duress of small groups of dominant men. . . .

Monopolies Cannot Change

I do not trust any promises of a change of temper on the part of monopoly. Monopoly never was conceived in the temper of tolerance. Monopoly never was conceived with the purpose of general development. It was conceived with the purpose of special advantage. Has monopoly been very benevolent to its employees? Have the trusts had a soft heart for the working people of America? Have you found trusts that cared whether women were sapped of their vitality or not? Have you found trusts who are very scrupulous about using children in their tender years? Have you found trusts that were keen to protect the lungs and the health and the freedom of their employees? Have you found trusts that thought as much of their men as they did of their machinery? Then who is going to convert these men into the chief instruments of justice and benevolence? . . .

I do not want to see the special interests of the United States take care of the workingmen, women, and children. I want to see justice, righteousness, fairness and humanity displayed in all the laws of the United States, and I do not want any power to intervene between the people and their government. Justice is what we want, not patronage and condescension and pitiful helpfulness. The trusts are our masters now, but I for one do not care to live in a country called free even under kind masters. I prefer to live under no masters at all. . . .

The reason that America was set up was that she might be different from all the nations of the world in this: that the strong could not put the weak to the wall, that the strong could not prevent the weak from entering the race. America stands for opportunity. America stands for a free field and no favor. America stands for a government responsive to the interests of all. And until America recovers those ideals in practice, she will not have the right to hold her head high again amidst the nations as she used to hold it.

Restoring Freedom

It is like coming out of a stifling cellar into the open where we can breathe again and see the free spaces of the heavens to turn away from such a doleful program of submission and dependence toward the other plan, the confident purpose for which the people have given their mandate. Our purpose is the restoration of freedom. We purpose to prevent private monopoly by law, to see to it that the methods by which monopolies have been built up are legally made impossible. We design that the limitations on private enterprise shall be removed, so that the next generation of youngsters, as they come along, will not have to become protégés of benevolent trusts, but will be free to go about making their own lives what they will; so that we shall taste again the full cup, not of charity, but of liberty,—the only wine that ever refreshed and renewed the spirit of a people.

VIEWPOINT 6

"If the anti-trust people . . . really had the power or the courage to do what they propose, they would be engaged in one of the most destructive agitations that America has known."

Antitrust Laws Are Harmful

Walter Lippmann (1889–1974)

The rapid industrialization of America following the Civil War created intense business growth and consolidation. Businessmen in many different industries sought to eliminate competition and control the market for their product by creating trusts and other legal arrangements under which separate corporations could effectively combine their operations and manipulate the production and pricing of a particular commodity. Responding to public discontent about the growing economic size and power of these industrial combinations, or "trusts," Congress passed the Sherman Antitrust Act in 1890. Under the act, "Every contract, combination in form of trust or otherwise, or conspiracy in restraint of trade among the several States" was declared illegal. However, the Supreme Court soon weakened the act by ruling in several cases that it applied only to interstate commerce and not to manufacturing. In 1911 the Court reversed itself somewhat and ordered the dissolution of the Standard Oil Company and the American Tobacco Company, in the process pronouncing a "rule of reason" principle; the Sherman Act was deemed to apply only to "unreasonable" combinations that restrained trade. Meanwhile, economic mergers and concentrations continued to take place. In 1904 financial analyst John Moody wrote that America had 318 trusts with total capital of $7.2 billion "covering every line of productive industry in the United States."

From Walter Lippmann, *Drift and Mastery* (New York: Mitchell Kennerley, 1914).

Not all people believed that big industrial combinations should be broken up. In the following viewpoint, Walter Lippmann argues that large business organizations are an essential component of America's industrial economy. He contends that antitrust laws, rather than the trusts themselves, pose a threat to the United States by crippling the ability of corporations to effectively operate. He criticizes the arguments made by leading American politicians who oppose trusts, including William Jennings Bryan, the unsuccessful Democratic presidential candidate of the 1896 and 1908 elections, and Woodrow Wilson, the successful Democratic candidate of 1912. Lippmann contends that these and other politicians, in attacking trusts and extolling the merits of self-employment and small businesses, are calling for an impossible return to a simpler past. Trusts, he asserts, are a necessary part of the changes industrialization has brought to American life. Lippmann, a recent Harvard University graduate, was just beginning a long career as a journalist, newspaper columnist, and political and social commentator. The following passages are excerpted from his 1914 book *Drift and Mastery*.

It has been said that no trust could have been created without breaking the law. Neither could astronomy in the time of Galileo. If you build up foolish laws and insist that invention is a crime, well—then it is a crime. That is undeniably true, but not very interesting. Of course, you can't possibly treat the trusts as crimes. First of all, nobody knows what the trust laws mean. The spectacle of an enlightened people trying in vain for twenty-five years to find out the intention of a statute that it has enacted—that is one of those episodes that only madmen can appreciate. You see, it is possible to sympathize with the difficulties of a scholar trying to decipher the hieroglyphics of some ancient people, but when statesmen can't read the things they've written themselves, it begins to look as if some imp had been playing pranks. The men who rule this country to-day were all alive, and presumably sane, when the Sherman Act was passed. They all say in public that it is a great piece of legislation—an "exquisite instrument" someone called it the other day. The highest paid legal intelligence has concentrated on the Act. The Supreme Court has interpreted it many times, ending with the enormous assumption that reason had something to do with the law. The Supreme Court was denounced for this: the reformers said that if there was any reason in the law, the devil himself had got hold of it. As I write, Congress is engaged in trying to define what it thinks it means by the Act. . . .

That uncertainty hasn't prevented a mass of indictments, injunctions, lawsuits. It has, if anything, invited them. But of course, you can't enforce the criminal law against every "unfair" business practice. Just try to imagine the standing army of inspectors, detectives, prosecutors, and judges, the city of courthouses and jails, the enormous costs, and the unremitting zeal—if you cannot see the folly, at least see the impossibility of the method. To work with it seriously would not only bring business to a standstill, it would drain the energy of America more thoroughly than the bitterest foreign war. . . .

The Stupidity of Anti-Trust Laws

If the anti-trust people really grasped the full meaning of what they said, and if they really had the power or the courage to do what they propose, they would be engaged in one of the most destructive agitations that America has known. They would be breaking up the beginning of a collective organization, thwarting the possibility of coöperation, and insisting upon submitting industry to the wasteful, the planless scramble of little profiteers. They would make impossible any deliberate and constructive use of our natural resources, they would thwart any effort to form the great industries into coordinated services, they would preserve commercialism as the undisputed master of our lives, they would lay a premium on the strategy of industrial war,—they would, if they could. For these anti-trust people have never seen the possibilities of organized industries. They have seen only the obvious evils, the birth-pains, the undisciplined strut of youth, the bad manners, the greed, and the trickery. The trusts have been ruthless, of course. No one tried to guide them; they have broken the law in a thousand ways, largely because the law was such that they had to.

At any rate, I should not like to answer before a just tribunal for the harm done this country in the last twenty-five years by the stupid hostility of anti-trust laws. How much they have perverted the constructive genius of this country it is impossible to estimate. They have blocked any policy of welcome and use, they have concentrated a nation's thinking on inessentials, they have driven creative business men to underhand methods, and put a high money value on intrigue and legal cunning, demagoguery and waste. The trusts have survived it all, but in mutilated form, the battered makeshifts of a trampled promise. They have learned every art of evasion—the only art reformers allowed them to learn.

It is said that the economy of trusts is unreal. Yet no one has ever tried the economies of the trust in any open, deliberate fashion. The amount of energy that has had to go into repelling stupid attack, the adjustments that had to be made underground—it is a wonder the trusts achieved what they did to bring order out of chaos, and forge an instrument for a nation's business. You have no more right to judge the trusts by what they are than to judge the labor movement by what it is. Both of them are in that preliminary state where they are fighting for existence, and any real outburst of constructive effort has been impossible for them. . . .

There has been no American policy on the trust question: there has been merely a widespread resentment. The small local competitors who were wiped out became little centers of bad feeling: these nationally organized industries were looked upon as foreign invaders. They were arrogant, as the English in Ireland or the Germans in Alsace, and much of the feeling for local democracy attached itself to the revolt against these national despotisms. The trusts made enemies right and left: they squeezed the profits of the farmer, they made life difficult for the shopkeeper, they abolished jobbers and travelling salesmen, they closed down factories, they exercised an enormous control over credit through their size and through their eastern connections. Labor was no match for them, state legislatures were impotent before them. They came into the life of the simple American community as a tremendous revolutionary force, upsetting custom, changing men's status, demanding a readjustment for which people were unready. Of course, there was anti-trust feeling; of course, there was a blind desire to smash them. Men had been ruined and they were too angry to think, too hard pressed to care much about the larger life which the trusts suggested.

William Jennings Bryan

This feeling came to a head in Bryan's famous "cross of gold" speech in 1896. "When you come before us and tell us that we shall disturb your business interests, we reply that you have disturbed our business interests by your action. . . . The man who is employed for wages is as much a business man as his employers. The attorney in a country town is as much a business man as the corporation counsel in a great metropolis. The merchant at the crossroads store is as much a business man as the merchant of New York. The farmer . . . is as much a business man as the man who goes upon the Board of Trade and bets upon the price of grain. The miners . . . It is for these that we speak . . . we are fighting in the defense of our homes, our families, and posterity." What Bryan was really defending was the old and, simple life of America, a life that was doomed by the great organization that had come into the world. He thought he was fighting the plutocracy: as a matter of fact he was fighting something much deeper than that; he was fighting the larger scale of human life. The Eastern money power controlled the new industrial system, and Bryan fought it. But what he and his people hated from the bottom of their souls were the economic conditions which had upset the old life of the prairies, made new demands upon democracy, introduced specialization and science, had destroyed village loyalties, frustrated private ambitions, and created the impersonal relationships of the modern world.

Bryan has never been able to adjust himself to the new world in which he lives. That is why he is so irresistibly funny to sophisticated newspaper men. His virtues, his habits, his ideas, are the simple, direct, shrewd qualities of early America. He is the true Don Quixote of our politics, for he moves in a world that has ceased to exist.

Roosevelt and Trusts

Theodore Roosevelt developed a reputation as a "trust buster" during his presidency, which lasted from 1901 to 1909. However, in an August 31, 1910, speech in Kansas, Roosevelt argues that trusts should be subjected to government regulation rather than dismantled. Roosevelt later campaigned on this position in his unsuccessful 1912 campaign for the presidency.

It has become entirely clear that we must have government supervision of the capitalization, not only of public-service corporations, including, particularly, railways, but of all corporations doing an interstate business. I do not wish to see the nation forced into the ownership of the railways if it can possibly be avoided, and the only alternative is thoroughgoing and effective regulation, which shall be based on a full knowledge of all the facts. . . .

Combinations in industry are the result of an imperative economic law which cannot be repealed by political legislation. The effort at prohibiting all combination has substantially failed. The way out lies, not in attempting to prevent such combinations, but in completely controlling them in the interest of the public welfare.

He is a more genuine conservative than some propertied bigot. Bryan stands for the popular tradition of America, whereas most of his enemies stand merely for the power that is destroying that tradition. Bryan is what America was; his critics are generally defenders of what America has become. And neither seems to have any vision of what America is to be.

Yet there has always been great power behind Bryan, the power of those who in one way or another were hurt by the greater organization that America was developing. The Populists were part of that power. [Robert] La Follette and the insurgent Republicans expressed it. It was easily a political majority of the American people. The Republican Party disintegrated under the pressure of the revolt. The Bull Moose gathered much of its strength from it. The Socialists have got some of it. But in 1912 it swept the Democratic Party, and by a combination of circumstances, carried the country. The plutocracy was beaten in politics, and the power that Bryan spoke for in 1896, the forces that had made muckraking popular, captured the government. They were led by a man who was no part of the power that he represented.

Woodrow Wilson

Woodrow Wilson is an outsider capable of skilled interpretation. He is an historian, and that has helped him to know the older tradition of America. He is a student of theory, and like most theorists of his generation he is deeply attached to the doctrines that swayed the world when America was founded.

But Woodrow Wilson at least knows that there is a new world. "There is one great basic fact which underlies all the questions that are discussed on the political platform at the present moment. That singular fact is that nothing is done in this country as it was done twenty years ago. We are in the presence of a new organization of society. . . . We have changed our economic conditions, absolutely, from top to bottom; and, with our economic society, the organization of our life." You could not make a more sweeping statement of the case. The President is perfectly aware of what has happened, and he says at the very outset that "our laws still deal with us on the basis of the old system . . . the old positive formulas do not fit the present problems."

You wait eagerly for some new formula. The new formula is this: "I believe the time has come when the governments of this country, both state and national, have to set the stage, and set it very minutely and carefully, for the doing of justice to men in every relationship of life." Now that is a new formula, because it means a willingness to use the power of government much more extensively.

But for what purpose is this power to be used? There, of course, is the rub. It is to be used to "*restore* our politics to their full spiritual vigor *again,* and our national life, whether in trade, in industry, or in what concerns us only as families and individuals, to its purity, its self-respect, and its *pristine* strength and freedom." The ideal is the old ideal, the ideal of Bryan, the method is the new one of government interference.

Wilson's Inner Contradiction

That, I believe, is the inner contradiction of Woodrow Wilson. He knows that there is a new world demanding new methods, but he dreams of an older world. He is torn between the two. It is a very deep conflict in him between what he knows and what he feels.

His feeling is, as he says, for "the man on the make." "For my part, I want the pigmy to have a chance to come out". . ."Just let some of the youngsters I know have a chance and they'll give these gentlemen points. Lend them a little money. They can't get any now. See to it that when they have got a local market they can't be squeezed out of it." Nowhere in his speeches will you find any sense that it may be possible to organize the fundamental industries on some deliberate plan for national service. He is thinking always about somebody's chance to build up a profitable business; he likes the idea that somebody can beat somebody else, and the small business man takes on the virtues of David in a battle with Goliath.

"Have you found trusts that thought as much of their men as they did of their machinery?" he asks, forgetting that few people have ever found competitive textile mills or clothing factories that did. There isn't an evil of commercialism that Wilson isn't ready to lay at the door of the trusts. He becomes quite reckless in his denunciation of the New Devil—Monopoly—and of course, by contrast the competitive business takes on a halo of light. It is amazing how clearly he sees the evils that trusts do, how blind he is to the evils that his supporters do. You would think that the trusts were the first oppressors of labor; you would think they were the first business organization that failed to achieve the highest possible efficiency. The pretty record of competition throughout the Nineteenth Century is forgotten. Suddenly all that is a glorious past which we have lost. You would think that competitive commercialism was really a generous, chivalrous, high-minded stage of human culture.

"We design that the limitations on private enterprise shall be removed, so that the next generation of youngsters, as they come along, will not have to become protégés of benevolent trusts, but will be free to go about making their own lives what they will; so that we shall taste again the full cup, not of charity, but of liberty,—the only wine that ever refreshed and renewed the spirit of a people." That cup of liberty—we may well ask him to go back to Manchester, to Paterson to-day, to the garment trades of New York, and taste it for himself.

The New Freedom

The New Freedom means the effort of small business men and farmers to use the government against the larger collective organization of industry. Wilson's power comes from them; his feeling is with them; his thinking is for them. Never a word of understanding for the new type of administrator, the specialist, the professionally trained business man; practically no mention of the consumer even the tariff is for the business man; no understanding of the new demands of labor, its solidarity, its aspiration for some control over the management of business; no hint that it may be necessary to organize the fundamental industries of the country on some definite plan so that our resources may be developed by scientific method instead of by men "on the make"; no friendliness for the larger, collective life upon which the world is entering, only a constant return to the commercial chances of young men trying to set up in business. That is the push and force of this New Freedom, a freedom for the little profiteer, but no freedom for the nation from the narrowness, the poor incentives, the limited vision of small competitors,—no freedom from clamorous advertisement, from wasteful selling, from duplication of plants, from unnecessary enterprise, from the chaos, the welter, the strategy of industrial war.

There is no doubt, I think, that President Wilson and his party represent primarily small business in a war against the great interests. Socialists speak of his administration as a revolution within the bounds of capitalism. Wilson doesn't really fight the oppressions of property. He fights the evil done by large property-holders to small ones. The temper of his administration was revealed very clearly when the proposal was made to establish a Federal Trade Commission. It was suggested at once by leading spokesmen of the Democratic Party that corporations with a capital of less than a million dollars should be exempted from supervision. Is that because little corporations exploit labor or the consumer less? Not a bit of it. It is because little corporations are in control of the political situation.

But there are certain obstacles to the working out of the New Freedom. First of all, there was a suspicion in Wilson's mind, even during the campaign, that the tendency to large organization was too powerful to be stopped by legislation. So he left open a way of escape from the literal achievement of what the New Freedom seemed to threaten. *"I am for big business,"* he said, *"and I am against the trusts."* That is a very subtle distinction, so subtle, I suspect, that no human legislation will ever be able to make it. The distinction is this: big business is a business that has survived competition; a trust is an arrangement to do away with competition. But when competition is done away with, who is the Solomon wise enough to know whether the result was accomplished by superior efficiency or by agreement among the competitors or by both?

The big trusts have undoubtedly been built up in part by superior business ability, and by successful competition, but also by ruthless competition, by underground arrangements, by an intricate series of facts which no earthly tribunal will ever be able to disentangle. And why should it try? These great combinations are here. What interests us is not their history but their future. The point is whether you are going to split them up, and if so into how many parts. Once split, are they to be kept from coming together again? Are you determined to prevent men who could coöperate from cooperating? Wilson seems to imply that a big business which has survived competition is to be let alone, and the trusts attacked. But as there is no real way of distinguishing between them, he leaves the question just where he found it: he must choose between the large organization of business and the small.

It's here that his temperament and his prejudices clash with fact and necessity. He really would like to disintegrate large business. "Are you not eager for the time," he asks, "when your sons shall be able to look forward to becoming not employees, but heads of some small, it may be, but hopeful business . . . ?" But to what percentage of the population can he hold out that hope? How many small but hopeful steel mills, coal mines, telegraph systems, oil refineries, copper mines, can this country support? A few hundred at the outside. And for these few hundred sons whose "best energies . . . are inspired by the knowledge that they are their own masters with the paths of the world before them," we are asked to give up the hope of a sane, deliberate organization of national industry brought under democratic control.

I submit that it is an unworthy dream. I submit that the intelligent men of my generation can find a better outlet for their energies than in making themselves masters of little businesses. They have the vast opportunity of introducing order and purpose into the business world, of devising administrative methods by which the great resources of the country can be operated on some thought-out plan. They have the whole new field of industrial statesmanship before them, and those who prefer the egotism of some little business are not the ones whose ambitions we need most to cultivate. . . .

Wilson is against the trusts for many reasons: the political economy of his generation was based on competition and free trade; the Democratic Party is by tradition opposed to a strong central government, and that opposition applies equally well to strong national business,—it is a party attached to local rights, to village patriotism, to humble but ambitious enterprise; its temper has always been hostile to specialization and expert knowledge, because it admires a very primitive man-to-man democracy. Wilson's thought is inspired by that outlook. It has been tempered somewhat by contact with men who have outgrown the village culture, so that Wilson is less hostile to experts, less oblivious to administrative problems than is Bryan. But at the same time his speeches are marked with contempt for the specialist: they play up quite obviously to the old democratic notion that any man can do almost any job. You have always to except the negro, of course, about whom the Democrats have a totally different tradition. But among white men, special training and expert knowledge are somewhat under suspicion in Democratic circles.

Hostility to large organization is a natural quality in village life. Wilson is always repeating that the old personal relationships of employer and employee have disappeared. He deplores the impersonal nature of the modern world. Now that is a fact not to be passed over lightly. It does change the nature of our problems enormously. Indeed, it is just this breakdown of the old relationships which constitutes the modern problem. . . .

The Promise of Big Business

Nobody likes the present situation very much. But where dispute arises is over whether we can by legislation return to a simpler and more direct stage of civilization. Bryan really hopes to do that, Wilson does too, but his mind is too critical not to have some doubts, and that is why he is against trusts but not against big business. But there is a growing body of opinion which says that communication is blotting out village culture, and opening up national and international thought. It says that bad as big business is to-day, it has a wide promise within it, and that the real task of our generation is to realize it. It looks to the infusion of scientific method, the careful application of administrative technique, the organization and education of the consumer for control, the discipline of labor for an increasing share of the management. Those of us who hold such a belief are pushed from behind by what we think is an irresistible economic development, and lured by a future which we think is possible.

We don't imagine that the trusts are going to drift naturally into the service of human life. We think they can be made to serve it if the American people compel them. We think that the American people may be able to do that if they can adjust their thinking to a new world situation, if they apply the scientific spirit to daily life, and if they can learn to coöperate on a large scale. Those, to be sure, are staggering *ifs*. The conditions may never be fulfilled entirely. But in so far as they are not fulfilled we shall drift along at the mercy of economic forces that we are unable to master. Those who cling to the village view of life may deflect the drift, may batter the trusts about a bit, but they will never dominate business, never humanize its machinery, and they will continue to be the playthings of industrial change.

CHAPTER 4

Industrial Workers and the Rise of Unionism

Chapter Preface

The industrial revolution and the technology it introduced not only increased the number of industrial workers in America (from 885,000 in 1860 to 3.2 million in 1900), but also brought new patterns of labor into the workplace. Mechanization and specialization decreased the demand for skilled workers. In the shoe industry, for example, skilled craftsmen who made shoes by hand were replaced by factory workers who just stitched one part of the shoe, or who operated machinery that did the work for them. Many of these unskilled jobs were filled by women and children. The relaxed atmosphere that had previously prevailed in small manufacturing workshops (where the owner of the shop was on a first-name basis with his employees) was replaced by a rigid discipline enforced by overseers who often felt greater responsibility to their corporate stockholders than for their employees.

Without land or property, workers were solely dependent on wages for their livelihood. Economic historians, factoring in declining prices during this period, have calculated that average real wages did rise 31 percent for unskilled workers and 74 percent for skilled workers between 1860 and 1890. Despite this general increase in average pay, however, workers often found their position in the new industrial economy to be a difficult and precarious one. The wages of many workers, especially unskilled ones, were usually low; families supported themselves by sending wives and children to work. Workers could be fired at will. Many worked sixty to eighty hours a week at jobs that were often exhausting and monotonous. Industrial accidents and periods of forced layoffs were common, but disability and unemployment insurance did not exist; such protection was not considered the employer's responsibility. Finally, as individuals the workers had little bargaining power against the corporations that hired them; companies in many cases could easily discharge unsatisfied workers and find willing replacements (often from the ranks of the millions of immigrants that came to America during this time).

In response to these changing and often difficult conditions, workers attempted to organize themselves in labor unions or similar organizations. Such labor activity had been part of American life since at least the early 1800s, but national organizations did not appear until after the Civil War. These labor groups differed in their composition and goals. The National Labor Union and the Knights of Labor, both begun in the 1860s, attempted to organize individual workers into a large political organization that would pursue political and social reforms, such as instituting an eight-hour workday for all workers. The American Federation of Labor, founded in 1886, eschewed advocacy of broad social reform and instead sought to improve worker conditions by enabling workers to bargain collectively, establish the principle of the "closed shop" (where only union members could be employed), and, if necessary, engage in strikes. Its federated craft unions generally limited their membership to skilled workers. The Industrial Workers of the World, founded in 1905, sought to overthrow capitalism and unite the masses of unskilled workers.

Between 1881 and 1905, nearly 7 million workers participated in more than thirty-seven thousand strikes. However, labor unions faced numerous obstacles in organizing workers and attaining their goals. Business executives believed that labor unions threatened the foundations of America's social order. Companies fired and blacklisted workers known to have participated in union activity. In their attempts to replace striking workers with nonunion "scabs," companies generally had the support of federal, state, and local governments; such support often took the form of police, state militia, or even federal troops dispatched to restore order and enforce court injunctions against strike activity. Many Americans, both within and outside the working class, were suspicious of unions and blamed them for the violence that often accompanied strikes. Divisions within the workers' ranks also hampered the rise of trade unionism. Most unions, for instance, excluded black and women workers.

Both because of strong opposition by businesses and because of internal divisions, labor unions represented only a small percentage of America's workforce by the beginning of the twentieth century. However, they did succeed by this time in drawing the public's attention to questions of workers' safety, wages, and other labor issues—issues that are debated in the viewpoints in this chapter.

Viewpoint 1

"[Labor organizations] stand discredited and distrusted before the community at large as impracticable, unjust, and reckless."

Labor Unions Are Harmful

Henry Clews (1834–1923)

Although labor unions and workers' strikes had existed in the United States in various localities since colonial times, they did not emerge on a nationwide basis until after the Civil War. Two major strikes made it clear to Americans that the problem of labor strife was now a national issue. First, in 1877 a strike by railway workers at the Baltimore and Ohio Railroad soon spread to other areas, eventually idling two-thirds of the nation's railroads. President Rutherford B. Hayes eventually mobilized federal troops to quell the strike, but not until after almost one hundred people had died in strike-related violence. Second, on May 1, 1886, 340,000 workers across the country walked off their jobs in support of a national campaign for an eight-hour workday. During this strike, an unidentified person threw a bomb at a Chicago, Illinois, labor rally and killed several policemen. Both the 1877 and 1886 actions generated fear of labor unions and their goals and tactics among the public.

The following viewpoint is by Henry Clews, a leading financier and investor during the Civil War and an economic adviser to President Ulysses S. Grant after the war. In the essay, first published in the June 1886 issue of the *North American Review*, Clews denounces the growth of unionism in the American labor force.

From Henry Clews, "The Folly of Organized Labor," *North American Review*, June 1886.

He argues that the May Day strike of 1886 has been a failure for workers and that workers in America have no real cause for complaint. Clews specifically attacks the Knights of Labor, a leading national organization of workers in the 1880s that many blamed for causing the disturbances of 1886.

The Knights of Labor have undertaken to test, upon a large scale, the application of compulsion as a means of enforcing their demands. The point to be determined is whether capital or labor shall, in future, determine the terms upon which the invested resources of the nation are to be employed.

To the employer, it is a question whether his individual rights as to the control of his property shall be so far overborne as to not only deprive him of his freedom but also expose him to interferences seriously impairing the value of his capital. To the employees, it is a question whether, by the force of coercion, they can wrest, to their own profit, powers and control which, in every civilized community, are secured as the most sacred and inalienable rights of the employer.

This issue is so absolutely revolutionary of the normal relations between labor and capital, that it has naturally produced a partial paralysis of business, especially among industries whose operations involve contracts extending into the future. There has been at no time any serious apprehension that such an utterly anarchical movement could succeed so long as American citizens have a clear perception of their rights and their true interests; but it has been distinctly perceived that this war could not fail to create a divided if not hostile feeling between the two great classes of society; that it must hold in check not only a large extent of ordinary business operations but also the undertaking of those new enterprises which contribute to our national progress, and that the commercial markets must be subjected to serious embarrassments.

This Labor Disease

From the nature of the case, however, this labor disease must soon end one way or another; and there is not much difficulty in foreseeing what its termination will be. The demands of the Knights and their sympathizers, whether openly expressed or temporarily concealed, are so utterly revolutionary of the inalienable rights of the citizen and so completely subversive of social order that the whole community has come to a firm conclusion that these pretensions must be resisted to the last extremity of endurance and authority; and that the present is the best opportunity for meeting the issue firmly and upon its merits.

In 1887 James Gibbons, the Roman Catholic archbishop of Baltimore, Maryland, issued a statement to the Vatican defending the rights of Catholic workers to join labor organizations, including the controversial Knights of Labor. His defense of labor unions was criticized by those who believed that unions were violent offenders of the social order—a view represented by this 1887 Puck *cartoon.*

The organizations have sacrificed the sympathy which lately was entertained for them on account of inequities existing in certain employments; they stand discredited and distrusted before the community at large as impracticable, unjust, and reckless; and, occupying this attitude before the public, their cause is gone and their organization doomed to failure. They have opened the floodgates to the immigration of foreign labor, which is already pouring in by the thousands; and they have set a premium on nonunion labor, which will be more sought for than ever, and will not be slow to secure superior earnings by making arrangements with employers upon such terms and for such hours as may best suit their interests. Thus, one great advantage will incidentally come out of this crisis beneficial to the workingman, who, by standing aloof from the dead-level system of the unions, will be enabled to earn according to his capacity and thereby maintain his chances for rising from the rank of the employee to that of the employer.

This result cannot be long delayed; because not only is loss and suffering following close upon the heels of the strikers, but the imprudences of their leaders are breeding dissatisfaction among the rank and file of the organizations, which, if much further protracted, will gravely threaten their cohesion. It is by no means certain that we may not see a yet further spread of strikes, and possibly with even worse forms of violence than we have yet witnessed; but, so long as a way to the end is seen, with a chance of that end demonstrating to the organizations that their aspirations to control capital are impossible dreams, the temporary evils will be borne with equanimity. The coolness with which the past phases of the strikes have been endured shows that the steady judgment of our people may be trusted to keep them calm under any further disturbance that may arise.

It is quite evident that the backbone of the strike is broken and that the worst is past, and that a general recovery of trade will assert itself, more or less, in spite of whatever obstacles may be raised by the labor organizations.

The labor movement inaugurated as a stupendous undertaking and announced to come off on the 1st of May, now past, has been a signal failure. The cause of justice and peace has achieved for itself new prestige sufficient to give it longevity, for the reason that the strike movement has been deprived of justification and right of existence. . . .

The timely and forcible action of Mayor Harrison, of Chicago, will put dynamiters and rioters where they belong, and thus divide the sheep from the goats in a very short time. If officials would sink political bias, the country would soon be rid of lawbreakers and disturbers of the peace. As this plan has now been adopted, it will be far-reaching in its effect, and stop mob gatherings, riotous speechmaking, and other such bad incentives which recently have been so conspicuous in Chicago, Milwaukee, St. Louis, and elsewhere. The laboring classes, who are parties to the strike, will now have an opportunity to retire to their homes, where there will be more safety than in the streets-which will bring to them reflection; they will then soon become satisfied that they are the aggrieved parties; and the not-unlikely result will be their turning upon the leaders who have deceived them.

Labor and Immigration

There have been numerous vacancies created by the strikers voluntarily resigning. There has been no difficulty in filling these vacancies by those that are equally capable, if not more so, from other countries flocking to our shores. The steam ferry which connects this country and Europe has demonstrated this by the steamer that arrived in six days and ten hours' time from European shores to our own. As the interval between the downtrodden and oppressed operatives of the Old World and America is thus reduced to hours, Europe will quickly send to us all the labor we need to meet the emergency. . . . Strikes may have been justifiable in other nations but they are not justifiable in our country, and there is where the mistake was in organizing such a movement. The Almighty has made this country for the oppressed of other nations, and therefore this is the land of refuge for the oppressed, and the hand of the laboring man should not be raised against it.

Wages Are Rising for Workers

Economist and writer W.A. Croffut, writing in the May 1886 issue of the Forum, *argues that the conditions of workers in America are improving.*

The laboring men of America were never so well off as they are to-day, considering both wages and the price of living.

The familiar maxim that "the poor are becoming poorer" is not true. In 1850 the average of wages in the United States was $248 per annum; in 1860 it was $272; in 1870 it was $310; in 1880 it was $346. The daily wage has increased from eighty cents to $1.16. During these thirty years, moreover, there has been a constant but not uniform decline in prices, so that seventy cents will buy in 1886 what it took $1 to buy in 1850. The accumulations of capital have also increased, but not in so great a proportion. All figures bearing on the subject show that the rich have not become relatively richer, and that workingmen could never buy so much of the necessaries of life with so few hours of labor as in the year 1886.

The laboring man in this bounteous and hospitable country has no ground for complaint. His vote is potential and he is elevated thereby to the position of man. Elsewhere he is a creature of circumstance, which is that of abject depression. Under the government of this nation, the effort is to elevate the standard of the human race and not to degrade it. In all other nations it is the reverse. What, therefore, has the laborer to complain of in America? By inciting strikes and encouraging discontent, he stands in the way of the elevation of his race and of mankind.

The tide of emigration to this country, now so large, makes peaceful strikes perfectly harmless in themselves, because the places of those who vacate good situations are easily filled by the newcomers. When disturbances occur under the cloak of strikes, it is a different matter, as law and order are then set at defiance. The recent disturbances in Chicago, which resulted in the assassination of a number of valiant policemen through some cowardly Polish nihilist firing a bomb of dynamite in their midst, was the worst thing that could have been done for the cause of the present labor agitation, as it alienates all sympathy from them. It is much to the credit, however, of Americans and Irishmen that, during the recent uprising of the labor classes, none of them have taken part in any violent measures whatsoever, nor have they shown any sympathy with such a policy.

America's Potential

If the labor troubles are to be regarded as only a transient interruption of the course of events, it is next to be asked: What may be anticipated when those obstructions disappear? We have still our magnificent country, with all the resources that have made it so prosperous and so progressive beyond the record of all nations. There is no abatement of our past ratio of increase of population; no limitation of the new sources of wealth awaiting development; no diminution of the means necessary to the utilization of the unbounded riches of the soil, the mine, and the forest. Our inventive genius has suffered no eclipse. In the practical application of what may be called the commercial sciences, we retain our lead of the world. As pioneers of new sources of wealth, we are producing greater results than all the combined new colonizing efforts which have recently excited the ambitions of European governments. To the overcrowded populations of the Old World, the United States still presents attractions superior to those of any other country; as is evidenced by the recent sudden revival of emigration from Great Britain and the Continent to our shores.

140

"The labor movement as represented by the trades unions stands for right, for justice, for liberty."

Labor Unions Are Necessary

Samuel Gompers (1850–1924)

Samuel Gompers cofounded the American Federation of Labor (AFL), an association of trade unions, in 1886 and served as the organization's president almost continuously thereafter until his death. Under his leadership the AFL grew to become the most important labor group in the country, representing 1.6 million of the 2 million union workers in the nation in 1904. Although sharing some basic goals, its structure and tactics differed somewhat from those of rival organizations such as the Knights of Labor. The AFL was organized as a federation of separate and largely independent unions, rather than as one big national union like the Knights of Labor. In addition, unlike the Knights, it eschewed calls for general social reform or support of a separate political party for workers, concentrating instead on gaining better wages, hours, and working conditions through collective bargaining and, if necessary, strikes.

Throughout his long career, Gompers remained a steadfast advocate of the rights of laborers to organize. The following viewpoint is taken from an 1894 open letter by Gompers to Peter Grosscup, a judge in the U.S. District Court of Illinois. During an 1894 strike against the Pullman Company that largely paralyzed the nation's railway system, Grosscup had presided over the indictment of American Railway Union president Eugene V. Debs for violating a federal court injunction against strikes (such in-

From Samuel Gompers, open letter to Peter Grosscup, reprinted in the *American Federationist*, vol. 1, September 1894.

junctions were frequently issued by the courts to stifle labor activities). In his charge to the jury, Grosscup argued that union organizing constituted an illegal conspiracy. Gompers responds in the letter by defending the right and necessity of workers to organize themselves and bargain collectively for better working conditions.

You say that, as you stated in your charge to the grand jury, you believe in labor organizations within such lawful and reasonable limits as will make them a service to the laboring man and not a menace to the lawful institutions of the country. I have had the pleasure of reading your charge to the grand jury, and have only partially been able to discover how far you believe in labor organizations.

What Workers Can Discuss

You would certainly have no objection officially or personally to workingmen organizing, and in their meetings discuss perhaps "the origin of man," benignly smiling upon each other and declaring that all existing things are right, going to their wretched homes to find some freedom in sleep from gnawing hunger. You would have them extol the virtues of monopolists and wreckers of the people's welfare. You would not have them consider seriously the fact that more than 2 million of their fellows are unemployed, and though willing and able, cannot find the opportunity to work in order that they may sustain themselves, their wives, and their children. You would not have them consider seriously the fact that [George] Pullman who has grown so rich from the toil of his workmen that he can riot in luxury, while he heartlessly turns these very workmen out of their tenements into the streets and leave to the tender mercies of corporate greed. Nor would you have them ponder upon the hundreds of other Pullmans of different names.

You know, or ought to know, that the introduction of machinery is turning into idleness thousands faster than new industries are founded, and yet, machinery certainly should not be either destroyed or hampered in its full development. The laborer is a man, he is made warm by the same sun and made cold-yes, colder-by the same winter as you are. He has a heart and brain, and feels and knows the human and paternal instinct for those depending upon him as keenly as do you.

What shall the workers do? Sit idly by and see the vast resources of nature and the human mind be utilized and monopolized for the benefit of the comparative few? No. The laborers must learn to think and act, and soon, too, that only by the power of organization and common concert of action can either their manhood be maintained, their rights to life (work to sustain it) be recognized, and liberty and rights secured.

Since you say that you favor labor organizations within certain limits, will you kindly give to thousands of your anxious fellow citizens what you believe the workers could and should do in their organizations to solve this great problem? Not what they should not do. You have told us that.

I am not one of those who regards the entire past as a failure. I recognize the progress made and the improved conditions of which nearly the entire civilized world are the beneficiaries. I ask you to explain, however, that if the wealth of the whole world is, as you say, "preeminently and beneficially the nation's wealth," how is it that thousands of able-bodied, willing, earnest men and women are suffering the pangs of hunger? We may boast of our wealth and civilization, but to the hungry man and woman and child our progress is a hollow mockery, our civilization a sham, and our "national wealth" a chimera.

Industrial Forces

You recognize that the industrial forces set in motion by steam and electricity have materially changed the structure of our civilization. You also admit that a system has grown up where the accumulations of the individual have passed from his control into that of representative combinations and trusts, and that the tendency in this direction is on the increase. How, then, can you consistently criticize the workingmen for recognizing that as individuals they can have no influence in deciding what the wages, hours of toil, and conditions of employment shall be?

You evidently have observed the growth of corporate wealth and influence. You recognize that wealth, in order to become more highly productive, is concentrated into fewer hands, and controlled by representatives and directors, and yet you sing the old siren song that the workingman should depend entirely upon his own "individual effort."

The school of laissez-faire, of which you seem to be a pronounced advocate, has produced great men in advocating the theory of each for himself and his Satanic majesty taking the hindermost, but the most pronounced advocates of your school of thought in economics have, when practically put to the test, been compelled to admit that combination and organization of the toiling masses are essential both to prevent the deterioration and to secure an improvement in the condition of the wage earners.

If, as you say, the success of commercial society depends upon

143

the full play of competition, why do not you and your confreres turn your attention and direct the shafts of your attacks against the trusts and corporations, business wreckers and manipulators in the food products-the necessities of the people. Why garland your thoughts in beautiful phrase when speaking of these modern vampires, and steep your pen in gall when writing of the laborers' efforts to secure some of the advantages accruing from the concentrated thought and genius of the ages? . . .

Progress and Poverty

One becomes enraptured in reading the beauty of your description of modern progress. Could you have had in mind the miners of Spring Valley or Pennsylvania, or the clothing workers of the sweatshops of New York or Chicago when you grandiloquently dilate,

> Who is not rich today when compared with his ancestors of a century ago? The steamboat and the railroad bring to his breakfast table the coffees of Java and Brazil, the fruits from Florida and California, and the steaks from the plains. The loom arrays him in garments and the factories furnish him with a dwelling that the richest contemporaries of his grandfather would have envied. With health and industry he is a prince.

Probably you have not read within the past year of babes dying of starvation at their mothers' breasts. More than likely the thousands of men lying upon the bare stones night after night in the City Hall of Chicago last winter escaped your notice. You may not have heard of the cry for bread that was sounded through this land of plenty by thousands of honest men and women. But should these and many other painful incidents have passed you by unnoticed, I am fearful that you may learn of them with keener thoughts with the coming sleets and blasts of winter.

You say that "labor cannot afford to attack capital." Let me remind you that labor has no quarrel with capital, as such. It is merely the possessors of capital who refuse to accord to labor the recognition, the right, the justice which is the laborers' due with whom we contend.

See what is implied by your contemptuous reference to the laborer when you ask, "Will the conqueror destroy his trophy?" Who ever heard of a conqueror marching unitedly with his trophy, as you would have them? But if by your comparison you mean that the conqueror is the corporation, the trust, the capitalist class, and ask then whether they would destroy their trophy, I would have you ask the widows and orphans of the thousands of men killed annually through the avarice of railroad corporations refusing to avail themselves of modern appliances in coupling and other improvements on their railroads.

Inquire from the thousands of women and children whose husbands or fathers were suffocated or crushed in the mines through the rapacious greed of stockholders clamoring for more dividends. Investigate the sweating dens of the large cities. Go to the mills, factories, through the country. Visit the modern tenement houses or hovels in which thousands of workers are compelled to eke out an existence. Ask these whether the conqueror (monopoly) cares whether his trophy (the laborers) is destroyed or preserved. Ascertain from employers whether the laborer is not regarded the same as a machine, thrown out as soon as all the work possible has been squeezed out of him.

Labor Legislation

Are you aware that all the legislation ever secured for the ventilation or safety of mines, factory, or workshop is the result of the efforts of organized labor? Do you know that the trade unions were the shield for the seven-year-old children from being the conqueror's trophy until they become somewhat older? And that the reformatory laws now on the statute books protecting or defending the trophies of both sexes, young and old from the fond care of the conquerors were wrested from congresses, legislatures, and parliaments despite the Pullmans, the Jeffries, the Ricks, the Tafts, the Williams, the Woods, or the Grosscups.

By what right, sir, do you assume that the labor organizations do not conduct their affairs within lawful limits, or that they are a menace to the lawful institutions of the country? Is it because some thoughtless or overzealous member at a time of great excitement and smarting under a wrong may violate under a law or commit an improper act? Would you apply the same rule to the churches, the other moral agencies and organizations that you do to the organizations of labor? If you did, the greatest moral force of life today, the trade unions, would certainly stand out the clearest, brightest, and purest. Because a certain class (for which you and a number of your colleagues on the bench seem to be the special pleaders) have a monopoly in their lines of trade, I submit that this is no good reason for their claim to have a monopoly on true patriotism or respect for the lawful institutions of the country.

But speaking of law reminds me of the higher law of the land. The Constitution prescribes that all rights not specifically granted to the general government are reserved to the states. There is another provision prohibiting the President from sending armed forces into any state except for the purpose of maintaining "a republican form of government," and then only upon the requisition of the legislature of the state, or of the governor when the legislature is not in session. Yet when, during the recent [1894 Pullman] railroad strike, the President [Grover Cleveland] sent the troops into Illinois, it was not in compliance with the request of the legislature of that state, nor of the governor, but in spite of his protest. Yes, even when the governor remonstrated he was practically told by the President to stop arguing the law upon the question. Pardon the simplicity of my inquiry, but does not the law require that its limits shall be observed by a president, a judge, equally as by a labor organization?

Labor Must Organize

John Peter Altgeld, governor of Illinois from 1892 to 1896, was more sympathetic to labor concerns than many other public officials at that time. The following passage is taken from an address observing Labor Day in Chicago in 1893, a time when America was suffering a severe economic depression. Altgeld argues that the working class must act together against the "giant combinations of power" that characterize the age.

In the industrial world, as well as in the political world, only those forces survive which can maintain themselves and which are so concentrated that their influence is immediately and directly felt. A scattered force, no matter how great, is of no account in the sharp contests of the age. This is an age of concentration. Everywhere there is concentration and combination of capital and of those factors which today rule the world. The formation of corporations has greatly accelerated this movement, and no matter what is said about it, whether we approve it or not, it is the characteristic feature of our civilization and grows out of increased invention, the speedy communication between different parts of the world, and the great industrial generalship and enterprise of the time. It is questionable whether this tendency to combination could have been stopped in any way. It is certain, without this concentration of force, the gigantic achievements of our times would have been an impossibility. Combination and concentration are the masters of the age.

Let the laborer learn from this and act accordingly. Faultfinding and idle complaint are useless. Great forces, like great rivers, cannot be stopped. You must be able to fight your own battles. For the laborer to stand single-handed before giant combinations of power means annihilation. The world gives only when it is obliged to and respects only those who compel its respect.

If I remember aright you based the injunctions recently issued by you upon the provisions of the [1887] Interstate Commerce Law, a law enacted by Congress upon the demand of the farmers and shippers of our country to protect them against the unjust and outrageous discriminations imposed by the railroads. Where in the law can you find one word to justify your course applying to workingmen organized and engaged in a strike?

Read the discussions in Congress when that law was under consideration. You will not find a remote reference to the application of the laws as you construe it. In fact, I am informed upon excellent authority that when the law was before the Senate in the form of a bill, Senator Morgan, of Alabama, proposed an amendment which, if adopted, would have had the effect of empowering judges to issue an order of the nature you have in the recent railroad strike; but it was not adopted; it was defeated. How then in the face of this you can issue your omnibus restraining order passes the comprehension of ordinary men. . . .

Year by year man's liberties are trampled underfoot at the bidding of corporations and trusts, rights are invaded, and law perverted. In all ages, wherever a tyrant has shown himself, he has always found some willing judge to clothe that tyranny in the robes of legality, and modern capitalism has proven no exception to the rule.

You may not know that the labor movement as represented by the trades unions stands for right, for justice, for liberty. You may not imagine that the issuance of an injunction depriving men of a legal as well as a natural right to protect themselves, their wives, and little ones must fail of its purpose. Repression or oppression never yet succeeded in crushing the truth or redressing a wrong.

In conclusion let me assure you that labor will organize and more compactly than ever and upon practical lines; and despite relentless antagonism, achieve for humanity a nobler manhood, a more beautiful womanhood, and a happier childhood.

"The owners of the mills had a perfect legal right to employ any necessary number of men to defend their property."

A Defense of the Acts of the Carnegie Steel Company Management at Homestead

George Ticknor Curtis (1812–1894)

Besides being an era of dramatic industrial growth, the decades following the Civil War were also a time of unprecedented labor unrest. Many labor disputes resulted in strikes, which often turned violent as employers sought to replace striking employees with scabs (substitute workers) while strikers attempted to prevent strikebreakers from working. Industrial employers, particularly those who refused to be reconciled to trade unions, often employed private guards, detectives, and other operatives to spy on suspected union activists and to break strikes by enabling scabs to work. In many cases companies received government assistance in defeating strikes. Between 1875 and 1910, state militia troops were called out nearly five hundred times to deal with strikes and labor unrest.

The Homestead strike of 1892, pitting the Amalgamated Association of Iron and Steel Workers against the Carnegie Steel Company, was one of the largest and most violent labor clashes of this period. The steel mill that was the site of the strike, one of three owned by Andrew Carnegie and the only one with union workers, was the largest employer in the small town of Homestead,

From George Ticknor Curtis, "The Homestead Strike: A Constitutional View," *North American Review*, September 1892.

Pennsylvania. Its 3,800 employees worked twelve-hour days, seven days a week. Most were unskilled workers who were not represented by unions and whose wages were generally low. Eight hundred of the more skilled laborers were represented by the union, which had won a favorable three-year contract in 1889. Negotiations over a new contract failed after the company proposed cutting wages. On June 24, 1892, plant manager and company chairman Henry Clay Frick announced that he would no longer recognize the union and would deal only with individual workers. On July 1, all the plant's workers, including those not in the union, went on strike. Frick planned on reopening the plant with replacement workers and hired three hundred guards from the Pinkerton Detective Agency to secure the mill. However, the striking workers and community supporters created an Advisory Committee and organized military-like divisions to guard the mill and the town and to prevent strikebreakers from working at Homestead.

Violence erupted on the morning of July 6, when Frick attempted to transport the Pinkerton agents by barge up the Monongahela River to Homestead. They were met by ten thousand strikers and supporters on the riverbank, many of them armed. After both sides exchanged gunfire, the Pinkerton agents eventually surrendered and agreed to leave the area and not return. Although guaranteed safe conduct by strike leaders, they were forced to run a gauntlet of mob clubbings and beatings before reaching safety. Most of the Pinkerton operatives were injured; several strikers and Pinkerton employees were killed.

Five days later the governor of Pennsylvania dispatched eight thousand state militia troops who took control of the town and enabled Frick to gradually reopen the plant with nonunion and replacement workers. More than one hundred strikers were indicted and arrested, some for murder. Most public sympathy for the strike evaporated when Alexander Berkman, a young anarchist, attempted to assassinate Frick on July 23, although there was no connection between Berkman and the strikers.

The following viewpoint is taken from an article by George Ticknor Curtis, an eminent patent attorney and author on history and the law. He presents a conservative view of the events at Homestead, arguing that the management at Carnegie Steel Company had every right to take steps to defend their property, including hiring the Pinkerton guards. Curtis contends that workers have an individual right to accept or reject employers' demands, but that unions have no collective right to dictate labor conditions or prevent other workers from replacing strikers.

The editor of *The North American Review* has requested me to give my opinion on "the legality of the employment of Pinkerton detectives in such cases as the Homestead strike." The inquiry relates to other cases similar in all material respects to the recent occurrences at Homestead, in Pennsylvania. It also involves the relations of employers and employed in all similar branches of manufactures; the relations between the owners of mills, factories, etc., and the workmen whom they employ. A great deal has been written on the relations of capital and labor, and written to very little purpose. It is, however, not difficult to define the rights of property owners or capitalists on the one hand, and of workmen on the other; nor is it difficult to determine what society—by which I mean the legislative power—owes to each of them respectively. . . .

Homestead is a borough on the Allegheny River, ten miles from Pittsburg. It contains about 10,000 inhabitants. Most of the male inhabitants are employed in one capacity or another, either as skilled or unskilled laborers, in the iron and steel manufacturing establishments. Their wages were exceptionally high. There exists among them, as there exists elsewhere, what is called a "trades-union." This is a body of workmen banded together for the purpose, among other things, of keeping up the price of labor, and, by means of a strike, of coercing their employers, when the latter do not accede to their terms. A strike is a concerted and sudden cessation of work at a given signal or order, issued by the authority of the union, in whom the power to issue it is vested by the members. Sometimes this authority is a single individual; sometimes it is an advisory committee. In all cases, when a strike is ordered, work ceases at once, to the great injury of employers and employed.

In the Homestead case, the existing agreement between the Carnegie Steel Company and their workmen about wages, had run out. Mr. [Henry Clay] Frick, the managing agent of the company, had an interview with the men, and offered a new scale of wages. This the men refused to accept. Mr. Frick then closed the mills. After this the workmen seized the mills, excluded the owners from their property by an overwhelming force, and prevented the employment of non-union men. Obviously, it was indispensable that something should be done to restore law and order, and to reinstate the owners of the mills in their property. The local officer of the law, whose duty it was to do this, was the sheriff of Allegheny County. His means consisted only of special deputy sheriffs appointed from the citizens at large, and sworn in as a temporary and extemporized force. In a population consisting largely of the striking workmen and their sympathizers, a force adequate to do what had to be done could not be obtained.

The Pinkerton Agents

Thereupon the Carnegie Steel Company applied to the Pinkerton agency for a body of watchmen to protect their property. The agency refused to supply the men unless they should be sworn in as deputy sheriffs before going to Homestead. . . .

The men were sent down the Allegheny River on barges. It is immaterial whether there is or is not a law of Pennsylvania which prohibits the sending of a body of armed men into the State for any purpose. I understand that there is no such law in Pennsylvania, although there is such a law in some of the New England States. But the Pinkerton men were within the limits of the State before they were armed or needed to be. The boxes containing arms and ammunition were shipped from Chicago, *and were to be delivered at the Homestead yards.* These boxes, on board the barges, were not opened and the contents distributed until after the strikers had begun firing from the shore on the watchmen and it had become an evident matter of self-defence. Klein, one of the Pinkerton watchmen, had been killed by the strikers, and about five other men shot and wounded before the Pinkerton men began their fire in self-defence. Then it was impossible to shoot those firing from the shore at the barges, because the strikers had made a breastwork for themselves by placing women and children in front and firing from behind them.

The Pinkerton men were obliged to capitulate before they were allowed to land and even then they were not permitted to go to the mills which they had been employed to protect. They were conducted by an overwhelming force of the strikers to Labor Hall, the place of meeting of the strikers. There they were made to promise to quit Homestead and never again to serve the mill owners. On their way from the hall they were insulted and brutally assailed by a mob, among whom the women were the most violent. They were withdrawn from the State by the agency, and thus the whole object for which they had been employed was prevented.

Under these circumstances, the sheriff of Allegheny County applied to the Governor of the State for a military force. The Governor declined to order out any of the troops of the State, until the sheriff had exhausted his means of restoring law and order by the appointment of special deputies. The sheriff made an ineffectual effort to do this, but the citizens responded in such few numbers that it would have been idle to rely on the civil arm alone. When the Governor was officially informed of this, he ordered out the entire division of the State militia, about 6,000 men, under General Snowden, a capable, prudent and experienced officer. The troops were marched to Homestead, and encamped on a hill that overlooks the town. It is only necessary to say, concerning this part of the history, that at the time at which I am writing there is every prospect that the strike will be completely put down, and thus the State of Pennsylvania will have rendered a great service to the whole country, employers and employed, capitalists and laborers.

Judgments on Homestead

On the indubitable facts of the Homestead case, which I have taken great pains to gather from authentic sources, I have no hesitation in expressing my opinion, as follows:

First, That the owners of the mills had a perfect legal right to employ any necessary number of men to defend their property.

Secondly, That all the acts of the Pinkerton men at Homestead were lawful; and that, as watchmen, they had a right to bear arms on the premises of the Carnegie company in order to protect life and property, whether they were or were not deputized by the sheriff of Allegheny County; and that the agency had the right to ship arms for such purposes from Chicago to the Carnegie yards at Homestead; and that, in view of the attack on the barges, the watchmen had the right to bear arms and defend themselves; and that all their acts in firing in self-defence from the barges after the attack on them were legally justifiable under the laws of the United States and the State of Pennsylvania.

Thirdly, That the killing of Klein by one or more of the riotous strikers was a murder.

Fourthly, That all who stood by, sympathizing with and encouraging the strikers, or not exerting themselves to prevent the strikers who were armed from firing on the barges, were accessories to the murder.

Having thus answered the question that was propounded to me, I shall devote the remainder of the space allotted for this article to the consideration of the duty of the legislative power in the States of this Union in reference to the whole subject of strikes. The stake that society has in all branches of manufacturing industries and in all the great lines of communication and travel is too vast to permit any body of men, large or small, on any pretext, to put a sudden stop to production, or to cause a sudden paralysis in the system of daily and hourly intercourse between different communities. . . .

The first duty of the legislative power is to emancipate the individual workman from the tyranny of his class. Unless this be done, capitalists can afford no aid to the solution of any labor problem whatever. Of what avail is it that a mill owner or a railroad company is willing to make fair terms with workmen if the state of things is such that they cannot employ whom they please, on such terms as will be agreed to by the men who want employment? It is only by making the individual laborer a perfectly free man that society can do its duty to him and to those who wish to buy his labor for a price that he is willing to take, and which it is for the interest of those who are dependent upon him to have him take.

In opposition to this view, it will be said that the individual workman is a free agent now, and that if he chooses to join a trades-union and bind himself not to work for wages less than

---

The Battle at Homestead

Congressman William C. Oates gave an account of the clash between Pinkerton agents and striking Homestead workers in the September 1892 issue of the North American Review.

When Capt. Rodgers's boat with the barges in tow was approaching Homestead, just as day was breaking, a small steamer used by the strikers for patrol purposes set up a whistle, which was responded to by all the engines in town under their control. This caused a crowd to at once assemble along the bank of the river, where it kept pace with the boat, discharging firearms. When the crowd on shore reached the fence around the works they were temporarily halted, but tearing down a part of it they rushed through. A part of the crowd on the shore came down near to the boat when the gang-plank was pushed out. A short war of words was followed by firing on each side, which resulted ultimately in the death of three of the Pinkerton men and seven of the workmen, and the wounding of many on each side. After a brief fusillade those on shore fled in various directions, and the Pinkerton men retreated into their barges. . . . The strikers on shore were endeavoring to use a piece of artillery upon the barges, but they could not depress it sufficiently and consequently fired over them. They also poured oil into the river above the barges and set it on fire, but this failed of its purpose, because the water in the river is slack at this point and the wind was blowing up instead of down the river. About five o'clock in the afternoon the Pinkertons displayed a white flag, and negotiated terms of surrender, by which they were allowed to take out their clothing, but their arms and everything else fell into the possession of the Homestead people. The barges were immediately set on fire and burned, and in their burning the pump-house belonging to the Carnegie company was also destroyed. The Pinkerton men now being practically prisoners of war, were marched up town to the skating rink for temporary imprisonment, and on their way, instead of receiving that protection which Mr. Hugh O'Donnell, the chairman of the Advisory Committee, in negotiating the terms of surrender had promised, they were brutally and outrageously maltreated. The injuries inflicted upon them, in some cases, were indecent as well as brutal. Whether these men were of good or bad character, the offence which they had committed against the feelings of the people of Homestead could in no degree justify the indignities with which they were treated.

what the union permits him to take, it is his own affair; he is acting in his own right. There is a wide distinction between the physical power to do a thing and the moral and legal right to do it. Men have the physical power to commit suicide, but society does not allow that they have a moral or a legal right to do it. On the same principle, the individual workman should not be allowed to commit moral suicide by surrendering his liberty to the control of his fellow workmen. His labor is his capital, all that he has in the world, all that he and his family have to depend upon for subsistence from day to day. It is to him and them what money invested in real estate, machinery, etc., is to the capitalist. Deprive the capitalist of the power to determine what remuneration he shall derive from the employment of his invested money, and you do the same wrong as when you deprive the laborer of the free power to determine what remuneration he will be content to take for the employment of his capital, which consists of his muscular power and his acquired skill.

These doctrines may not be popular. They may not meet at once with universal acceptance. But until they are accepted and carried out in legislation, there can be no successful reconcilement between the interests of capital and the interests of labor; no adjustment of the rights of society and the rights of employers and employed.

What Workers Can Do

In order that I may not be misunderstood, I will now draw the line between what it may and what it may not be permitted to workmen to do. Associations of workmen, formed for the purpose of discussing the subject of wages with their employers, of obtaining and diffusing information about the price of labor in different places, and of mutual assistance in time of sickness, are beneficial and should be encouraged. But the trades-unions do not confine themselves to these objects. They transcend the line which divides what they may from what they may not rightfully do. In this respect they do a double wrong:

First, They bind their members to strike when ordered to do so by the governing authority of the union. Now the right to renounce an employment is an individual and not a corporate right. The corporate body of a trades-union should not be permitted to bind their members to quit work, as a body, when ordered to do so by the governing authority of the association.

Secondly, The trades-unions, as most of them are now organized, prevent non-union men from getting employment, by every species of intimidation, even by personal violence, and sometimes by murder.

This coercion of non-union men, however attempted and in whatever it ends, should be made a crime, and be punished with

154

severity. It is contrary to the fundamental principles of our institutions. The Declaration of Independence says "we hold these truths to be self-evident, that all men are created equal; that they are endowed by their Creator with certain inalienable rights; that among these are life, liberty and the pursuit of happiness. That, to secure these rights, governments are instituted among men, deriving their just powers from the consent of the governed."

Be it observed that these are individual rights; that they are inalienable by the individual himself. We should not permit a man to sell himself into slavery or to sell his own life. He cannot alienate his right to life or his right to liberty. No more should he be permitted to alienate his right to the pursuit of happiness, by giving up his power to consult his own individual welfare, in obtaining the means of happiness; and by putting it in the power of those who are engaged in the same employment to take the bread out of his mouth. We have emancipated the colored race from slavery; certain portions of our own race need emancipation from a slavery that is just as bad.

"Those who harshly criticise the workmen of Homestead should put themselves in the place of these workmen for a few brief moments of thought."

A Defense of the Actions of Strikers at Homestead

Terence V. Powderly (1849–1924)

Terence V. Powderly was a railroad machinist who joined the Knights of Labor in 1874 and was the chief executive of that labor organization from 1879 to 1893. He dispensed with earlier rules of secrecy and committed the organization to broad social reforms, including the eight-hour day, bans on immigration, and equal pay for women. In its peak year of 1886, the nationwide labor union topped 700,000 members. Powderly was more of a social reformer than a union activist. He personally opposed strikes, although they were sometimes utilized by local Knights of Labor unions. Powderly later worked for the federal government's Bureau of Immigration.

In the following viewpoint, taken from a September 1892 article in the *North American Review*, Powderly gives his views about the Homestead strike. The struggle between steelworkers and the Carnegie Steel Company in Homestead, Pennsylvania, had become violent on July 6, when company management attempted to bring in three hundred hired Pinkerton guards to safeguard the plant; the private security force was met and defeated by thousands of armed strikers and their supporters in a bloody engagement. Powderly argues that the company was wrong to bring in the Pinkerton guards and defends the actions of the strikers. He rejects the argument that workers have the right to bargain individually, but not collectively, for better working conditions. Workers must form unions to protect and manage their interests, Powderly

From Terence V. Powderly, "The Homestead Strike: A Knight of Labor's View," *North American Review*, September 1892.

insists, just as capitalists create corporations to manage theirs.

At the time Powderly wrote the article, the strike at Homestead was still in progress. However, with the help of state militia troops, the company was successfully reopening the steel mill with nonunion workers. By November 1892 workers called off the strike; none of their demands had been met and their union, the Amalgamated Association of Iron and Steel Workers, had been effectively destroyed. Unions would not gain a strong foothold in the steel industry until the 1930s.

The principle involved in the Homestead trouble is the same as that by which the founders of this republic were governed in rebelling against the British government. To have accepted decisions, decrees, and laws without question, and without a voice in their making, would have stamped the colonists as slaves. To accept, without inquiring the why or wherefore, such terms and wages as the Carnegie Steel Company saw fit to offer would stamp the brand of inferiority upon the workmen of Homestead. Independence is worth as much to the workingman as it can be to the employer. The right to sell his labor in the highest market is as dear to the workman as the right of the manufacturer to sell the product of that labor can possibly be to the latter. It is folly to assert that the workman has no right to a voice in determining what the minimum rate of compensation shall be. If the manufacturer is permitted to invade the market place and undersell competitors a reduction in the wages of his employees must inevitably follow. It was to protect the manufacturer as well as the workman that the Amalgamated Association insisted on a minimum rate of pay. The fixing of that rate imposed no hardship on the manufacturer; it gave no competitor the advantage over him, for the majority of mills were operated under the Amalgamated scale, and this of itself fixed a rate below which manufacturers would not sell. The minimum rate was therefore as advantageous to the manufacturer as to the workman in the steel trade. The question at issue between the Carnegie Steel Company and the steel workers does not so much concern the price as the right to a voice in fixing that price.

Unions and Corporations

Individual employers no longer exist; the day no longer dawns on the employer taking his place in the shop among the men. When that condition of workshop life existed employer and employee experienced a feeling of lasting friendship for each other; the interests of each were faithfully guarded by the other. Now the employer of men may be three thousand miles away from the workshop; he may be a part of a syndicate or corporation which deals with the employees through a special agent or superintendent, whose desire to secure the confidence and good will of the corporation may cause him to create friction in order to demonstrate that he is vigilant in looking after the interests of those to whom he looks for favors. The corporation, composed of many men, is an association of capital which delegates its authority to an agent whose duty it is to deal with the workmen and make terms with them. The Amalgamated Association, and all other bodies of organized workmen, stand in the same relation to the men as the corporation does to the capitalists whose money is invested. One invests money, that is, his capital; the other invests his labor, which to him is not only his capital but his all. That the workman should have the same right to be heard through his legitimately appointed agent, the officer of the labor organization, that the corporation has to be heard through the superintendent or agent, is but equity. This is the bone of contention at Homestead, and in fact everywhere else where a labor organization attempts to guard the rights of its members.

Every law, every right, every concession which the workingmen now enjoy has come to them through the labor organization. Philanthropists have spoken honeyed words for the laboring man, but he has always been forced to knock, and knock hard, with his organization in order to take what equity would have accorded him without a struggle if greed had not entered its protest. Equality of rights is what the workmen are contesting for, and because of its immense wealth the Carnegie Steel Company denies that right. It is argued that this trouble is between the employer and the employed and that no other has the right to interfere. That is a doubtful position to take. In a store, in a small shop, or where but a few persons are interested, a strike or lockout may be said to affect only those directly engaged in it, but in the present instance the case presents a different aspect to the thoughtful person. If the great steel plant were not just where it is the town of Homestead would would not be the flourishing place that it is. The establishment of that plant attracted workmen to the spot; they built homes, raised their families, and invested every dollar of their earnings there. Business men, professional men, and clergymen followed them, and a community of well-behaved, respectable citizens surrounds the steel works. The workmen by their labor made the steel works prosperous and great; on the other hand they made Homestead what it is. The men depend for their support on steady work, and the community back of them depends on their steady employment. Three parties are interested in this struggle, the Carnegie Steel Company, the employees of that concern, and the community. By community I mean the whole people. Other towns have grown up as Homestead grew, by the labor of workmen, and each one is to a certain extent interested in the welfare of the other. The articles manufactured in one place are sold in another, and a mutuality of interests exist to-day which did not, and could not, exist years ago when men required but few things to serve the every-day needs of life. The manager of the Carnegie Steel Company in asserting that he has the right to turn the makers of a prosperous town out of employment and out of the town,—for that naturally follows,—stands upon treacherous ground, for the makers of towns have equally as good a right to be heard as have the investors of money. If we go to a higher law than that of the land, the moral law, there will be no disputing the assertion that flesh and blood should receive more consideration than dollars and cents.

North Wind Picture Archives

This illustration of the Homestead strike depicts the scene following the Pinkertons' surrender and disembarkment from the river barge they had arrived on. The workers' triumph shown here proved to be temporary, however, as state militia troops were subsequently used to break the strike.

The Carnegie Steel Company and like concerns owe their prosperity to the protective [tariff] laws of the United States. These laws were passed in the interest of labor. During discussion on the tariff laws it was never advanced as a reason why they should be passed, that capital would be protected,—the argument was always that labor would be protected. The workman has not been protected from foreign competition by the government. He has had to fight the battle for himself through the labor organization. Not only has he had to fight against foreign competition, largely attracted by our delusive tariff laws, but he has had to wage war with the employer for a share of that protection which his government decreed by law that he should have. Our government has enacted protective legislation in the interest of labor, if we read congressional speeches aright, but it quiescently allows the manufacturer to absorb the bulk of protection, and then throws its armies around the establishment at the slightest provocation when the workmen ask for what their government admitted that they had a right to enjoy.

How Violence Could Have Been Prevented

What would have averted this trouble at Homestead, is asked? Industries which are protected by tariff laws should be open to inspection by government officials. When the managers of such concerns seek to absorb all of the protection the government should interfere on behalf of the workingmen. If we must have protection let us see to it that it protects the man who works.

At the hands of the law-making power of State and nation the Knights of Labor demand "the enactment of laws providing for arbitration between employers and employed, and to enforce the decision of the arbitrators." It should be a law in every State that in disputed cases the employer should be obliged to select two arbitrators and the employees two, these four to select the fifth; this arbitration commission to have access to all books, papers, and facts bearing on the question at issue from both sides. It goes without saying that the commission should be made up of reasonable, well-disposed men, and that publicity would not be given to such information as they might become possessed of.

An established board of arbitration, appointed by a governor or other authority, is simply no board of arbitration at all, for the reason that the workmen would have no voice in its selection, and the other side, having all the money and influence, would be tempted to "fix" such a board preparatory to engaging in a controversy with workingmen. For either side to refuse to appoint its arbitrators should be held to be cause for their appointment by the Governor of the State. No strike or lockout should be entered upon before the decision of the board of arbitrators. Provisions for appeal from the decision of the arbitrators should be made in order to prevent intimidation or money from influencing the board.

In no case should the introduction of an armed force, such as the Pinkerton detective agency arms and equips, be tolerated. The system which makes one man a millionaire makes tramps and paupers of thousands. The thousands go down to the brothels and slums, where they sprout the germs of anarchy and stand ready for any deed of desperation. The millionaire becomes more arrogant and unreasonable as his millions accumulate. Victimizing and blacklisting are the concomitants of the rule of industrial establishments by our millionaire "lords of industry," and these measures furnish recruits for the army of greed when organized labor enters its protest against such acts of injustice as has made tramps of other men under like circumstances. The employer who is satisfied with a reasonable profit will not fear to intrust his case to such a board of arbitrators as I have described. The employer who refuses arbitration fears for the justice of his cause. He who would acquire legitimately need not fear investigation; he who would steal must do it in the dark in order to be successful.

The Mood of the Homestead Men

John Fitch, a special investigator, describes the mood of the Homestead workers and what led to their battle with the three hundred Pinkerton guards sent to secure the plant.

The Homestead men had been working in the mill at that place, many of them since it was first built. They had seen it grow from a small beginning to one of the finest and best equipped plants in the world. They were proud of that plant and proud of the part that they had had in its progress.

Over the hills rising from the river were their cottages, many of them owned by the workingmen . . . and now these homes were in jeopardy. They could have gone back to work. . . . But that meant giving up their union . . . self-disenfranchisement. So when the Pinkerton men came, the Homestead steel workers saw in their approach an attempt at subjugation at the hands of an armed force of unauthorized individuals. A mob of men with guns coming to take their jobs . . . to take away the chance to work, to break up their homes—that is what passed through the minds of the Homestead men that morning.

Those who harshly criticise the workmen of Homestead should put themselves in the place of these workmen for a few brief moments of thought. Picture the skill required to turn out faultless work, the loss of eyesight which follows a few years of toil before the seething furnace, the devotion to duty which must be shown in order to succeed. Then step outside of the mill and witness the erection of a high fence and its armament. Consider what it means and that it is being erected before a threat has been made or a disagreement considered among the possibilities. Think of the stigma which the erection of that fence casts on the man who works, the builder of the town; and then reflect that it is being built to serve as a prison-pen for those who must work so cheap that they will not be able to erect homes or maintain families in respectability. Ponder over the fact that when cheap men take the places of well-paid men, they do not buy carpets, organs, pianos, decent, respectable furniture or raiment, and that the makers of these articles elsewhere will be thrown out of employment, and that other manufacturers will be driven to bankruptcy because of a falling off in the demand for their product. Then read what Mr. [Andrew] Carnegie said six short years ago in speaking of the question of employing non-union, cheap men:

> To expect that one dependent upon his daily wage for the necessaries of life will stand by peaceably and see a new man employed in his stead is to expect much. This poor man may have a wife and children dependent upon his labor. Whether medicine for a sick child, or even nourishing food for a delicate wife, is procurable, depends upon his steady employment. In all but a very few departments of labor it is unnecessary, and, I think, improper, to subject men to such an ordeal. In the case of railways and a few other employments it is, of course, essential for the public wants that no interruption occur, and in such cases substitutes must be employed; but the employer of labor will find it much more to his interest, wherever possible, to allow his works to remain idle and await the result of a dispute than to employ the class of men that can be induced to take the place of other men who have stopped work. Neither the best men as men, nor the best men as workers, are thus to be obtained. There is an unwritten law among the best workmen: "Thou shalt not take thy neighbor's job." No wise employer will lightly lose his old employees. Length of service counts for much in many ways. Calling upon strange men should be the last resort.

The introduction of an armed body of men at the outset was an indication that some man would be expected to "take his neighbor's job," and at once. The arbitrament of the sword was the first thought with the Carnegie Steel Company. The laws of Pennsylvania were disregarded in arming citizens of other States and assigning them to duty at Homestead. In that awful spectacle to which the eyes of humanity turned on the 6th of July could be seen the final abolition of brute force in the settlement of strikes and lockouts. What the law will not do for men they must do for themselves, and by the light of the blazing guns at Homestead it was written that arbitration must take the place of "Pinkertonism."

CHAPTER 5

Social Effects of the Industrial Revolution

Chapter Preface

The rise of industry to a dominant position in America's economy had a significant impact on U.S. society during the last third of the nineteenth century. Big business corporations supplanted smaller concerns, people moved from rural to urban areas, and the number of women who worked outside the home in factories and offices increased as more jobs became available. The new industries were manufacturing products ranging from electric lights and sewing machines to ready-made clothing and processed foods, items that were changing the way people lived at home. Chain stores and mail-order catalogs helped spark the rise of a new consumer consciousness by offering convenient ways to obtain mass-produced wares. Even notions of time were altered by the industrial economy; strict factory schedules replaced the rising and setting sun in regulating working hours, while in 1883 railroads replaced varying local times with a standardized national system of four time zones.

The many changes brought about by industrialization caused some people to question whether existing political institutions and economic theories needed to be changed as well. A central consideration was whether the government should take greater responsibility in regulating big business and in helping the class of poor unemployed workers that the industrial revolution seemed to have helped to create.

The doctrine of laissez-faire ("hands-off") that was dominant in business, government, and academic circles decreed that government should not attempt to control economic activity. The "invisible hand" of the marketplace described by British economist Adam Smith would regulate supply and demand for goods and services to the satisfaction of all. Inequalities in wealth produced necessary incentives for progress, in this view, and efforts by the government to curb poverty or to regulate wages and working hours would stunt the natural development of society. Banking and business crashes that periodically resulted in economic slowdowns and large-scale unemployment (such as the "Panics" of 1873 and 1893) were considered to be inevitable occurrences in which the government should not interfere.

Many historians have noted that business leaders were often inconsistent in their application of the doctrine of laissez-faire; while they objected to government regulation and social legislation, they often asked for and received government assistance in the form of protective tariffs, land grants for railroads, and government investments in roads and harbors. However, such government aid to business did not diminish the prevailing belief that laissez-faire was a proper government policy and that anyone in America could rise "from rags to riches" through individual effort.

However, in the late 1800s, a growing number of Americans began to question the doctrine of laissez-faire and to criticize some of the ramifications of the industrial revolution. Social reformers, "muckraking" journalists, and political leaders all lent their efforts to various social and political reforms during the late 1800s and the early 1900s, many of which were a direct response to the perceived abuses of major corporations and the social changes generated by industrialization. Among these reforms were limiting the hours that constituted a workday, passing laws designed to improve labor conditions in industry (especially for women and children), creating funds for workmen's compensation in response to industrial accidents, and effecting measures to alleviate the poor conditions found in the slums of America's growing cities. Other reforms dealt with the control of large corporations, including railroad regulation and public control and ownership of power utilities.

The industrial revolution that followed America's Civil War thus became the ultimate source for a wide array of social reforms, debates, and controversies that stretched into the early decades of the twentieth century. The viewpoints in this chapter examine some of the arguments surrounding the state of American society and the changes brought by industrial expansion following the Civil War.

VIEWPOINT 1

*"The economic changes of the last quarter of a century
. . . [have] been, for mankind in general, movement
upward and not downward."*

The Industrial Revolution Has Benefited American Society

David A. Wells (1828–1898)

David A. Wells was an economist, author, and government official. His books include *The Silver Question* and *Practical Economics*. In his 1889 book *Recent Economic Changes*, from which the following viewpoint is excerpted, he examines the impact industrialization and advances in technology have made on American society in the years following the Civil War. He compares the United States with nations such as Great Britain that have undergone similar economic developments as well as with other nations and peoples who have not yet industrialized. Among the changes attributable to the industrial revolution, Wells argues, are declining death rates, lower prices and greater availability of goods and foodstuffs, improved communication and transportation for much of the world, and rising living standards for most Americans. Wells acknowledges that some observers have decried the social effects of the industrial revolution, blaming industrialization for such ills as inequality and labor disruption. He concludes, however, that the benefits industrialization has brought to the lives of Americans outweigh its drawbacks.

From David A. Wells, *Recent Economic Changes*, 1889.

The predominant feeling induced by a review and consideration of the numerous and complex economic changes and disturbances that have occurred since 1873 . . . is undoubtedly, in the case of very many persons, discouraging and pessimistic. The questions which naturally suggest themselves, and in fact are being continually asked, are: Is mankind being made happier or better by this increased knowledge and application of the forces of nature, and a consequent increased power of production and distribution? Or, on the contrary, is not the tendency of this new condition of things, as Dr. Siemens, of Berlin, has expressed it, "to the destruction of all of our ideals and to coarse sensualism; to aggravate injustice in the distribution of wealth; diminish to individual laborers the opportunities for independent work, and thereby bring them into a more dependent position; and, finally, is not the supremacy of birth and the sword about to be superseded by the still more oppressive reign of inherited or acquired property?"

What many think, but hesitate to say, finds forcible expression in the following extract from a letter addressed to the author by a large-hearted, sympathetic man, who is at the same time one of the best known of American journalists and leaders of public opinion. After referring to his great interest in the exhibit that has been made of the extraordinary economic disturbances since 1873 and their effect on persons, production, distribution, and prices, he says:

> But what a deplorable and quite awful picture you suggest of the future! The wheel of progress is to be run over the whole human race and smash us all, or nearly all, to a monstrous flatness! I get up from the reading of what you have written scared, and more satisfied than ever before that the true and wise course of every man is to get somewhere a piece of land, raise and make what he can for himself, and try thus to get out of the crushing process. It seems to me that what we call civilization is to degrade and incapacitate the mass of men and women; and how strange and incongruous a state it is! At the same time these masses of men are thrown out of their accustomed employments by the introduction or perfection of machinery—at that very time the number of women and children employed in factories rapidly increases; an unprecedented cheapness of all necessaries of life is coincident with an intensification of the bitter struggle for bread and shelter. It is a new form of slavery which, it seems to me, projects itself into view—universal slavery—not patriarchal, but mercantile. I get yearly more tired of what we call civilization. It seems to me a preposterous fraud. It does not give us leisure; it does not enable us to be clean except at a monstrous cost; it affects us with horrible diseases—like diphtheria and typhoid fever—poisoning our water and the air

we breathe; it fosters the vicious classes—the politicians and the liquor-sellers—so that these grow continually more formidable; and it compels mankind to a strife for bread, which makes us all meaner than God intended us to be. Do you really think the "game pays for the candle"?

From another, occupying high position as an economic thinker and writer, come also these questions:

What are the social and political results to follow the sweeping reconstruction of our material prices and our labor system? Are we not unconsciously, and from the sheer force of these new elements, drifting fast into a form of actual socialism—if not exactly such as the *doctrinaire* reformers preach, yet a form which in respect to material interests swallows up individualism in huge combinations? Does not the economizing of the new methods of production necessitate this tendency? And, if so, to what sort of social reconstruction is it likely to lead? Does it mean a future of industrial kings and industrial slaves? How far does the new situation harmonize with current aspirations of labor? Are these aspirations a reflex effect of the new conditions of industry?

To form now any rational opinion concerning the present and future influences of the causes of the recent and existing economic disturbances, and to be able to return any intelligent answers to the questions and impressions which they have prompted or created, there is clearly but one practical, common-sense method to adopt, and that is to review and analyze the sociological sequences of these disturbances so far as they have been developed and determined. . . .

That many of the features of the situation are, when considered by themselves, disagreeable and even appalling, can not be denied. When one recalls, for example, through what seemingly weird power of genius, machinery has been summoned into existence—machinery which does not sleep, does not need rest, is not the recipient of wages; is most profitable when most unremittingly employed—and how no one agency has so stimulated its invention and use as the opposition of those whose toil it has supplemented or lightened—the first remedial idea of every employer whose labor is discontented being to devise and use a tool in place of a man; and how in the place of being a bond-slave it seems to be passing beyond control and assuming the mastery; when one recalls all these incidents of progress, the following story of Eastern magic might be almost regarded in the light of a purposely obscured old-time prophecy: A certain man, having great learning, obtained knowledge of an incantation whereby he could compel inanimate objects to work for him, commanded a stick to bring him water. The stick at once obeyed. But when water sufficient for the man's necessities had been brought, and there was threatened danger of an oversupply, he desired the stick to stop working. Having, however, omitted to learn the words for revoking the incantation, the stick refused to obey. Thereupon, the magician in anger caught up an axe, and, with a view to diminish or destroy the power of the stick to perform work, chopped it into several pieces; whereupon, each piece immediately began to bring as much water as one had formerly done; and in the end not only the magician but the whole world was deluged and destroyed.

The proposition that all transitions in the life of society, even those to a better stage, are inevitably accompanied by human suffering, is undoubtedly correct. It is impossible, as an old-time writer (Sir James Stewart, 1767) has remarked, to even sweep a room without raising a dust and occasioning temporary discomfort. But those who are inclined to take discouraging and pessimistic views of recent economic movements, seem not only to forget this, but also to content themselves with looking mainly at the bad results of such movements, in place of the good and bad together. . . . No one . . . can familiarize himself with life as it exists in the slums and tenement-houses of all great cities in countries of the highest civilization; or in sterile Newfoundland, where all Nature is harsh and niggardly; or in sunny Mexico and the islands of the West Indies, where she is all bountiful and attractive, without finding much to sicken him with the aspects under which average humanity presents itself. But even here the evidence is absolutely conclusive that matters are not worse, but almost immeasurably better, than formerly; and that the possibilities for melioration, through what may be termed the general drift of affairs, is, beyond all comparison, greater than at any former period.

The first and signal result of the recent remarkable changes in the conditions of production and distribution, which in turn have been so conducive of industrial and societary disturbances, has been to greatly increase the abundance and reduce the price of most useful and desirable commodities. If some may say, "What of that, so long as distribution is impeded and has not been correspondingly perfected?" it may be answered, that production and distribution in virtue of a natural law are correlative or reciprocal. We produce to consume, and we consume to produce, and the one will not go on independently of the other; and although there may be, and actually is, and mainly through the influence of bad laws, more or less extensive maladjustment of these two great processes, the tendency is, and by methods to be hereafter pointed out, for the two to come into closer and closer harmony.

Next in order, it is important to recognize and keep clearly in view in reasoning upon this subject, what of good these same agencies, whose influence in respect to the future is now regarded by so many with alarm or suspicion, have already accomplished.

A Century of Progress

A hundred years ago the maintenance of the existing population of Great Britain, of the United States, and of all other highly-civilized countries, could not have been possible under the then imperfect and limited conditions of production and distribution. . . .

All the resources of the population of the United States, as they existed in 1840, would have been wholly inadequate to sow or harvest the present average annual corn or wheat crops of the country; and, even if these two results had been accomplished, the greater proportion of such a cereal product would have been of no value to the cultivator, and must have rotted on the ground for lack of any means of adequate distribution; the cost of the transportation of a ton of wheat, worth twenty-five dollars at a market, for a distance of a hundred and twenty miles over good roads, and with good teams and vehicles, entirely exhausting its initial value.

Fifty years ago corn (maize) was shelled in the United States by scraping the ears against the sharp edge of a frying-pan or shovel, or by using the cob of one ear to shell the corn from another. In this way about five bushels in ten hours could be shelled, and the laborer would have received about one fifth of the product. The six great corn States are Illinois, Indiana, Missouri, Iowa, Ohio, and Kansas. They produce more than one half the corn raised in the country. These States, by the census of 1880, had 2,056,770 persons engaged in agriculture, and it would have been necessary for this entire community to sit astride of shovels and frying-pans for one hundred and ten days out of three hundred and sixty-five to shell their corn-crop for the year 1880 by the old processes.

In 1790, before the grain-"cradle" was invented, an able-bodied farm-laborer in Great Britain could with a sickle reap only about a quarter of an acre of wheat in a day; at the present time a man with two horses can cut, rake, and bind in a day the wheat-product of twenty acres.

Forty years ago a deficient harvest in any one of the countries of Europe entailed a vast amount of suffering and starvation on their population. To-day the deficiency of any local crop of wheat is comparatively of little consequence, for the prices of cereals in every country readily accessible by railroad and steamships are now regulated, not by any local conditions, but by the combined production and consumption of the world; and the day of famines for the people of all such countries has passed forever. The extent to which all local advantages in respect to the supply and prices of food have been equalized in recent years through the railway service of the United States, is demonstrated by the fact that a full year's requirement of meat and bread for an adult person can now be moved from the points of their most abundant and cheapest production, a thousand miles, for a cost not in ex-

Wealth and Technology

Steel magnate Andrew Carnegie, in his 1886 book The Triumph of Democracy, *described some of the material advances made by the United States the previous two decades.*

In 1850 the total wealth of the United States was but $8,430,000,000 (£1,686,000,000), while that of the United Kingdom exceeded $22,500,000,000 (£4,500,000,000), or nearly three times that sum. Thirty short years sufficed to reverse the positions of the respective countries. In 1882 the Monarchy was possessed of a golden load of no less than eight thousand, seven hundred and twenty millions sterling. . . . But stupendous as this seems, it is exceeded by the wealth of the Republic, which in 1880, two years before, amounted to $48,950,000,000 (£9,790,000,000). What a mercy we write for 1880; for had we to give the wealth of one year later another figure would have to be found, and added to the interminable row. America's wealth today greatly exceeds ten thousand millions sterling. Nor is this altogether due to her enormous agricultural resources, as may at first glance be thought; for all the world knows she is first among nations in agriculture. It is largely attributable to her manufacturing industries, for, as all the world does not know, she, and not Great Britain, is also the greatest manufacturing country. . . .

In the application of science to social and industrial uses, she is far in advance of other nations. Many of the most important practical inventions which have contributed to the progress of the world during the past century originated with Americans. No other people have devised so many labor-saving machines and appliances. The first commercially successful steamboat navigated the Hudson, and the first steamship to cross the Atlantic sailed under the American flag from an American port. America gave to the world the cotton-gin, and the first practical mowing, reaping, and sewing machines. In the most spiritual, most ethereal of all departments in which man has produced great triumphs, viz.: electricity, the position of the American is specially noteworthy. He may be said almost to have made this province his own, for, beginning with [Benjamin] Franklin's discovery of the identity of lightning and electricity, it was an American who devised the best and most widely used system of telegraphy, and an American who boldly undertook to bind together the old and the new land with electric chains. In the use of electricity for illuminating purposes America maintains her position as first wherever the subtile [subtle] agent is invoked. The recent addition to the world's means of communication, the telephone, is also to be credited to the new land.

cess of the single day's wages of an average American mechanic or artisan. . . .

The existence of the present populations of Europe and the United States—nay, more, the continuance and progress of civilization itself—has therefore been made possible solely through the invention and use of the same labor-saving machinery which not a few are inclined to regard as likely to work permanent injury to the masses in the future. It is still easy to avoid all trouble arising out of the use of labor-saving machinery by going to the numerous countries—many of which are rich in the bounties of Nature—which do not possess it. But these are the very countries to which no person of average intelligence desires to go.

Restless and progressive humanity generally believes also that the continued betterment of the race is largely conditioned on the extension of free government based on popular representation and constitutional safeguards; and also on the successful continuation of the experiment under such conditions which was entered upon by the people of the United States just a hundred years ago. But the Government of the United States, under its existing Constitution, has been made possible only through the progress which man has made in recent years in his knowledge and control of the forces of nature. Without the perfected railroad and telegraph systems, the war for the maintenance of the Federal Union under the existing Constitution could not probably have been prosecuted to a successful conclusion; and even if no domestic strife had intervened, it is more than doubtful whether a federation of numerous States, sovereign in many particulars—floating down the stream of time like an elongated series of separate rafts, linked together—could have been indefinitely perpetuated, when the time necessary to overcome the distance between its extremities for the mere transmission of intelligence amounted to from twenty to thirty days. . . .

Finally, an absolute demonstration that the progress of mankind, in countries where the new economic conditions have been most influential in producing those disturbances and transitions in industry and society which to many seem fraught with disaster, has been for the better and not for the worse, is to be found in the marked prolongation of human life, or decline in the average death-rate, which has occurred within comparatively recent years in these same countries. Thus, the average annual death-rate in England and Wales, during the period from 1838 to 1875, was 22.3 per thousand. From 1876 to 1880, it was 20.08. But, for the six years from 1880 to 1887, the average has not exceeded 19.3; which means that about 500,000 persons in England and Wales were alive at the close of the year 1886 who would have been dead if the rate of mortality which prevailed between 1838 and 1875 had been maintained. . . . The average death-rate for the whole United States, for the census year 1880, was between 17 and 18 per thousand; which is believed to be a less mean rate than that of any European country except Sweden. . . .

Causes of Discontent

The causes of the almost universal discontent of labor, which has characterized the recent transitions in the world's methods of production and distribution, and which, intensified by such transitions, have been more productive of disturbances than at any former period . . . would seem to be mainly these:

1. *The displacement or supplanting of labor through more economical and effective methods of production and distribution.* . . .

Of the injury thus occasioned, and of the suffering attendant, no more pitiful and instructive example of recent date could be given than the following account, furnished to the United States Department of State, of the effect of the displacement of hand-loom weaving in the city of Chemnitz, Saxony, by the introduction and use of the power-loom:

> In 1875 there were no less than 4,519 of the so-called *"master-weavers"* in Chemnitz, each of whom employed from one to ten journeymen at hand-loom weaving in his own house. The introduction of machinery, however, imposed conditions upon these weavers which they found the more difficult to meet the more the machinery was improved. The plainer goods were made on power-looms, and work in the factories was found to be more remunerative. Instead of giving work to others, they were gradually compelled to seek work for themselves. The independent "master" soon fell into ranks with the dependent factory-hand, but as he grew older and his eye-sight failed him he was replaced by younger and more active hands, and what once promised to become a well-to-do citizen in his old age now bids fair to become a burden upon the community. Those who had means of procuring the newer Jacquard contrivance, or even the improved "leaf" or "shaft-looms," managed to eke out a subsistence; but the prospects of the weavers who have learned to work only with the hand-looms are becoming more hopeless every day.

Now, while such cases of displacement of labor appeal most strongly to human sympathy, and pre-eminently constitute a field for individual or societal action for the purpose of relief, it should be at the same time remembered that the world, especially during the last century, has had a large experience in such matters, and that the following points may be regarded as established beyond the possibility of contradiction: 1. That such phases of human suffering are now, always have been, and undoubtedly always will be, the inevitable concomitants of the progress of civilization, or the transitions of the life of society to a higher and better stage. They seem to be in the nature of "growing-pains," or of penalty which Nature exacts at the outset, but for once only, whenever mankind subordinates her forces in greater degree to its own will and uses. 2. That it is not within the power of statute enactment to arrest such transitions, even when a large and immediate amount of human suffering can certainly be predicated as their consequent, except so far as it initiates and favors a return of society toward barbarism; for the whole progress in civilization consists in accomplishing greater or better results with the same or lesser effort, physical or mental. 3. All experience shows that, whatever disadvantage or detriment the introduction and use of new and improved instrumentalities or methods of production and distribution may temporarily entail on individuals or classes, the ultimate result is always an almost immeasurable degree of increased good to mankind in general. . . . There is little foundation for the belief largely entertained by the masses, and which has been inculcated by many sincere and humane persons, who have undertaken to counsel and direct them, that the amount of remunerative work to be done in the world is a fixed quantity, and that the fewer there are to do it the more each one will get; when the real truth is, that work as it were breeds work; that the amount to be done is not limited; that the more there is done the more there will be to do; and that the continued increasing material abundance which follows all new methods for effecting greater production and distribution is the true and permanent foundation for increasing general prosperity. . . .

Attention is next asked to the *second* (assumed) cause for the prevailing discontent of labor, namely:

Changes in the character or nature of employments consequent upon the introduction of new methods—machinery or processes—which it is claimed have tended to lower the grade of labor, impair the independence, and restrict the mental development of the laborer.

That such changes have been in the nature of evil, can not be questioned. . . . Happily, however, the number of industries, in which the division of labor and its subordination to machinery has been productive of such extreme results, is not very large; the manufacture of boots and shoes by modern machine methods, in which every finished shoe is said to represent sixty-two distinct mechanical employments or products, being perhaps the most notable. And yet even here there is not a little in way of compensating benefit to be credited to such a system. Thus, for example, it is stated that "the use of machinery has compelled employés to apply themselves more closely to their work; and, being paid by the piece, has enabled them to make better wages." When shoe-making was a handicraft, "the hours of labor were very irregular;

the workmen, who decided their own hours of labor, working some days only a few hours, and then working far into the night for a few days to make up for lost time. It was once customary for shoemakers (in New England) to work on an average fifteen hours a day," now the hours of labor in the shoe-factories are not in excess of ten hours. It is also claimed that the introduction of the sewing-machine into the manufacture of boots and shoes has greatly increased the opportunities for the employment of women, at better rates of wages. . . .

The third cause which has especially operated in recent years to occasion discontent on the part of labor has been undoubtedly *the increase in intelligence or general information on the part of the masses in all civilized countries.*

The best definition, or rather statement, of the essential difference between a man and an animal, that has ever been given is, that a man has progressive wants, and an animal has not. Under the guidance of what is termed instinct, the animal wants the same habitat and quantity and quality of food as its progenitors, and nothing more. And the more nearly man approaches in condition to the animal, the more limited is the sphere of his wants, and the greater his contentment. A greater supply of blubber and skins to the Eskimo, more "pulque" to the native Mexican, to the West Indian negro a constant supply of yams and plantains without labor, and the ability to buy five salt herrings for the same price that he has now to give for three, would, in each case, temporarily fill the cup of individual happiness nearly to repletion. And, among civilized men, the contentment and also sluggishness of those neighborhoods in which the population come little in contact with the outer world and have little of diversity of employment open to them, are proverbial.

Increasing Wants

Now the wonderful material progress which has been made within the last quarter of a century has probably done more to overcome the inertia, and quicken the energy of the masses, than all that has been hitherto achieved in this direction in all preceding centuries. The railroad, the steamship, and the telegraph have broken down the barriers of space and time that formerly constituted almost insuperable obstacles in the way of frequent intercourse between people of different races, countries, and communities, and have made the civilized world, as it were, one great neighborhood. Every increased facility that is afforded for the dissemination of intelligence, or for personal movement, finds a marvelously quick response in an extended use. The written correspondence—letters and cards—exchanged through the world's postal service, more than doubled between the years 1873 and

1885, while in the United States the number of people annually transported on railroads alone exceeds every year many times the total population of the country, the annual number for the New England States being more than sixteen times greater than their population. Under these powerful but natural educating influences, there has been a great advance in the intelligence of the masses. They have come to know more of what others are doing; know better what they themselves are capable of doing; and their wants have correspondingly increased, not merely in respect to quantities of the things to which they have always been accustomed, but very many articles and services which within a comparatively recent period were regarded as luxuries, are now almost universally considered and demanded as necessaries. At the same time, the increased power of production and distribution, and the consequent reduction in the cost of most commodities and services, have also worked for the satisfaction of these wants in such a degree that a complete revolution has been effected during recent years in the every-day life of all classes of the people of the great industrial and commercial countries. Let any one compare the condition of even the abject poor of London, as described in recent publications, with the condition of English laborers as described by writers of acknowledged authority not more than forty years ago, and he can not resist the conclusion that the very outcasts of England are now better provided for than were multitudes of her common laboring-men at the period mentioned.

The widening of the sphere of one's surroundings, and a larger acquaintance with other men and pursuits, have long been recognized as not productive of content. Writing to his nephew more than one hundred years ago, Thomas Jefferson thus concisely expressed the results of his own observation: "Traveling," he says, "makes men wiser, but less happy. When men of sober age travel they gather knowledge, but they are, after all, subject to recollections mixed with regret; their affections are weakened by being extended over more objects, and they learn new habits which can not be gratified when they return home." Again, as the former few and simple requirements of the masses have become more varied and costly, the individual effort necessary for the satisfaction of the latter is not relatively less, even under the new conditions of production, than before, and in many instances is possibly greater. Hence, notwithstanding the large advance in recent years in the average rates of wages, and a greatly increased purchasing power of wages, there is no less complaint than ever of the cost of living. . . .

There is, therefore, unquestionably in these facts an explanation in no small part of what to many has seemed one of the greatest puzzles of the times—namely, that with undoubtedly greater and increasing abundance and cheapness of most desirable things, popular discontent with the existing economic condition of affairs does not seem to diminish, but rather to greatly increase. And out of such discontent, which is not based on anything akin to actual and unavoidable poverty, has originated a feeling that the new conditions of abundance should be further equalized by some other methods than intelligent individual effort, self-denial, and natural, progressive material and social development (the actuality of which is proved by all experience); and that the state could, if it would, make all men prosperous; and therefore should, in some way not yet clearly defined by anybody, arbitrarily intervene and effect it. And this feeling, so far as it assumes definiteness of idea and purpose, constitutes what is called "socialism.". . . .

Conclusion

Finally, a comprehensive review of the economic changes of the last quarter of a century, and a careful balancing of what seems to have been good and what seems to have been evil in respect to results, would seem to warrant the following conclusions: That the immense material progress that these changes have entailed has been, for mankind in general, movement upward and not downward; for the better and not for the worse; and that the epoch of time under consideration will hereafter rank in history as one that has had no parallel, but which corresponds in importance with the periods that successively succeeded the Crusades, the invention of gunpowder, the emancipation of thought through the Reformation, and the invention of the steam-engine; when the whole plane of civilization and humanity rose to a higher level, each great movement being accompanied by social disturbances of great magnitude and serious import, but which experience has proved were but temporary in their nature and infinitesimal in their influence for evil in comparison with the good that followed. . . . The time has come when the population of the world commands the means of a comfortable subsistence in a greater degree and with less of effort than ever before.

"Industrial progress necessarily involves . . . growing relative inequalities in society, which constitutes one of the most serious of social problems."

The Industrial Revolution Has Created Inequality and Other Social Ills

W.D. Dabney (1853–1899)

Many people debated whether the economic changes brought about by industrialization following the Civil War in America were of ultimate benefit to American society. Among those who studied and wrote about the social effects of industrialization was W.D. Dabney, an economist and the author of *The Public Regulation of Railways*. In the following viewpoint, excerpted from an 1892 article published in the *Annals of the American Academy of Political and Social Science*, Dabney examines the social impact of the "industrial operations of modern society." He argues that before industrialization, most people lived on farms or in small communities and were largely self-sufficient in providing for their basic needs and wants through their own labor and capital—a situation he asserts was conducive to stability, economic equality, and social contentment. He contends, however, that a driving feature of "industrial progress" has been the loss of economic self-sufficiency for individuals as more and more people are instead employed in factories performing specific tasks (or on farms that produce just one or two cash crops). The livelihoods of many people, he states, have become dependent to a greater degree on impersonal market forces and on large corporations and other organizations over which individuals have little control. Dabney

From W.D. Dabney, "The Basis of the Demand for Public Regulation of Industries," *Annals of the American Academy of Political and Social Science*, January 1892.

writes that because of this growing specialization of labor and its attendant erosion of people's economic self-sufficiency, the industrial revolution, while it has provided many material advances in American society, has also created inequality, class conflict, and widespread discontent. Dabney states that one manifestation of this discontent is a growing popular demand for public regulation, or even government takeover, of certain key industries.

In the industrial operations of modern society no tendency is more observable—none, it may be said, has advanced so far—as that towards specialization of function. The result has been that the needs of civilized life have been far more perfectly met and supplied than would otherwise have been possible. This separation of functions is, in fact, a manifestation of a general law of social evolution. It is the imperative requirement, and the necessary condition of advanced human society. Hand in hand, step by step with advancing civilization, the division of labor—differentiation of function—has proceeded, furnishing at once the most striking phenomenon of industrial progress, and the most powerful aid to its further achievements.

And yet, incalculable as have been the benefits to mankind hence resulting, impossible as human advancement would have been under other conditions, and undeniable as has been the improvement in the conditions of the masses of society as compared with former times, it cannot escape observation that what constitutes the strength and progressive power of society, as a whole, constitutes also, in a sense, the weakness of the individual, and often involves unfortunate disparity between man and man. Different industrial classes have arisen, and the dependence of class upon class has increased almost beyond conception; but the reciprocity of dependence between individuals of different classes has in many cases been well-nigh destroyed.

Under social conditions which would now be called primitive, but which, nevertheless, supply all the necessities and many of the enjoyments of life, the circle of dependencies, if the expression may be used, is often very limited. For illustrations of this fact it is not necessary to revert to a remote past, or to an early and primitive period of civilized life. In many of our older states may be found, to-day, communities remote from contact with the throbbing energies and insatiable aspirations of modern progress, isolated by physical barriers from the great world beyond them, living for the most part in simple independence of the rest of mankind. In such communities specialization has made but little progress. The tastes of the people are simple and their wants are few. The soil, rudely cultivated with antiquated implements, yields a sufficiency of vegetable food for man and beast. The product of the chase and the tribute of the stream supplement the scanty stock of domestic animal food. The neighboring forest, yielding to the blows of the axe—no other implement is needed—furnishes the logs and the rudely riven boards for the construction of the dwelling. A patch of cotton or of flax and half a dozen sheep to each family yield the raw material which hand-cards, spinning-wheels, and ancestral hand-looms convert into ample clothing for the people. Usually, with the occasional aid of a neighbor, each household can perform, within and for itself, most of the simple functions which are necessary for the maintenance of such a life as is here described. Every man is his own farmer, herdsman, huntsman, clothier, builder. Such food, shelter and raiment as he has are the product of his own, almost unaided, exertions. The functions of such a society are but slightly differentiated. Such interdependencies as exist, exist directly between man and man. Each individual clearly perceives his own equal dependence upon, or independence of, other individuals. The industrial equilibrium is maintained by forces operating directly between individuals, and class distinctions are almost unknown. Among the most striking characteristics of such a community are the social equality of its members and the comparatively equal distribution of its wealth.

Lost Industrial Independence

And this condition of industrial independence contains within itself elements of contentment, of individual happiness, and of good citizenship, which, in the march of progress and the advance of civilization, have vanished away. Strikes and lock-outs, labor organizations and trusts, those inevitable and unhappy concomitants of progress, have no place in a simple society. The very sense of industrial independence, the knowledge of every man that within himself, or at most within a small circle of known, equal, and mutual dependencies, exists the means of supporting life, and supplying at least its more elementary wants, is the most substantial basis of social contentment and stability.

But however desirable in itself industrial independence may be, it is incompatible with high industrial development. He who attempts the performance of many functions will perform none of them in a complete and satisfactory manner. "Jack at all trades and master of none" is the popular proverb which expresses the general appreciation of this fact. And the smaller the circle of dependencies, the greater the number of functions each member of the circle must perform, and the more unsatisfactory and incomplete will be the performance.

Hence, industrial progress necessarily involves the continued expansion of the circle of dependencies, and from this results the growing relative inequalities in society, which constitutes one of the most serious of social problems. . . .

Inequality in Industrial Society

The principle which underlies and explains individual inequality in industrial society, broadly stated, is that certain functions necessary to all can be best discharged, and are in fact discharged by a few, while other functions necessary to all are in fact discharged by many. Equality of dependence exists between the few collectively on the one side and the many on the other. But consequent disparity exists between the average individual of the few and the average individual of the many. Combination among the few increases the relative dependence of the many, and can only be counteracted by combination among the many, or by something equivalent thereto. But combination among a few is easy, and combination among many is difficult. Moreover, combination of class against class implies antagonism, and itself frequently engenders still further antagonism between the classes. And antagonism between classes whose co-operation is essential to the proper discharge of any function implies a failure of that function; and apart from the merits of the controversy as between the immediate parties to it, other and vastly larger classes may suffer from the failure of the function upon whose proper discharge they have become dependent.

How to harmonize industrial progress, with a reasonable degree of security, in the masses against the arbitrary action of a few, who, in every advanced society, inevitably acquire exclusive control of industrial functions of great consequence to all is, then, a problem well worthy of consideration. Before venturing any suggestion as to the direction in which a solution seems likely to be sought (and without meaning to imply that it is the right direction), it will be well to illustrate the foregoing general observations by reference to a few salient features in the industrial situation of our own country. . . .

Observe, then, in connection with what has been said, the three great divisions of industrial society in the United States—the Agricultural, the Commercial, and Manufacturing—and a few of their most distinct and conspicuous subdivisions. . . .

Agriculture is, of course, the fundamental and primary function upon the efficacy and adequate discharge of which all classes are ultimately dependent. It is the largest of the industrial segments, and has made the least progress in specialization. The 7,670,493

181

persons engaged in agriculture in the United States in 1880, are by the census of that year divided into only twelve classes, some of which are very insignificant; the most important being "farmers and planters," numbering 4,225,925, and "agricultural laborers," numbering 3,323,876.

Commerce, or the exchange of products, with all the agencies and instrumentalities of exchanges, is an industrial function of the highest importance, yet less essential than agriculture. It implies an advance in industrial evolution, and is more highly differentiated than agriculture. The persons engaged in commerce in the United States under the head of "trade and transportation," numbering 1,810,256, are, by the census of 1880, subdivided into seventy-one classes.

"Manufacturing, mining and mechanical industries," denoting still further industrial advancement, occupy in the United States (or did, in 1880) 3,137,812 persons, and are by the same authority subdivided into one hundred and thirty-six classes.

The tendency towards specialization, it is thus seen, has grown with industrial progress, and is strongest in the segment of most complex functions. In commerce and manufactures the specialization is often so complete that some distinct branches of industry, under one or the other of those heads, though controlled by a comparatively small number of persons, appear to constitute in themselves separate and essential industrial segments, upon which all, or very many others, are dependent. Illustrations are found in warehouse and storage facilities, under certain circumstances, in telegraphic service, in railroad transportation, in the production of "dressed meats," in the production of illuminating oil, in sugar refining, in the production of iron and steel, and in many manufactures thereof, and to a considerable extent in the manufacture of other articles essential to the due welfare of advanced industrial society.

The Agricultural Segment

Recurring now for a moment to the agricultural segment, this striking fact is noticeable, that the "farmers and planters" in the country at large outnumber the "agricultural laborers"; the employer class is numerically greater than the employe class. Under these circumstances, oppressive conduct of employer towards employe must, as a general rule, be impossible, and a fair share of the average product is assured to the latter for his services. "Agricultural laborers" outnumber "farmers and planters" only in the South Atlantic and Gulf States from Maryland to Louisiana, inclusive, and in Tennessee. This, at least, was the case in 1880. Even at that time the numbers of each class were nearly balanced in several of these states, and as a considerable subdivision of landed property has taken place since then, the census just taken will probably show a reversal of majorities in some of them. In no state does the proportion of laborers to farmers reach three to one, and in the leading agricultural states of the West, the proportion is something like one to two. Hence, except where race constitutes an indestructible basis of social distinction, the farmer and his hired laborers are usually found associating on terms of equality, and the reciprocity of dependence between them is sufficiently manifest. Even where difference of race creates social distinction between the planter and his hireling it is doubtful whether it is at all more pronounced than that existing between the factory owner and the factory operative of his own race.

And whatever the occasion or the degree of social distinction between employer and employe in agricultural communities, the directness and frequency of personal contact, and the evident mutuality and equality of dependence between them, contribute in the highest degree to reciprocal goodwill.

But carrying the comparison between the employer and employe classes into commercial industries, and selecting at once that subdivision of commerce where the numerical disparity between those classes is most conspicuous—that of railroad transportation—a situation of the utmost gravity is disclosed. Of the railroads of the United States, other than mere street railroads, a mileage of about 160,000 miles is controlled and operated by less than 600 independent companies who give employment to three-fourths of a million, or more, of persons. The employes of some of the principal railroad systems number high into the thousands, all under the same control and direction, and most of them dependent upon the action of a single man, or at most a limited number of individuals for their very daily bread.

The mutuality of dependence between a great railroad corporation and any single one of its hundreds of machinists, engineers, firemen, brakemen, switchmen, trackmen or other employes is absolutely inappreciable. The dependence is altogether one-sided.

Labor Relations in Industry

The same is true of the relations between the proprietors of large manufacturing establishments and their employes. The average number of employes to each manufacturing establishment in the United States in 1880, was nearly eleven. It is doubtless larger at the present time, as the tendency is plainly noticeable towards concentration of labor and capital into large establishments. This average numerical relation between employers and employes in manufacturing industries is very striking when compared with the same relation in agricultural occupations. In the principal manufacturing states of New England—Massachusetts,

183

Connecticut and Rhode Island—the ratio of employes to establishments is about 25 to 1; in some cities of other states it is nearly as high, and in Pittsburgh, notably, the great centre of iron manufacture, it is more than 33 to 1.

From Workshop to Factory

Many people observed that the industrial revolution was changing old patterns of work. Speaking before a congressional committee in 1899, a witness describes how two essential parts of the industrial revolution—mechanization and specialization—changed the lives and working conditions of shoemakers.

In these old shops, years ago, one man owned the shop; he took in work and three, four, five, or six others, neighbors, came in there and sat down and made shoes right in their laps, and there was no machinery. Everybody was at liberty to talk; they were all politicians. . . . Of course, under these conditions, there was absolute freedom and exchange of ideas, they naturally would become more intelligent than shoe workers can at the present time, when they are driving each man to see how many shoes he can handle, and where he is surrounded by noisy machinery. And another thing, this nervous strain on a man doing just one thing over and over again must necessarily have a wearing effect on him and his ideals, I believe, must be lowered.

These figures are sufficiently suggestive of the inequality of dependence between the employer and employe classes in manufacturing industries; but they represent averages merely. It is well known that many single establishments both in manufactures and mining, give occupation to thousands of employes each, and here the disparity between the classes is yet more aggravated and conspicuous. The discontent of a few unorganized factory operatives or miners, or their refusal to accept a reduction of wages, is a matter of supreme indifference to the employer of a thousand men, so long as the vast majority of them remain faithful and fresh applicants for work are always on hand; but a frown of displeasure from the employer may well strike terror into any one of the thousand, to whom dismissal from service means the loss of the means of subsistence for himself and perhaps a dependent family.

It appears to be the sense of this dependence among the laboring classes, rather than the urgency of actual want, or actual exercise of oppressive conduct towards them, that has given rise to labor organizations; for the solicitude of large employers for the welfare of their employes, and the practical manner in which it is manifested, are matters of daily observation.

It can hardly be doubted that a very large majority of the members of these associations receive in their regular occupations wages which enable them to live in a state of comfort to which the great mass of agricultural laborers, and many of the small farmers, of the country are utter strangers. Yet agricultural laborers are rarely connected with labor organizations, and apparently feel but little interest in them. Their comparative independence, however, and the liberal share of the average agricultural product which they receive, seems to more than compensate for their far greater discomforts.

In controversies between labor and capital, public sympathy in the beginning is usually on the side of the former, but the sense of power arising from organization is apt to inspire unreasonable demands; and the coercive and retaliatory methods of labor organizations—the strike and the boycott—apart from the merits of the controversy in which they may be employed, are frequently grossly tyrannical in their character, result often in serious public inconvenience, and have seldom accomplished the object of their originators. Such antagonisms can not but be fraught with the most dangerous tendencies to social tranquillity and safety.

The loss from them resulting to both sides and often to innocent third parties is usually very great. Due co-operation between the railway companies and their employes, for example, is essential to the commercial interests of the country, which are dependent upon railroad transportation. The idleness of multitudes of laborers and of a vast capital, consequent upon an extensive strike of railroad employes, implies an enormous loss to both the labor and capital directly involved, but the consequent paralysis of the function of transportation entails still further loss upon a multitude of persons who can in no way be held responsible for the controversy and who are entitled to protection against its incidental results.

Class Distinctions

These brief illustrations suffice to show the serious and general evils that may result from glaring class distinctions *within* the several industrial segments of society. Observe, now, the inequalities existing between members of different industrial segments. The farmer, occupied with the primary functions of civilized society, claims first attention. His, of all the industrial occupations, is the one most nearly capable of maintaining existence without extraneous aid. Yet agriculture, even in its widest forms, is to some extent dependent on other occupations, and for the development of its highest capacities and greatest productive powers its dependence upon other occupations is simply incalculable. Improved farm machinery is an essential factor in the agricultural

185

product of the country, and the adequate distribution of the surplus is no less important. Many, it is true, are engaged in tillage on a small scale, who use but few and simple implements, yet their product is usually no more than sufficient for their own incomplete and stinted subsistence. Those who aspire to a share of the comforts and enjoyments which modern progress has made possible must do so at the cost of a proportionate part of their natural independence.

But see how unequal are the relative situations of the average farmer, on the one hand, and on the other, of those in commercial and manufacturing industries on whom he is dependent. Railroad facilities for example, are indispensable in the transportation of his surplus product. Usually he has no choice of routes or of markets, and not the slightest voice in fixing the price he must pay for the service. He is but one of many thousand patrons of the carrier, while the latter has practically complete control of the means by which he may market his produce. His indignation and his protests against apparent injustice count for nothing; his ruin even is a master of indifference, so long as the carriers' revenues are maintained from other sources. Mutuality of dependence between the average farmer and the railroad company is inappreciable, for while the latter performs exclusively the essential function of transportation, the former is but one of many thousands who perform the reciprocal function of supplying commodities for carriage.

Another operation is frequently essential in the distribution of agricultural products; that is their aggregation in large quantities, and reassortment according to quality. This requires facilities on a large scale, usually of an exclusive character, and concentrated in a very few hands. The grain elevators of Chicago and other large cities furnish examples. Nothing is more natural or easier, in the absence of legal restrictions, than for the proprietors of these establishments to combine and prescribe prices and regulations for the storage of grain, regardless of the views of those to whom their service is indispensable. There is no reciprocity of dependence between the proprietor on one side and the individual patron on the other.

The manufacture of those implements of husbandry so necessary to the achievement of the best results in agriculture, such, for example, as mowers, reapers, and other harvesting machines, is also usually confined to a few extensive establishments. This is partly due to the fact that they are generally patented inventions, in the manufacture and sale of which the patentees have a legal monopoly. But there is a more fundamental economic reason which underlies the tendency towards concentration and monopoly in manufacturing industries. This is the diminished cost of production in proportion to capital invested. When the operation of this principle has gradually centered in a few great establishments the control of any important branch of manufacture or commerce, the facility of combination among them, and the danger of injury likely to follow upon independent and competitive action, are very apt to result in a mutually protective alliance between them, more or less complete and effective.

Such alliances, whether or not they necessarily involve (as the popular belief is) the practice of extortion upon a helpless public, do certainly constitute in themselves a real and a serious social danger, because they strikingly manifest the great inequality of dependence, between the few who are thus combined on the one side and the unorganized masses of the common people on the other. The feeling of dependence, when evidently not reciprocated, is a powerful element of social discontent. The organization of the "Farmers' Alliance" is largely based on these considerations. . . .

Monopolies and the Public

Popular denunciation of "monopolies" and the vague but irrepressible dread with which the masses regard the enterprises of associated wealth, are often met and sought to be allayed by the assertion, which statistics frequently sustain, that every step towards industrial centralization has resulted in cheapening to the public the product or the service which is the subject of the monopoly.

That this is in some cases true is beyond question; yet it is but half the truth. The other half consists in the fact that the cost of production to the producer, and the cost of service to him who renders it, are by virtue of the monopoly enjoyed by them, cheapened in far greater ratio than are the prices of the products or the services to those who purchase or employ them. Hence, while the actual condition of all classes may be improved, their relative condition becomes far more unequal. And it is a fact never to be lost sight of, that the conception of the terms "good" and "bad" as applied to social conditions, is always relative, never absolute. It may well admit of question, whether the gross inequality of different industrial classes, resulting from highly differentiated industrial conditions, does not often outweigh as a social evil the general benefits conferred by the existence of those conditions.

Competition may be no less essential as a principle of limitation upon private fortunes than as a safeguard against extortion. The actual prices of the product of a monopolized industry may be less than those prevailing where the same industry is carried on under competitive conditions. Yet these conditions tend strongly to prevent the amassment in a few hands of vast proportions of the entire wealth of the community, and the creation of glaring and dangerous inequalities between its component members.

There are, however, certain functions of the highest public consequence, which can be so much better performed under exclusive than under competitive conditions, that the latter, if they ever prevail at all, are soon eliminated, and monopoly holds full sway. In some instances the government has itself assumed or been intrusted with the discharge of this class of functions, and private parties are strictly excluded from participating in them. The mail service of the country is in point. If left to private enterprise and competition, doubtless the price of the service would be much less in densely populated commercial communities than even it is now, but in sparsely settled regions the price would be practically prohibitory of communication by mail. Under government monopoly all sections are equalized. The principle of the service is to this extent communistic, but its general results are admirable. The building of highways for transportation has always been regarded as a public function, though in the matter of railroad building in the United States, the function is usually delegated by the states to corporations.

It is, however, a well-known fact that the original conception of the railroad was (by analogy to the turnpike) that of a highway open for the use of all carriers upon equal terms. That every railroad company has now become practically the exclusive carrier over its own line is due perhaps more to economic than to physical causes. The bulk of the traffic is unquestionably carried cheaper under exclusive, than it would be under competitive conditions.

The Option of Government Takeover

Of course, where private monopoly of any industrial function prevails, its object will be to extract from the public the largest possible net gains for its products or services. This does not necessarily mean that the highest possible prices are charged. High prices very often defeat their object and diminish profits by driving off patronage. Still the cost to the public is apt to be more than is necessary to secure to the owners of the monopoly a reasonable net return upon capital invested. Under these circumstances, there is a growing disposition in the public to assume to itself (by delegation to government) some functions which, for their proper discharge, must necessarily be of an exclusive nature.

This disposition is most often manifested in municipal ownership of water works and gas or electric plants for the supply of the city with water and light. The success of governmental discharge of a few industrial functions has suggested to many the still further extension of the government's sphere of industrial action. A large and increasing number of conservative persons who would indignantly resent the imputation to themselves of a spirit of socialism, are convinced of the necessity—not of absolute public control, perhaps—but of stringent public regulation of many industries. And it is in this direction that the solution of the problem of industrial monopoly seems likely to be attempted. The limits of this article forbid any explanation of the methods of public regulation of industries or any reference to the attempts toward public intervention between employers and employes which have been, or are likely to be, made.

In conclusion, it may be said that the further extension of the principle of governmental regulation of private business in the United States, where practically unlimited manhood suffrage prevails, will in all probability be attended with serious dangers and evils; but that it will be resorted to as an attempted remedy for the existing evils of private monopoly is hardly to be doubted.

VIEWPOINT 3

"That the employment of so many women in factories must have disastrous effects upon the home cannot be questioned."

The Industrial Revolution Has Harmed Society by Encouraging Women to Work Outside the Home

Washington Gladden (1836–1918)

Washington Gladden was a minister who led the First Congregational Church of Columbus, Ohio, for many years. He was a proponent of the Social Gospel, a late-nineteenth-century movement within American Protestantism whose leaders sought to apply Christian teachings to the problems of industrial society. A frequent lecturer and prolific writer on social issues, Gladden's books include *Working People and Their Employers* and *Social Salvation*. The following viewpoint is taken from *Social Facts and Forces*, an 1897 book composed of previous lectures that, as he writes in his introduction, are "an attempt to discover in what manner the well-being of the people is affected by the changes which are taking place in our industrial and social life."

The following excerpts from this book focus on the effect of industrialism on "home life" and especially on women, many of whom had found employment in the textile, food processing, and garment industries. Gladden argues that the rise in the number of working women is a worrisome social development that subverts what he views to be the "natural order" in which men are employed outside the home and women are homemakers.

From Washington Gladden, *Social Facts and Forces*, 1897.

The effect of the factory system upon the home life is a great inquiry to which I can give but a cursory glance. If we study the factory proper, in the great textile industries—the cotton and woollen mills of New England—we shall find, I think, that its influence upon family life has been, on the whole, injurious. Colonel [Carroll D.] Wright disputes this conclusion, but my own observation supports it. The great majority of these manufacturing corporations own the tenements in which the work-people live. As a general rule, these tenements are comfortable, and the rent is cheap; the external conditions of the home are not untoward, except that the houses in these factory villages are sometimes too closely packed together. But the home life of people who live in hired houses is never deeply rooted. When you come upon a whole village, as you often do in New England, in which the people are almost all renters; in which the houses are all owned by the proprietors of the mill about which they are grouped, you need not expect to find in these households the sentiment of home blooming very luxuriantly. These people are not, as a general rule, attached to the houses that they live in, nor to the neighborhood in which they live. They cannot afford to form such attachments. The uncertainty of employment makes it highly probable that they will be compelled to move on, before many months, to some other locality. Home life will not flourish under such conditions. . . .

[The] fact . . . that married women are employed to so large an extent in many of our factories, must, as a matter of course, have injurious effects upon the home life. Under the old domestic system the women workers wrought at home. The spinner or the weaver performed her daily task with her children round about her, and could turn, in the pauses of her toil, to attend to the wants of her household. The home was not deserted, nor were the children neglected. But the mother of many a household in a factory village leaves her home before seven o'clock in the morning, and returns to it, if at all, only for a few minutes in the middle of the day, until after six o'clock in the evening. You can judge for yourselves what home must be without any more mother in it than that.

But the influence of the factory upon the home begins even earlier. Tens of thousands of girls spend all their girlhood within the walls of the factory. The hours are so long and the work so laborious that they have no time nor strength to study and practise the fine art of housewifery; nor is it generally true that the schooling of the mill develops grace and gentleness. Most of these girls are married, sooner or later—and they are quite as apt to be married

191

sooner as later. They are wholly destitute, of course, of domestic tastes and aptitudes. You can imagine the kind of homes that they will make.

Now I am well aware that the opportunity of self-support which the factory offers is to some women a great boon; and doubtless the comfort of many households is increased by the earnings of women in such places. It is difficult to see how some families could subsist if the opportunity were withdrawn. Nevertheless, the fact that the factory invites women to enter so numerously into the ranks of the bread-winners, is a fact that must be well considered in making up our estimate of it as a social force. In the natural order, as I believe, man is the bread-winner and woman is the home-builder. An industrial arrangement that tends to subvert this natural order is of doubtful benefit. Many men, it is true, are quite willing to let the women of their households go out and earn wages to support the family, and are willing themselves to live on what their wives and daughters bring in; but it is not clear that a system which encourages this ought to be unreservedly commended. That the factory system, under purely economic forces, does produce this precise result cannot be denied. The constant tendency is to replace male by female labor. Mr. [J.A.] Hobson gives figures covering the leading industries of Great Britain for the fifty years between 1841 and 1891; and they show that while the number of male workers increased during this period from 1,030,600 to 1,576,100, the number of female workers increased from 463,000 to 1,447,500. That is, while the number of male workers had increased 53 per cent., the number of female workers had increased 221 per cent. And his conclusions [in *The Evolution of Modern Capitalism*], drawn from a full survey of the field, are "(1) that the tendency of modern industry is to increase the quantity of wage work given to women as compared with that given to men; (2) that the tendency is specially operative in manufacturing industries; (3) that in the manufacturing industries the increased rate of female employment is greatest in those industries where machinery has been most largely developed." All this is just as true of America as of England. The tendency of the factory system, when it is left to the control of purely economic forces, is to the displacement of men by women in the manufacturing industries. Every year some work that was formerly done by men falls into the hands of women and children. In many of the planing mills and sash and blind factories of Chicago and of Wisconsin, women are now employed at from 30 to 60 cents a day, to do work for which men in some States receive $2.50 a day.

It may be supposed that the earnings of the women and children are added to the earnings of the men and thus increase the family income; but the fact is that the women and children generally drive the men out of business; and, even when this is not the case, their competition brings down his wages, so that the entire earnings of the family, when husband, wife, and children are all employed, are apt to be less than are the earnings of the man in employments which have not been invaded by the competition of women and children.

An Assault on the Home

Some of the strongest opponents of women in the workplace were trade union organizations. Edward O'Donnell, a union activist from Boston, wrote about the topic in the October 1897 issue of the American Federationist, *the publication of the American Federation of Labor.*

The invasion of the crafts by women has been developing for years amid irritation and injury to the workman. The right of the woman to win honest bread is accorded on all sides, but with craftsmen it is an open question whether this manifestation is of a healthy social growth or not.

The rapid displacement of men by women in the factory and workshop has to be met sooner or later, and the question is forcing itself upon the leaders and thinkers among the labor organizations of the land.

Is it a pleasing indication of progress to see the father, the brother and the son displaced as the bread winner by the mother, sister and daughter?

Is not this evolutionary backslide, which certainly modernizes the present wage system in vogue, a menace to prosperity—a foe to our civilized pretensions? . . .

The growing demand for female labor is not founded upon philanthropy, as those who encourage it would have sentimentalists believe; it does not spring from the milk of human kindness. It is an insidious assault upon the home; it is the knife of the assassin, aimed at the family circle—the divine injunction. It debars the man through financial embarrassment from family responsibility, and physically, mentally and socially excludes the woman equally from nature's dearest impulse. Is this the demand of civilized progress; is it the desire of Christian dogma?

On the whole, therefore, I am inclined to believe that the replacement of men by women in factories works economic injury. But what we are now specially considering is its effect upon the home. That the employment of so many women in factories must have disastrous effects upon the home cannot be questioned.

"Factory life for women," says Mr. Hobson,

> save in extremely rare cases, saps the physical and moral health

of the family. The exigencies of factory life are inconsistent with the position of a good mother, a good wife, or the maker of a home. Save in extreme circumstances, no increase of the family wage can balance these losses, whose values stand upon a higher qualitative level.

Still it must be remembered that the employment of women and girls in factories is *no essential part of the factory system.* It is a feature of the present administration of this system, but it might be eliminated. I am inclined to think that the perfected society of the New Jerusalem will find higher and finer work for women to do than tending machinery. And I hope that the progress of the ages will steadily lift from their shoulders the heavier burdens of physical toil.

VIEWPOINT 4

"It is not intended to argue that every woman should leave the home and go into business, but only that those who wish to do so shall have the opportunity."

Society Is Not Harmed by Women's Working Outside the Home

Ida Husted Harper (1851–1931)

One change the industrial revolution brought upon American society in the late nineteenth century was an increase in the number of women working outside the home. In 1900 the number of women entering the workforce reached five million, a number roughly triple that of 1870. Women in the workforce had diverse occupations and backgrounds. They included college-educated journalists and social workers, high-school-educated stenographers and office workers, and immigrant laborers in sweatshops and factories. Some Americans warned that the employment of women harmed society by undermining traditional gender roles. Others welcomed the employment of women as a positive step away from restrictive traditions.

The following defense of working women is taken from a 1901 article in *Independent* magazine by Ida Husted Harper. An author, journalist, and social reformer, Harper was editor of the *New York Sunday Sun* and *Harper's Bazaar* and author of *The Life and Work of Susan B. Anthony*. This article was written partly in response to an earlier *Independent* article on working women by music critic Henry T. Finck. Although she agrees that mothers of young children should not work outside the home, Harper argues that the entrance of women into the workforce has been a positive development and that women of all economic classes should have the opportunity to pursue careers in business.

From Ida Husted Harper, "Women Ought to Work," *Independent*, May 16, 1901.

The moment we accept the theory that women must enter wage-earning occupations only when compelled to do so by poverty, that moment we degrade labor and lower the status of all women who are engaged in it. This theory prevailed throughout past ages, and it placed a stigma upon working women which is only beginning to be removed by the present generation. As long as a woman advertised her dire necessity by going outside the home to work, she could not avoid a feeling of humiliation and the placing of a barrier between herself and her more favored sisters. The fact that only a few insignificant employments with the most meager wages were permitted added still further to the disgrace of her position.

When, however, in the rapid evolution of the last third of a century, practically all occupations were thrown open and into these poured women of education and social standing belonging to families of ample means, the barriers at once began to fall and the stigma to fade out of sight. The great organizations of women which have been formed during this period freely admit wage earners; all meet on common ground; and frequently, by reason of their superior ability, women engaged in business are elected to the offices. There never was a time when there was such fraternity between women of the leisure and the working classes. To destroy this by barring out from remunerative vocations all except those who must earn their daily bread or become paupers would be a calamity, and this long backward step never will be taken....

Those who insist that all the women of the family should confine their labors to the household wholly ignore the vital fact that most of its duties have been carried outside. They note with regret that "while a century ago there were no women in our factories, now 45 percent of their employees are women," but omit to state that far more than 45 percent of the work now done in factories has been taken directly away from the women of the household. They have not left their legitimate work; they simply have followed it from the home to the factory,

The charge is continually made that the entrance of women into the industrial world has lowered men's wages to a ruinous degree. As a matter of fact, there are very few departments of work where men are not receiving higher wages now than ever before. If, however, these were placed at the same figure as before women entered into competition, and the 4 million women now engaged in breadwinning employments were withdrawn and set down in the home, the results would be most disastrous. From necessity they would constitute a vast body of consumers depending upon an inadequate body of producers. It would mean a life of idleness and privation for women, of added labor and sacrifice for men, a situation equally undesirable for both.

Nothing could more effectually destroy the stimulus to exertion in the girls of the high schools and colleges than the knowledge that all progress was to stop on commencement day, that it was to be the end instead of the beginning, that because their fathers were able to support them therefore they must make no use of this education. It is in the households of such that usually there is the least demand for domestic service on their part, as paid servants supply all that is necessary.

Shall these highly trained girls be restricted to the narrow round of social life? Shall they be directed to church, or charity, or reform work, for which they may have neither taste nor capacity? Shall they be forbidden any kind of business because they will take the bread out of the mouth of some poor woman? Why, then, such commendation when the *son* of a Vanderbilt, a Rockefeller, or a Morgan enters actively into business pursuits? Shall only those girls with the good luck to be poor have the chance to develop their talents? How shall the world ever know the capabilities of woman if she is to be restricted rigidly to one line of action, except when starvation stares her in the face?

Those girls who have the advantage of a home are not wholly responsible for the low wages of the clerks, factory hands, etc. If all such would withdraw from the market it still would be flooded with those capable only of the simplest kind of cheap labor. There is no such thing as a "family standard" or an "individual standard" of wages. It is gauged only by the service performed. A certain price is paid for a certain kind of work. No employer ever asks a man if he has a family, and, if so, pays him more, or if he is unmarried, pays him less. If there were a "family standard," vast numbers of wage-earning women should be paid by it, for they also are supporting others. Women do not "offer themselves cheaply" to employers; they do not underbid; they take all they possibly can get. If they held out for more they would get nothing. Men cannot hope to raise their own wages by driving out this competing element—it has come to stay. They must make common cause with it and both advance together.

Work and Marriage

If the ranks of bachelors were recruited only from the wage-earning classes, there might be some force in the charge that by lowering wages women made it impossible for men to marry. But the proportion of bachelors is equally as large among the well-to-do and wealthy classes. If the percent of marriage is decreasing, one of the most conspicuous causes is that women themselves are not so anxious to marry as they used to be. This is not on account of any change in the nature of woman, but only because with freedom of industrial opportunity has come that greatest of blessings, freedom of choice in marriage.

Under the old regime the poor girl married because she was obliged to be taken care of; the rich girl because her life was without aim or occupation and was considered by herself and everybody else a failure until she secured a husband. The necessity was practically the same in both cases. Now the one is enabled to take care of herself, and the other is permitted to follow whatever pursuit she finds most congenial; and, while each expects to marry, each intends to wait until the husband comes whom she can love, respect, and honor until death doth part. Under no other condition should any woman wed.

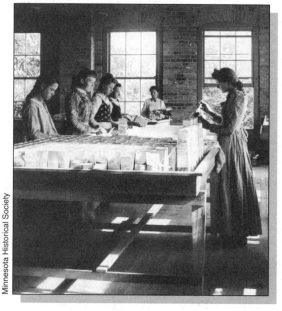

Minnesota Historical Society

By 1900 women comprised 17 percent of the American workforce. Many were employed in factories such as the one pictured.

Marriage should bear the same relation to her life that it does to a man's. She should fit herself to be a useful and agreeable member of society; she should select a vocation—the management of the household, a profession, philanthropy, stenography, factory work—whatever she is best adapted for, and follow it cheerfully and conscientiously. When an offer of marriage comes, she should balance it carefully against the work she has chosen, and if it bring down the scale, as it never will fail to do when the right man makes it, she should accept it with pride and happiness.

Under these circumstances the husband may feel infinitely

more honored than if he had been made a choice between two evils—merely preferred to wage earning or an idle, useless existence in a home which had become wearisome. Nothing could be more demoralizing than the injunction to women to "regard their employment as a necessary evil to be cured in as many cases as possible by marriage." It is a sorry compliment to a man to be taken like a dose of medicine.

As a rule, husband and wife should found a home to be supported by the joint labor of both—his without, hers within—each considered of the same value and the proceeds belonging equally to both. Where there are young children, it is most unfortunate for the mother to be compelled to work outside the home. It is even more deplorable for these children themselves to be employed in the mills and factories. There is no difference of opinion on these two points, and a civilization must be striven for which will make such sacrifices unnecessary.

There is not, there never has been, an effort "to create a sentiment that home is no place for a girl." A good home is the one place above all others for a girl, as it is for a boy. It is her rest, her haven, her protection, but this does not necessarily imply that she must not engage in any work outside its limits. Nevertheless, it is a far stretch of the imagination to assume that all girls "leave the refining atmosphere of a home where they might cultivate the graces" to go into ill-smelling, disease-breeding shops and factories. Very few who are employed in such places have homes of refinement, or even of comfort and decency, and oftentimes the factories and stores are far more cheerful and hygienic than the so-called homes they leave. Women among the poor must work if they would live honestly, and the drudgery of factory and shop is no harder than that of the washtub, the scrubbing brush, and the needle; but seldom does the statistician or sociologist devote his time and sympathy to the victims of the heavy and never-ending household tasks. . . .

Suitable Employments for Women

It is wholly impracticable to draw a dividing line between the employments which are suitable and those which are unsuitable for women. They have just as much right as men have to decide this question for themselves. Their decision may impose some loss upon man, but this will be compensated by the gain to woman. Nobody can decide just where moral or physical risks are involved. . . .

The countless thousands who have listened to the eloquence of a [Frances] Willard or an [Susan B.] Anthony, and have seen the great reforms they have accomplished, would take issue with him who would characterize them as "stump speakers, misguided and unseemly," or would name theirs as a calling which makes women "bold, fierce, muscular, and brawny in body or mind." It is a mistaken kindness which would doom a woman to inhale the poisonous fumes of "artificial flower making," or to bend her back over a sewing machine, or to depend on the poor rewards of the artist's pencil, rather than engage in some employment which will develop "muscle."

It is no new thing, however, for men to insist that women shall remain physically soft and inactive because it pleases their own aesthetic taste. This was the constant refrain of the Rousseaus and Voltaires of a century ago. In that book of advice which the good old English Dr. Gregory left as a *Legacy to My Daughters*, toward the close of the 18th century, he said: "Should you be so unfortunate as to possess a robust constitution by nature, simulate such sickly delicacy as is necessary to keep up the proper female charm." The Dr. Gregorys of today have advanced a step beyond "sickly delicacy," but they implore women to "show their gratitude to men for relieving them of the heavy work by becoming more and more unmistakably and delightfully feminine." There is simply a difference in expression, but none in the sentiment behind it.

The progressive portion of mankind, however, is beginning to forget sex occasionally and regard woman as a human being entitled to the same opportunity for healthy physical development as man; and, from the kindergarten to the university, girls now are receiving thorough, scientific training in athletics. The time is past when women can be frightened by an appeal not to become "muscular and brawny," and if it is not objectionable for them to become so by college athletics and outdoor exercise, it certainly is not wrong for them to develop their muscles by work. If, for the good of the world, it should become necessary to decide between "vegetables and flowers, the ox and the antelope," the flowers and the antelope would have to go. But the world needs all of them. It demands men and women of muscle in some departments, and men and women of mind in others. Even in marriage it would be a great sacrifice to hand over to certain classes of men women "whose strength lies in beauty and gentleness."

Neither can women be frightened at the warning that by engaging in occupations outside the home they decrease their chances of marrying. Whatever brings men and women into close association promotes marriage, which is largely the result of propinquity. Those who remain in the seclusion of home find no rivals so dangerous as those who in various outside employments have an opportunity to meet the men, and whom they continually see marrying not only their fellow workmen but frequently their employers. The latter, in all kinds of business, declare that the greatest objection to employing women is that they marry after a few years' service.

It is not intended to argue that every woman should leave the home and go into business, but only that those who wish to do so shall have the opportunity, and that men shall no longer monopolize the gainful occupations. The pleasure of earning money and of enjoying financial independence is just as sweet to a woman as to a man. If men would look upon the household service performed by the women of their family as a wage-earning occupation, entitled to a fixed remuneration, there would be infinitely less desire on their part to engage in outside work. When, however, they receive only board and lodging and must ask for every dollar required for clothes and other necessities, they naturally gaze with longing eyes into more fruitful fields of labor. When men cannot afford to pay their daughters or sisters a fixed sum, then at once the argument falls to the ground that "by studying domestic economy women save as much money at home as they can earn in outside occupations."

It may be that in selecting a wife "men want a girl who has not rubbed off the peach bloom of innocence by exposure to a rough world," but it is not permitted all girls to stay at home and take care of their peach bloom. Those women who make it the object of life to cultivate "refined allurements and soft blandishments to render themselves desirable to future husbands" are not many degrees removed from their sisters who practise the same arts upon the street with a less permanent object. It is no longer practicable to shut women up within four walls to preserve their virtue, and, instead of demanding a return to that medieval custom, it is the duty of society to recognize the new order and, through individual effort, public sentiment, and law, to improve the conditions which surround wage-earning women; to invest them with every right and privilege possessed by workingmen; and in every possible way help them develop strength of character to resist temptation and to fix a higher standard not only for themselves but also for the men with whom they come in contact.

"The modern metropolis is an enormity, and must be decentralized."

The Growth of Cities Must Be Reversed

Anna R. Weeks (dates unknown)

The industrial revolution in America resulted in the growth of the nation's cities, which became centers of industry and magnets for people from American rural areas and Europe. The rapid growth in both the number and size of America's cities was viewed with alarm by many Americans. Some echoed the beliefs of Thomas Jefferson and others who idealized the self-sufficient farmer as the American ideal and viewed cities as places of corruption and vice. Others looked warily at the millions of American immigrants, many from southern and eastern Europe, who lived in run-down housing in densely populated, impoverished, dirty, and crime-ridden slums. Yet others idealized nature and decried the fact that American children were growing up in urban environments.

The following viewpoint is taken from an 1894 article by poet and writer Anna R. Weeks that was published in *Arena*, a Boston-based journal that featured articles on social issues. Weeks contends that the growth of cities has deprived Americans of the joys of nature. She envisions a future in which cities will be abolished but in which Americans will continue to enjoy the benefits of technology.

From Anna R. Weeks, "The Divorce of Man from Nature," *Arena*, January 1894.

Man's love of nature, their divorce, and the wickedness of a social scheme which causes this, have haunted me all through a long summer and autumn. Until I speak my mind the ghost cannot rest.

If theories of evolution are true, if the new belief of life in all things be true, then is man, as to earth, "bone of her bone, flesh of her flesh." That wonderful allegory in Genesis once more flashes a response to science and the inner light when it says, "And the Lord God formed man of the dust of the ground." And it is that which is dear to man, whenever he has been allowed to come in contact with it in its pristine state.

There is no time of year in which one may get away from the city that this love of nature does not assert itself.

Go out in January and see how the heart thrills at the purity of the snow, unsoiled by city grime; how the eye feasts upon the grace and tints of the bare tree branches, and on the tasseled pines beplumed with snow; what velvet in the mosses, what peace under the stars.

Watch the leaves come out in May; call to the answering chipmunk, hide to watch the birds at their love making and nest building.

> Each little form celestial seems,
> Untouched, unspoiled, a harp with wings;
> Each little sprite a message brings,
> A glimpse of heaven while he sings.

The flashing gulls above like silver stars on wing, the snow of the rabbit's breast, the flirt of the squirrel's plume, the rain on the cottage roof, the rustle of the wren, the warm breath of the pines, the rattle of the nuts on the crisp brown leaves, the chatter of departing blackbirds;—what are all these but messages of brotherhood from the humbler of God's creation to the higher?

Go to the Great Lake beaches in midsummer and autumn; press joyful feet upon them, breathe full and free in unison with the jubilant waves; read ancient stories in the stones they toss you. But ever between all this and you comes the face of the proletariat; it dims the sunrise, it gazes from the incandescent sumach, from the soft glory of the maple. When lingering cottagers sat on the grassy bluff that September Sabbath eve, when the moon rose from the lake, when they sang soft evensongs to her, where were the toilers? *Not there.* Have they, then, no ear for these lofty tidings from nature? Alas! only those at the court may receive the envoy. Man is in the great city, struggling with his brother. What to him can all this beauty bring? Can a fighting man stop to enjoy the sunrise? To him it means only another heroic day; it is but his battle reveille.

The child who should be like the squirrel peers through the grime of the factory window to envy the sparrow. Even the field mice are happier than the poor babes in Chicago; they gather their seeds and berries, they lack not for acorns and nuts, they sip the dew from the fallen leaf. The very cows are better cared for than is the poverty-stricken mother in Babylon. While the summer was in its glow it came to her only as a fierce fiend of fire on the attic roof; it made a place of death of her miserable alley rooms when the steam of her washing stifled her. Or mayhap she sat with her babe on her lap to watch it die, while her faith in man—and so in God—went slowly out.

Some spirits are blind and some are heartless; either of these will dismiss the complaint with the *ipse dixit* [dogmatic assertion], "But the poor flock incessantly to the cities." Aye, they do. Is it not better to starve with one's fellows than alone? But thoughtful and gentle hearts will continue to ask, "Whence come these wrongs?"

Why People Move to the City

The competitive system is responsible. The man of the peasant class or middle class is compelled by misfortune to mortgage his little farm, and never is able to get ahead enough to redeem it; at last the mortgage is foreclosed, and his means of production gone. Or his place was paid for, and he does not mortgage, but the ground becomes a millstone round his neck; the crops fail, or he can get no market, or the usurpers of the public highway exact such freight tribute as leaves him to famish. At the same time the chicane of the "village promoter" puts a fictitious value on his land; the tax becomes excessive and yet he cannot sell. Then he "strikes for his altars and his fires" by a desperate flight to the city. Surely there is much work where there are so many to be served.

But there is another force which makes exiles of the farmer class; that is, the barrenness of their lives as regards music, literature, the drama, pictorial art, and society. All love these things more or less, in the degree that they are aware of their existence; but to pursue them in the country costs much, and is only possible to a limited degree, as country life now is. In the city the young man or woman who has these tastes can find libraries and night schools, and he supposes that he will also find choice society. He has heard of the charms of that great centre; he dreams of the parks, the boulevards, the theatres, palaces, schools, picture galleries; neighbors all about one, instead of half a mile away. He has seen but the hard side of nature and is as yet somewhat unconscious of her beauty, or, associating it with his Dead Sea life, he really hates it. The gregarious instinct masters him, and the "earth longing" is for the moment eclipsed. He, too, embarks in the municipal whirlpool.

Here, then, are the two classes of men and women who are so rapidly shifting from prairie and village to the city, and it is poverty which drives them both; in one bodily hunger, and in the other soul hunger. But they soon discover that one cannot enjoy even the public parks, the drives, the schools, unless he has at least a little money; even a car fare is frequently more than they dare to take from the rent coming due; it takes time to go to those distant fairy fields—they do not live in a quarter near them. Only the prosperous can do that. To the children of these families the schools are naught, for the child, too, must toil in Vanity Fair.

The writings and photographs of social reformer Jacob Riis, including his 1890 book How the Other Half Lives, *helped focus public attention on the living conditions found in the slums of American cities. This photograph, taken by Riis in New York City in 1888, depicts a bleak urban environment that many believed to be characteristic of cities.*

And society? One place opens its doors—aye, two; the saloon and the house of hell. These are always filled with light, music, games, and gayety. Neighbors? He finds that in cities people seldom have neighbors, unless on those magnificent streets where wealth allows one to live a lifetime. His dearest may die, and those on the other side of the wall may not know it until they see the hearse. He seems not to understand that, while every man is at war with his brother, Ishmael cannot guard his munitions too carefully. And so in the urban maelstrom he is more pitifully alone than on the bitter barrens of the Dakotas. He sees at last that he is driven not only from agrarian life, but even from human relations. Thus does the two-edged flaming sword of industrial war bar the gate of his Eden, from whence he becomes doubly exiled.

Is man, then, to be permanently separated from the earth? Not only has he left the pasture and wood, but in the towns his shelter lifts higher and higher, nearer the stars, but surely not nearer heaven. He helplessly talks of roof gardens, he accepts for his little ones the pitiful dole of the Fresh Air Fund [a charity organization that took New York City children on excursions and vacations to the countryside].

"The Fresh Air Fund"! Can the successful class imagine what that means? Had we not once a phrase, "as free as air"? It is obsolete. Few commodities now cost as much as air. The monster office buildings increase in number and in grotesque want of symmetry. They shut out the air and light of day from adjoining houses and from the street. Men work constantly by artificial light till they

> Scarce can hold it true
> That in distant lanes the lilies blossom under skies of blue.

The herding goes on. The crowds in the street congest travel until local transportation seems a Sphinx riddle. Citizens' committees are appointed to consider it; every solution but the right one is tried, and proved ineffectual or palliative only. And yet in all that throng there is scarcely a man who does not dream of a little home under the skies, with trees and vines and birds! Should the masses at last conclude that this dream is but a phantasm, then may our *quasi* civilization beware. But let us hope that ere the giant awakes he will be restored to that which he loves, the society of nature.

The City Must Go

There is but one way to do this with absolute success, and that is, the great city of to-day must go. This is to be brought to pass by a socialistic order which shall conduct its manufactures, its schools, its society, on such a basis as will for a time convert centripetal forces into centrifugal; an order which shall set the stream of life flowing back again in its natural channel, and make it possible for men to live without this dragnet huddling. The modern metropolis is an enormity, and must be decentralized; as there should be no vast wastes untrodden by man, neither should there be any wilderness of masonry where myriads of prisoners stay out their weary years. Says August Bebel:—

> No one can regard the development of our large towns as a healthy product. The present economic and industrial system is

constantly attracting great masses of the population hither. . . .
All round the towns and immediately adjoining them, the villages are also assuming the character of towns, and an enormous mass of proletariat is collecting within them. Meanwhile
the villages increase in the direction of the town and the town
in the direction of the villages, until at length they fall into the
town, like planets that have come too near the sun. But their
mutual conditions of existence are not improved thereby. On
the contrary these aggregations of masses, these centres of revolution, as one might call them, were a necessity during the present phase of development; when the new community is constituted, their object will have been fulfilled. Their gradual
dissolution becomes inevitable.

To those who have never thought that the capitals of the competitive age could vanish, the suggestion of such a thing may
seem as a foolish dream. Certainly none of us shall see it in the
flesh, but there are conditions foreshadowed which, if considered,
will lend to this conception an air of feasibility.

Cumulative modern invention and cumulative psychic light are
intensely unifying the race. To be in and of the world it will not
always be necessary that we shall be piled above one another in
brick and mortar, or that we shall every day behold the tangible
faces of the crowd. Electricity, aluminum, and the thought force
promise to serve us far more in the future than as yet.

The Adam and Even of the new Eden will have a home for life,
with its plot of ground or its share in the common park about the
dwellings. Factories will be, not in a few congested, barren spots,
but wherever the raw material is produced. Improved roads, the
bicycle, the telegraph, the telephone, the ocean cable, pneumatic
tubes, air ships, electric cars, and telepathy will keep us near one
another and near our needs. Immense concourses of people can
in an hour unite in great auditoriums scattered here and there,
but they need not gather thus for daily work. Each public building will be not a tower but a palace; its harmony will be restored,
and the space about it will allow its proportions to be understood
at a glance. Its inner beauty, too, will be increased by the freedom
with which shall enter light, air, and odors of flowers.

The prophet of humanity still insists that there shall be a New
Jerusalem, but it will have neither walls nor gates; its streets shall
be not of gold but of grass; flowing through it no stream of filth,
death laden, but "the river of the water of life, clear as crystal."

"Cities as places of human habitation have vastly improved within half a century."

The Growth of Cities Is Inevitable and Beneficial

F.J. Kingsbury (1823–1910)

Between 1860 and 1900 the percentage of America's population who lived in cities doubled from 20 percent to 40 percent. The urbanization of America alarmed some who viewed cities as centers of crime, squalor, and transportation gridlock that were populated by alien immigrants and run by corrupt political machines. Many questioned the attractiveness of city life. "It is a striking characteristic of our period," stated an 1895 editorial in *Forum*, "that it is a period of universal transition, in which large masses of people, apparently against their own interests, leave the country where homes are cheap, the air pure, all men equal, and extreme poverty unknown, and crowd into cities where all these conditions are reversed."

A more positive picture of city life appears in the following viewpoint, excerpted from an 1895 article by social scientist F.J. Kingsbury. Kingsbury attributes the growth of cities both to the human need for companionship and to the economic effects of industrialization, which promote the concentration of businesses and workers and the clustering of certain industries in particular cities. He also argues that urban living conditions have improved in recent years and that city dwellers are often better off than people in isolated rural areas. Those who seek to improve the lot of the urban poor should concentrate on improving the conditions in cities where they reside rather than attempt to remove them to the countryside, he concludes.

From F. J. Kingsbury, "The Tendency of Men to Live in Cities," *Journal of Social Sciences*, vol. 32, November 1895.

One would think after reading all . . . about the evils of cities from the time of Cain to the last New York election that nothing short of the treatment applied to Sodom and Gomorrah will meet the necessities of the case, that every sane man and woman should flee without stopping for the open country; and nothing should induce them to turn their faces cityward again.

Now, in spite of all this, precisely the reverse is true; and, while there has always been a strong tendency in humanity cityward, this nineteenth century sees it intensified beyond all former experience. . . .

Industrial Life and Cities

Perhaps you are familiar with the story of the kind lady who found a widow with a great family of children living in the depths of poverty and dirt in the city, and moved them all to a comfortable country home where, with a moderate amount of exertion, they were sure of a living. At the end of six weeks her country agent reported that the family had suddenly disappeared, no one knew where. Going back to the neighborhood of their old haunts, she found them all re-established there in the same circumstances of dirt and destitution as of old. "Why *did* you leave that comfortable home, and come back here?" was her astonished inquiry. "Folks is more company nor sthoops, anyhow," was the answer. Poor food and little of it, dirt and discomfort, heat and cold—all count as nothing in competition with this passion of gregariousness and desire for human society, even where that means more or less of a constant fight as the popular form of social intercourse. All modern industrial life tends to concentration as a matter of economy. It has long been remarked that the best place to establish or carry on any kind of business is where that business is already being done. For that reason we see different kinds of manufactures grouping themselves together—textiles in one place, metals in another; and, of the textiles, cottons in one place, woollens in another; and of the metals, iron in one place, copper in another; and so on. The reason of this is obvious. In a community where a certain kind of business is carried on the whole population unconsciously become, to a certain extent, experts. They know a vast deal more of it than people who have had no such experience. Every man, woman, and child in a fishing village is much superior in his or her knowledge of fish, bait, boats, wind, and weather to the inhabitants of inland towns. This is true of all the arts, so that besides the trained hands which may be drawn upon when needed, there is a whole population of half-trained ones ready to be drawn upon to fill their places. Then every kind of business is partly dependent of several other kinds. There must be machine-makers, blacksmiths, millwrights, and dealers in supplies of all sorts. Where there is a large business of any kind, these subsidiary trades that are supported by it naturally flock around it; whereas in an isolated situation the central establishment must support all these trades itself or go a considerable distance when it needs their assistance. Fifty or sixty years ago small manufacturing establishments in isolated situations and on small streams were scattered all through the Eastern States. The condition of trade at that time rendered this possible. Now they have almost wholly disappeared, driven out by economic necessity; and their successors are in the cities and large towns. We must remember, too, that cities as places of human habitation have vastly improved within half a century. About fifty years ago neither New York nor Boston had public water, and very few of our cities had either water or gas, and horse railroads had not been thought of. When we stop to think what this

City Growth Inevitable

Noted economist and social reformer Richard T. Ely, in an 1889 lecture entitled "The Needs of the City," asserted that further city growth was inevitable and argued against "utopian schemes" of ending urbanization.

We are considering the needs of the city. But this means an increasing proportion of the population, and, on the whole, I think we may rejoice that it does mean an ever increasing proportion of the population. The statistics of the increasing urban population throughout the civilized world have often been presented. We all know that one hundred years ago a thirtieth of the population of our country lived in cities, that now one-fourth live in cities, and that presently half of our population will be urban. This movement is inevitable. It is not due, as some think, in any considerable degree to the inclinations and desires of the people, but it is due to an economic force which is well-nigh as irresistible as the movements of the tide.

Let us cherish no utopian schemes of turning people back to the rural districts. Every new good road, every new canal, every new railway, every new invention, every economic improvement, in short, nearly all industrial progress centralizes the population in cities. It is on the whole good because man finds his welfare in association with his fellows; by nature, as Aristotle says, he is a social being; and city life makes a higher degree of association possible. This means progress of all kinds, if we are but equal to the increasing strains city life puts upon our civilization.

really means in sanitary matters, it seems to me that the increase of cities is no longer a matter of surprise.

City vs. Rural Life

I have been fairly familiar with the streets of New York and Boston for the last fifty years, and there is no fact in that connection with which I have been more impressed than the physical improvement which has taken place in both men and women during that period. The men are more robust and more erect, the women have greatly improved both in feature and in carriage; and in the care and condition of the teeth in both sexes a surprising change has taken place. In Boston streets and street-cars it seems to me that you see a hundred good-looking women where you formerly saw one. Whether this would hold good in the slums and low parts of the town may be doubted, but there, of course, one looks for the refuse and cast-off material of society.

I think isolated rural life, where people seldom come in contact with dwellers in large towns, always tends to barbarism. I believe that poorer people in our cities, if planted in isolated situations in the country, would deteriorate and grow barbaric in habit and thought, even though they might be physically in better condition. What very unattractive people most of our rural population are!

It would seem, then,

(1) That for economic reasons a large part of the work of the world must be done in cities, and the people who do that work must live in cities.

(2) That most everything that is best in life can be better had in the city than elsewhere, and that, with those who can command the means, physical comforts and favorable sanitary conditions are better obtained there.

(3) That a certain amount of change from city to country is desirable, and is also very universally attainable to those who desire it and is constantly growing more so.

(4) That the city is growing a better place to live in year by year; that in regard to the degenerate portion of mankind, the very poor, the very wicked, or the very indifferent, it is a question whether they are better off in the country; but, whether they are or not, their gregarious instincts will lead them to the city, and they must be dealt with there as part of the problem.

(5) That efforts to relieve the congested conditions of the city poor are good and praiseworthy, but only touch the surface of things, and that city degeneration must mainly be fought on its own ground.

"Do we ever think of the over two million children who—in free America—are pushed out as little burden bearers to share the toils and strains and dangers of the world of battling men?"

An Attack on Child Labor Practices in Industry

Edwin Markham (1852–1940)

A significant portion of the workers that powered America's industrial revolution were children. Boys and girls from five to sixteen worked in textile plants, cigar factories, glass factories, and other industrial enterprises. Others worked at home in the "sweatshop" system under which assembly and sewing work was subcontracted to families working in tenements. The 1900 U.S. census counted 1.75 million children in the labor force, about 18 percent of the total child population. Of this number—which many believed understated the true extent of child labor—about 40 percent worked in factories, mines, and tenement workshops.

Beginning around 1900, social reformers made the abolition of child labor in the United States one of the their leading goals. In earlier times child labor was not a controversy. Children in America had traditionally worked in farms or handicrafts; boys who became apprentices in a certain trade typically began their apprenticeships between ages ten and fourteen. However, many reformers argued that the industrial revolution had changed the nature of child labor and that children in factories and mines were exploited, victimized by terrible working conditions, and deprived of education. Although by the turn of the century some states had passed laws mandating school attendance and forbid-

From Edwin Markham, "The Hoe Man in the Making," *Cosmopolitan*, September 1906.

ding the employment of children under twelve, enforcement was often lax and evasion of these laws was common.

The following viewpoint is excerpted from a September 1906 article by journalist and poet Edwin Markham. A former school-teacher and principal, Markham was one of the "muckrakers" of the Progressive era who wrote numerous exposés in newspapers and magazines about political corruption, consumer fraud, and other social and economic ills of American society. This essay, one of a series of articles on child labor Markham wrote for *Cosmopolitan* magazine, focuses on children working in textile mills in the southern states. Markham strongly attacks the practice of child labor and calls for laws prohibiting it.

Once, so the story goes, an old Indian chieftain was shown the ways and wonders of New York. He saw the cathedrals, the skyscrapers, the bleak tenements, the blaring mansions, the crowded circus, the airy span of the Brooklyn Bridge. "What is the most surprising thing you have seen?" asked several comfortable Christian gentlemen of this benighted pagan whose worship was a "bowing down to sticks and stones." The savage shifted his red blanket and answered in three slow words, "Little children working."

It has remained, then, for civilization to give the world an abominable custom which shocks the social ethics of even an unregenerate savage. For the Indian father does not ask his children to work, but leaves them free till the age of maturity, when they are ushered with solemn rites into the obligations of their elders. Some of us are wondering why our savage friends do not send their medicine men as missionaries, to shed upon our Christian darkness the light of barbarism. Child labor is a new thing in human affairs. Ancient history records no such infamy. "Children," says the Talmud, "must not be taken from the schools even to rebuild the temple." In Greece and Rome the children of both slave and master fared alike in a common nursery. The trainers worked to build up strong and beautiful bodies, careless of the accident of lineage or fortune. But how different is our "Christian civilization"! Seventeen hundred thousand children at work! Does the enumeration bring any significance to our minds when we say that an army of one million seven hundred thousand children are at work in our "land of the free"? This was the figure in 1900; now there are hundreds of thousands more. And many of them working their long ten or fourteen hours by day or by night, with only a miserable dime for a wage! Can the heart take in the enormity?

Picture the procession of them all—enough to people a modern Babylon—all held from the green fields, barred from school, shut out of home, dragged from play and sleep and rest, and set tramping in grim, forced march to the mills and mines and shops and offices in this our America—the land whose name we have been told is Opportunity! We of the "upper crust" give our children books and beauty by day, and fold them into white beds at night; and we feel all this caretaking to be only the natural order of things. Do we ever think of the over two million children who—in free America—are pushed out as little burden bearers to share the toils and strains and dangers of the world of battling men?

Let us glance into the weaving rooms of the cotton mills and behold in the hot, damp, decaying atmosphere the little wan figures flying in hideous cotillion among looms and wheels—children choked and blinded by clouds of lint forever molting from the webs, children deafened by the jar and uproar of an eternal Niagara of machines, children silenced utterly in the desert desolation in the heart of the never-ceasing clamor, children that seem like specter-shapes, doomed to silence and done with life, beckoning to one another across some thunder-shaken Inferno.

Is it not shameful, is it not astounding that this craft . . . should now, after all the advance of the ages, be loaded in any degree upon the frail, half-formed bodies of little children? To what purpose then is our "age of invention"? Why these machines at all, if they do not help to lift care from the soul and burden from the back? To what purpose is our "age of enlightenment," if, just to cover our nakedness, we establish among us a barbarism that overshadows the barbarism of the savage cycle? Is this the wisdom of the wise? Is this the Christianity we boast of and parade in benighted Madagascar and unsaved Malabar? Is this what our orators mean when they jubilate over "civilization" and "the progress of the species"?

Cotton Mills

After all these ages, more children are crowded into this limbo of the loom than into any other cavern of our industrial abyss. In the southern cotton mills, where the doors shut out the odor of the magnolia and shut in the reeking damps and clouds of lint, and where the mocking bird outside keeps obbligato to the whirring wheels within, we find a gaunt goblin army of children keeping their forced march on the factory floors—an army that outwatches the sun by day and the stars by night. Eighty thousand children, mostly girls, are at work in the textile mills of the United States. The South, the center of the cotton industry, happens to have the eminence of being the leader in this social in-

214

famy. At the beginning of 1903 there were in the South twenty thousand children at the spindles. *The Tradesman*, of Chattanooga, estimates that with the springing up of new mills there must now be fifty thousand children at the southern looms. This is 30 per cent of all the cotton workers of the South—a spectral army of pygmy people sucked in from the hills to dance beside the crazing wheels.

Let us again reckon up this Devil's toll. In the North (where, God knows, conditions are bad enough), for every one thousand workers over sixteen years of age there are eighty-three workers under sixteen (that young old-age of the working-child); while in the South, for every one thousand workers in the mills over sixteen years of age there are three hundred and fifty-three under sixteen. Some of these are eight and nine years old, and some are only five and six. For a day or a night at a stretch these little children do some one monotonous thing—abusing their eyes in watching the rushing threads; dwarfing their muscles in an eternity of petty movements; befouling their lungs by breathing flecks of flying cotton; bestowing ceaseless, anxious attention for hours, where science says that "a twenty-minute strain is long enough for a growing mind." And these are not the children of recent immigrants, hardened by the effete conditions of foreign servitude. Nor are they Negro children who have shifted their shackles from field to mill. They are white children of old and pure colonial stock. Think of it! Here is a people that has outlived the bondage of England, that has seen the rise and fall of slavery—a people that must now fling their children into the clutches of capital, into the maw of the blind machine; must see their latest-born drag on in a face of servility that reminds us of the Saxon churl under the frown of the Norman lord. For Mammon is merciless.

Fifty thousand children, mostly girls, are in the textile mills of the South. Six times as many children are working now as were working twenty years ago. Unless the conscience of the nation can be awakened, it will not be long before one hundred thousand children will be hobbling in hopeless lock-step to these Bastilles of labor. It will not be long till these little spinners shall be "far on the way to be spiders and needles."

Deadly Drudgery

Think of the deadly drudgery in these cotton mills. Children rise at half-past four, commanded by the ogre scream of the factory whistle; they hurry, ill fed, unkempt, unwashed, half dressed, to the walls which shut out the day and which confine them amid the din and dust and merciless maze of the machines. Here, penned in little narrow lanes, they look and leap and reach and tie among acres and acres of looms. Always the snow of lint

215

in their faces, always the thunder of the machines in their ears. A scant half hour at noon breaks the twelve-hour vigil, for it is nightfall when the long hours end and the children may return to the barracks they call "home," often too tired to wait for the cheerless meal which the mother, also working in the factory,

How Child Labor Has Changed

Journalist John Spargo traveled the country investigating conditions of child laborers; the results of his studies were published in his 1907 book The Bitter Cry of Children. *In the following excerpt from that book, Spargo describes how the industrial revolution has changed the nature of child labor.*

Children have always worked, but it is only since the reign of the machine that their work has been synonymous with slavery. Under the old form of simple, domestic industry even the very young children were assigned their share of the work in the family. But this form of child labor was a good and wholesome thing. There may have been abuses; children may have suffered from the ignorance, cupidity, and brutality of fathers and mothers, but in the main the child's share in the work of the family was a good thing. In the first place, the child was associated in its work with one or both of its parents, and thus kept under all those influences which we deem of most worth, the influences of home and parental care. Secondly, the work of the child constituted a major part of its education. And it was no mean education, either, which gave the world generation after generation of glorious craftsmen. The seventeenth-century glassblower of Venice or Murano, for instance, learned his craft from his father in this manner, and in turn taught it to his son. There was a bond of interest between them; a parental pride and interest on the part of the father infinitely greater and more potent for good than any commercial relation would have allowed. On the part of the child, too, there was a filial pride and devotion which found its expression in a spirit of emulation, the spirit out of which all the rich glory of that wonderfully rich craft was born. So, too, it was with the potters of ancient Greece, and with the tapestry weavers of fourteenth-century France. In the golden age of the craftsman, child labor was child training in the noblest and best sense. The training of hand and heart and brain was the end achieved, even where it was not the sole purpose of the child's labor.

But with the coming of the machine age all this was changed. The craftsman was supplanted by the tireless, soulless machine. The child still worked, but in a great factory throbbing with the vibration of swift, intricate machines. In place of parental interest and affection there was the harsh, pitiless authority of an employer or his agent, looking, not to the child's well-being and skill as an artificer, but to the supplying of a great, ever widening market for cash gain.

must cook, after her factory day is over. Frequently at noon and at night they fall asleep with the food unswallowed in the mouth. Frequently they snatch only a bite and curl up undressed on the bed, to gather strength for the same dull round tomorrow, and tomorrow, and tomorrow.

When I was in the South I was everywhere charmed by the bright courtesy of the cultured classes, but I was everywhere depressed by the stark penury of the working people. This penury stands grimly out in the gray monotonous shells that they call "homes"—dingy shacks, or bleak, barnlike structures. And for these dirty, desolate homes the workers must pay rent to the mill owner. But the rent is graded according to the number of children sent to work in the mill. The more the children, the less the rent. Mammon is wise: he knows how to keep a cruel grip upon the tots at the fireside.

And why do these children know no rest, no play, no learning, nothing but the grim grind of existence? Is it because we are all naked and shivering? Is it because there is sudden destitution in the land? Is it because pestilence walks at noonday? Is it because war's red hand is pillaging our storehouses and burning our cities? No, forsooth! Never before were the storehouses so crammed to bursting with bolts and bales of every warp and woof. No, forsooth! The children, while yet in the gristle, are ground down that a few more useless millions may be heaped up. We boast that we are leading the commercialism of the world, and we grind in our mills the bones of the little ones to make good our boast.

Rev. Edgar Murphy of Montgomery, Alabama, has photographed many groups of these pathetic little toilers, all under twelve. Jane Addams saw in a night-factory a little girl of five, her teeth blacked with snuff, like all the little girls about her—a little girl who was busily and clumsily tying threads in coarse muslin. The average child lives only four years after it enters the mills. Pneumonia stalks in the damp, lint-filled rooms, and leads hundreds of the little ones out to rest. Hundreds more are maimed by the machinery, two or three for each of their elders. One old mill hand carries sixty-four scars, the cruel record of the shuttles.

The labor commissioner of North Carolina reports that there are two hundred and sixty-one cotton mills in that state, in which nearly forty thousand people are employed, including nearly eight thousand children. The average daily wage of the men is fifty-seven cents, of the women thirty-nine cents, of the children twenty-two cents. The commissioner goes on to say: "I have talked with a little boy of seven years who worked for forty nights in Alabama, and with another child who, at six years of age, had been on the night shift eleven months. Little boys turned out at two o'clock in the morning, afraid to go home, would beg a clerk in the mill for permission to lie down on the office floor. In one city mill in the South, a doctor said he had amputated the fingers of more than one hundred children, mangled in the mill machinery, and that a horrible form of dropsy occurs frequently among the overworked children.". . . .

These little white children often begin work in the mill with no fragment of education. And often after a year of this brain-blasting labor they lose the power to learn even the simple art of reading. There is sometimes a night school for the little workers, but they often topple over with sleep at the desks, after the long grind of the day. Indeed they must not spend too many wakeful hours in the night school, shortening their sleep-time; for the ogre of the mill must have all their strength at full head in the morning. The overseer cannot afford to be sending his mounted "poker-up" to their homes to rout them out of bed day after day, nor can he be continually watching lest they fall asleep on the mill floor while working or eating. Nor can he afford to keep a clerk busy docking the wages of these little sleep-starved workers for the constant mistakes and accidents of the fatigued and fumbling fingers. For these little drudges are fined for their lacks and lapses; and they are sometimes in debt to the concern at the week's end.

But worse than all is the breakdown of the soul in these God-forgetting mills. Here boys and girls are pushed into the company of coarse men who are glib with oaths and reeking jests. Torrents of foul profanity from angry overseers wash over the souls of the children, till they, too, grow hardened in crusts of coarseness. Piled on all these are the fearful risks that the young girls run from the attentions of men "higher up," especially if the girls happen to be cursed with a little beauty.

Treasons Against God

What avail our exports, our tariffs, our dividends, if they rise out of these treasons against God? All gains are losses, all riches are poverties, so long as the soul is left to rot down. What the friends of mercy are pleading, is the old, old plea of the Friend of Children—the plea of him who cried out, "Be not afraid of them which kill the body, but are not able to kill the soul: but rather fear him which is able to destroy both body and soul in hell."

The poor remnant of these young toilers, they who do not crumble down in an early death, or drift to the gutter or the brothel, are left, alas! to become fathers and mothers. Fathers and mothers, forsooth! What sort of fatherhood and motherhood can we hope for from these children robbed of childhood, from these children with the marrow sucked out of their bones and the beauty run out of their faces? Tragical is it beyond words to think that any of these poor human effigies should ever escape to engender their kind and to send on a still more pitiable progeny. What child worthy of the name can spring from the loins of these withered effigies of men? What babe worthy of the name can be mothered in the side of this wasted and weakened woman who has given her virgin vitality to the Moloch of the mill? And what wonder that, if expelled from the factory as no longer competent to be a cog or a pulley in the vast machine, they have no ambition but to sit idly in the sun? What wonder that the commonwealth, having fostered these dull degenerates, should be forced to care for them in her almshouses, her jails, her asylums? What wonder that only the cheapest and coarsest pleasures can stir their numb spirits? The things of the soul which they have missed, they will never know that they have missed. They sit idly in the sun, a sorrowful type of the savage created by civilization, and sad protest against civilization—the starved, the stunted, the stunned, who speak no protest! . . .

What boots a social order that makes thousands of degenerates as the by-product of its exquisite linens and delicate muslins? Must we take our civilization on such terms as this? Must thousands fall and perish that a few may soar and shine? Let us rather go back to the clout of the savage, for "the body is more than raiment." The savage, the grim son of the forest, has at least a light step, a sound body, a brood of lusty children and a treasure of poetic legend and song. But our savage of civilization, what of him? Look at his wasted body, his empty face, his beauty-robbed existence. Men are such cravens before custom that they often think a thing right because it has been long in existence. But child labor has about it no halo of antiquity. It is a thing of yesterday—a sudden toadstool in the infernal garden. It shot up with the coming of steam and loom at the end of the eighteenth century. England began to fight the villainy in 1802, yet today the black shadow of it lies wide upon America.

Driven by Profit

The factory, we are told, must make a certain profit, or the owners (absentee proprietors generally, living in larded luxury) will complain. Therefore the president is goaded on by the directors. He in turn whips up the overseer; the overseer takes it out on the workers. So the long end of the lash cuts red the backs of the little children. Need we wonder, then, that cotton-factory stock gives back portly profits—25, 35, yes, even 50 per cent? It pays, my masters, to grind little children into dividends! And the silks and muslins do not show the stain of blood, although they are splashed with scarlet on God's side. . . .

"Rob us of child labor and we will take our mills from your state." This is the frequent threat of the mill owners in the chambers and lobbies of legislation. And, alas! we are in a civilization where such a threat avails. Still, in spite of the apathy of the church, in spite of the assault of the capital, the friends of mercy have in all but four states forced some sort of a protective law: no child under twelve years of age shall work for longer than eight hours, nor any without a common-school education. This reads fairly well; but a law on the statute book is not always a law on the factory-floor. The inspectors are often vigilant and quick with conscience. Some mills desire to keep the law. But others are crooked: they have their forged and perjured certificates, their double payrolls—one for the inspector, another for the counting-house. They have, also, the device of bringing children in as "mothers' helps," giving the mothers a few more pennies for the baby fingers.

Hard masters of mills, shiftless or hapless parents, even misguided children themselves, all conspire to hold the little slaves to the wheel. Yes, even the children are taught to lie about their age, and their tongues are ever ready with the glib rehearsal. Some mills keep a lookout for the inspector, and at the danger signal the children scurry like rats to hide in attics, to crouch in cellars, behind bales of cotton, under heaps of old machinery. But God's battle has begun. Still there must be a wider unification of the bands of justice and mercy, a fusing and forcing of public opinion. Let the women of America arise, unite, and resolve in a great passion of righteousness to save the children of the nation. Nothing can stand against the fire of an awakened and banded womanhood.

VIEWPOINT 8

"At the mills, children over 12 years old, after they learn their job, can make more than men can make on farms."

A Defense of Child Labor Practices in Industry

Thomas L. Livermore and
a North Carolina Mill Worker (dates unknown)

In 1870, the Census Bureau established a separate category of workers who were between the ages of ten and fifteen; the bureau ascertained that one out of eight American children in this age group were employed. By 1900 that number had risen to one in six, and the practice of child labor had come under increasing attack from political leaders and social reformers.

The following two-part viewpoint presents the opinions of two people intimately involved with child labor in factories. The first part is excerpted from testimony by Thomas L. Livermore, a manager of a textile factory in New Hampshire, before an 1883 congressional committee investigating labor conditions. Responding to questions from the committee's chairman, New Hampshire senator Henry W. Blair, Livermore concedes that children need some classroom education, but asserts that factory employment is a worthwhile source of "practical" education for many children. The second part of the viewpoint is taken from a handbill that was circulated in cotton mills in North Carolina around 1906. In it, the anonymous author states that he and his family, including his two boys and three girls, are much better off employed together in a cotton mill than they had been previously on a two-hundred-acre farm.

Part I: From testimony of Thomas L. Livermore, *Report of the Committee of the Senate Upon the Relations Between Labor and Capital* (Washington, DC: GPO, 1885). Part II: From August Kohn, *The Cotton Mills of South Carolina* (Columbia, SC: 1907).

I

Senator Henry W. Blair. Won't you please tell us your experience with the question of child labor; how it is and to what extent it exists here; why it exists, and whether, as it is actually existing here, it is a hardship on a child or on a parent; or whether there is any evil in that direction that should be remedied?

Livermore. There is a certain class of labor in the mills which, to put it in very common phrase, consists mainly in running about the floor—where there is not as much muscular exercise required as a child would put forth in play, and a child can do it about as well as a grown person can do it—not quite as much of it, but somewhere near it—and with proper supervision of older people, the child serves the purpose. That has led to the employment of children in the mills, I think. . . .

Now, a good many heads of families, without any question in my mind, were not sufficiently considerate of the mental and physical welfare of their children, and they put them to work in the mills, perhaps too early, and certainly kept them there too much of the time in former years, and the legislature had to step in and protect the children against the parents by requiring that they should go to school a certain number of months or weeks in a year, or else they should not be allowed to work in the mills; and at the present time there is a very severe law in this state applicable to children—I think some under twelve and some under sixteen. I do not remember the terms of it, but the child has to have a certificate of the authorities in control of the schools that he has been to school the time required by the statute before the mill manager is able to employ him. I think the mill manager is subject to a very considerable penalty for noncompliance with that law.

In this city in our mills, and as far as I know in the rest of the mills, we have been very particular to observe the statute. I do not know how it is outside of the city. I suppose that it may depend a good deal upon public sentiment. If public sentiment supports the law, it will be enforced; if it does not, it will not be. I think public sentiment does support it here to an extent, although I think it extends a little too far in preventing children up to sixteen working in mills more than a given time. . . . The city authorities here have an officer who makes it his business to go through the mills to see whether the law is complied with or not.

Work and Education

Now, I think that when it is provided that a child shall go to school as long as it is profitable for a workman's child (who has got to be a workingman himself) to go to school, the limit has been reached at which labor in the mills should be forbidden. There is such a thing as too much education for working people sometimes. I do not mean to say by that that I discourage education to any person on earth, or that I think that with good sense any amount of education can hurt anyone, but I have seen cases where young people were spoiled for labor by being educated to a little too much refinement.

A photograph of a young textile worker. Many of the workers at American factories at the turn of the century were under sixteen years of age.

Q. You have known something of farm life and the necessity that a boy is put under of learning to farm while he is still a boy?
A. Yes.
Q. Now, with reference to the acquirement of the necessary skill to earn a living, without which an education would amount to little—a man having enough knowledge to starve upon has not much advantage—do you think that the child should be withheld from the educating idea in the industrial line to so large an extent as the law now requires?
A. I do not.
Q. Is there danger of too much abstention from that sort of practical education which enables a child when grown to earn his living?
A. I think so. I will state that in our machine shops we take apprentices to learn the trade of a machinist, which is one of the

best trades that any man in this country can have. We agree that if they will agree to serve three years for pay which enables them to live, we will teach them the trade of a machinist; and it is a curious illustration of the effect of very advanced common schools that our foremen prefer for apprentices boys from the country, who have worked on farms and been to a district school a little while, to boys that have been educated in the city. They say that the city boys do not stick to their work as the others do. They are a little above the employment.

Q. Is this employment that you speak about in the mills in which children are engaged of a character to tax their muscular or physical frame more than it ought to during their growing period?

A. No, sir; I don't know of any such employment in the mills being put upon children.

II

Three years ago I owned a little mountain farm of two hundred acres. I had two good horses, two good cows, plenty of hogs, sheep and several calves. I had three girls and two boys; ages run from 11 to 21. On my little farm I raised about four hundred bushels of corn, thirty to forty bushels of wheat, two hundred to three hundred dozen oats, and cut from four to eight stacks of hay during the summer. After I clothed my family, fed all my stock during the winter, I had only enough provisions and feed to carry me through making another crop, and no profit left. I sold my farm and stock, paid up all my debts and moved my family to a cotton mill. At that time green hands had to work for nothing til they learned their job, about one month, but now my youngest daughter, only 14 years old, is making $6 per week, my other two are making $7.50 each per week and my two boys are making $8 per week and I am making $4.50 per week; a total of $166 per month. My provisions average $30, house rent $2, coal and wood $4, total $36; leaving a balance of $130, to buy clothes and deposit in the bank.

My experience is that, while you are on the farm toiling in rain and snow, feeding away what you have made during the summer and making wood to keep fires to keep your family from freezing, you could at the same time be in a cotton mill and in a good, comfortable room, making more than you can make in the summer time on the farm, and there is no stock to eat up what you make. At the mills, children over 12 years old, after they learn their job, can make more than men can make on farms. It is not every family that can do as well as the above family, but it only shows what a family can do that will try and work. Most any family can do half as well—so divide the above number of workers' wages by two and see if you would not still be doing well.

Give this matter your careful thought.

CHAPTER 6

Historians Debate the Role of Robber Barons in the Industrial Revolution

Chapter Preface

The American entrepreneurs who led America's post–Civil War industrial revolution—people such as steel magnate Andrew Carnegie, oil industrialist John D. Rockefeller, and railroad owners Cornelius and William Vanderbilt—continue to provoke debate regarding their character, social contributions, and their impact on America's economy. This perennial controversy is reflected in the different names they have been called. Some historians, such as Charles and Mary Beard and Allan Nevins, have referred to them as "captains of industry" or "industrial statesmen" and have argued that they were essential to America's industrial development. Through their creative powers of business organization, their ability to grasp the implications of changing industrial technologies, and their drive (even ruthlessness), these individuals helped America become the world's leading industrial power.

However, other journalists and historians have called the same group of people "robber barons" (a term coined in a 1934 book by journalist Matthew Josephson) whose actions in building and running industrial companies were detrimental to American society and American workers. Josephson and others contend that these businessmen made their fortunes by bribing politicians to obtain favors, manipulating the stock market, paying workers poor wages, and using unscrupulous means to crush competitors. To their critics, these individuals were more exploiters than creators of America's industrial development and should not receive undue credit.

The following pair of viewpoints present sharply contrasting pictures of America's nineteenth-century business leaders and their relationship to American society.

VIEWPOINT 1

"And so it went, in industry after industry—shrewd, efficient businessmen building empires, choking out competition, maintaining high prices, keeping wages low, using government subsidies."

Robber Barons Contributed to Social Problems

Howard Zinn (b. 1922)

Howard Zinn is professor emeritus of political science at Boston University. He has also been involved in social and political activism including the civil rights movement and protests against the Vietnam War. Zinn's books include *Disobedience & Democracy* and *Declarations of Independence: Cross-Examining American Ideology*. The following viewpoint is excerpted from the 1995 revised edition of his book *A People's History of the United States*, which was nominated for an American Book Award when it was published in 1980. The book surveys American history from the point of view of the poor, blacks, Native Americans, women, and other minorities and disadvantaged classes.

In the viewpoint, Zinn examines economic developments in America following the Civil War, with particular emphasis on the owners and presidents of large industrial and business enterprises—notably John D. Rockefeller, J.P. Morgan, and Andrew Carnegie—who led the country into a new industrial age. Zinn argues that many of these industrialists, who are commonly referred to as "robber barons," attained their wealth in unscrupulous, illegal, and socially costly ways. Their riches, he asserts, were the product of ruthless business tactics, cozy and self-

From Howard Zinn, "Robber Barons and Rebels," in *A People's History of the United States*, ©1980 by Howard Zinn. Reprinted by permission of HarperCollins Publishers, Inc.

serving deals with politicians and bankers, and the harsh treatment of millions of working Americans who were not permitted to share the wealth their labor helped to create. Zinn further contends that during this era, the federal and state governments and the Supreme Court established policies that favored business interests and the rich. In addition, according to Zinn, many of the philanthropy projects created by Carnegie and others were designed to discourage or stifle public discontent and thus maintain the status quo.

In the year 1877, the signals were given for the rest of the century: the black would be put back; the strikes of white workers would not be tolerated; the industrial and political elites of North and South would take hold of the country and organize the greatest march of economic growth in human history. They would do it with the aid of, and at the expense of, black labor, white labor, Chinese labor, European immigrant labor, female labor, rewarding them differently by race, sex, national origin, and social class, in such a way as to create separate levels of oppression—a skillful terracing to stabilize the pyramid of wealth.

Between the Civil War and 1900, steam and electricity replaced human muscle, iron replaced wood, and steel replaced iron (before the Bessemer process, iron was hardened into steel at the rate of 3 to 5 tons a day; now the same amount could be processed in 15 minutes). Machines could now drive steel tools. Oil could lubricate machines and light homes, streets, factories. People and goods could move by railroad, propelled by steam along steel rails; by 1900 there were 193,000 miles of railroad. The telephone, the typewriter, and the adding machine speeded up the work of business.

Machines changed farming. Before the Civil War it took 61 hours of labor to produce an acre of wheat. By 1900, it took 3 hours, 19 minutes. Manufactured ice enabled the transport of food over long distances, and the industry of meatpacking was born.

Steam drove textile mill spindles; it drove sewing machines. It came from coal. Pneumatic drills now drilled deeper into the earth for coal. In 1860, 14 million tons of coal were mined; by 1884 it was 100 million tons. More coal meant more steel, because coal furnaces converted iron into steel; by 1880 a million tons of steel were being produced; by 1910, 25 million tons. By now electricity was beginning to replace steam. Electrical wire needed copper, of which 30,000 tons were produced in 1880; 500,000 tons by 1910.

To accomplish all this required ingenious inventors of new processes and new machines, clever organizers and administrators of the new corporations, a country rich with land and minerals, and a huge supply of human beings to do the back-breaking, unhealthful, and dangerous work. Immigrants would come from Europe and China, to make the new labor force. Farmers unable to buy the new machinery or pay the new railroad rates would move to the cities. Between 1860 and 1914, New York grew from 850,000 to 4 million, Chicago from 110,000 to 2 million, Philadelphia from 650,000 to 1½ million.

The Horatio Alger Myth

In some cases the inventor himself became the organizer of businesses—like Thomas Edison, inventor of electrical devices. In other cases, the businessman compiled other people's inventions, like Gustavus Swift, a Chicago butcher who put together the ice-cooled railway car with the ice-cooled warehouse to make the first national meatpacking company in 1885. James Duke used a new cigarette-rolling machine that could roll, paste, and cut tubes of tobacco into 100,000 cigarettes a day; in 1890 he combined the four biggest cigarette producers to form the American Tobacco Company.

While some multimillionaires started in poverty, most did not. A study of the origins of 303 textile, railroad, and steel executives of the 1870s showed that 90 percent came from middle- or upper-class families. The Horatio Alger stories of "rags to riches" were true for a few men, but mostly a myth, and a useful myth for control.

Most of the fortune building was done legally, with the collaboration of the government and the courts. Sometimes the collaboration had to be paid for. Thomas Edison promised New Jersey politicians $1,000 each in return for favorable legislation. Daniel Drew and Jay Gould spent $1 million to bribe the New York legislature to legalize their issue of $8 million in "watered stock" (stock not representing real value) on the Erie Railroad.

Building the Railroads

The first transcontinental railroad was built with blood, sweat, politics and thievery, out of the meeting of the Union Pacific and Central Pacific railroads. The Central Pacific started on the West Coast going east; it spent $200,000 in Washington on bribes to get 9 million acres of free land and $24 million in bonds, and paid $79 million, an overpayment of $36 million, to a construction company which really was its own. The construction was done by three thousand Irish and ten thousand Chinese, over a period of four years, working for one or two dollars a day.

The Union Pacific started in Nebraska going west. It had been given 12 million acres of free land and $27 million in government bonds. It created the Credit Mobilier company and gave them $94 million for construction when the actual cost was $44 million. Shares were sold cheaply to Congressmen to prevent investigation. This was at the suggestion of Massachusetts Congressman Oakes Ames, a shovel manufacturer and director of Credit Mobilier, who said: "There is no difficulty in getting men to look after their own property." The Union Pacific used twenty thousand workers—war veterans and Irish immigrants, who laid 5 miles of track a day and died by the hundreds in the heat, the cold, and the battles with Indians opposing the invasion of their territory.

Both railroads used longer, twisting routes to get subsidies from towns they went through. In 1869, amid music and speeches, the two crooked lines met in Utah.

The wild fraud on the railroads led to more control of railroad finances by bankers, who wanted more stability—profit by law rather than by theft. By the 1890s, most of the country's railway mileage was concentrated in six huge systems. Four of these were completely or partially controlled by the House of Morgan, and two others by the bankers Kuhn, Loeb, and Company.

J.P. Morgan

J.P. Morgan had started before the war, as the son of a banker who began selling stocks for the railroads for good commissions. During the Civil War he bought five thousand rifles for $3.50 each from an army arsenal, and sold them to a general in the field for $22 each. The rifles were defective and would shoot off the thumbs of the soldiers using them. A congressional committee noted this in the small print of an obscure report, but a federal judge upheld the deal as the fulfillment of a valid legal contract.

Morgan had escaped military service in the Civil War by paying $300 to a substitute. So did John D. Rockefeller, Andrew Carnegie, Philip Armour, Jay Gould, and James Mellon. Mellon's father had written to him that "a man may be a patriot without risking his own life or sacrificing his health. There are plenty of lives less valuable."

It was the firm of Drexel, Morgan and Company that was given a U.S. government contract to float a bond issue of $260 million. The government could have sold the bonds directly; it chose to pay the bankers $5 million in commission.

On January 2, 1889, as Gustavus Myers reports:

> . . . a circular marked "Private and Confidential" was issued by the three banking houses of Drexel, Morgan & Company, Brown Brothers & Company, and Kidder, Peabody & Company. The most painstaking care was exercised that this document should not find its way into the press or otherwise become public. . . . Why this fear? Because the circular was an invitation . . .

to the great railroad magnates to assemble at Morgan's house, No. 219 Madison Avenue, there to form, in the phrase of the day, an iron-clad combination . . . a compact which would efface competition among certain railroads, and unite those interests in an agreement by which the people of the United States would be bled even more effectively than before.

There was a human cost to this exciting story of financial ingenuity. That year, 1889, records of the Interstate Commerce Commission showed that 22,000 railroad workers were killed or injured.

In 1895 the gold reserve of the United States was depleted, while twenty-six New York City banks had $129 million in gold in their vaults. A syndicate of bankers headed by J.P. Morgan & Company, August Belmont & Company, the National City Bank, and others offered to give the government gold in exchange for bonds. President Grover Cleveland agreed. The bankers immediately resold the bonds at higher prices, making $18 million profit.

A journalist wrote: "If a man wants to buy beef, he must go to the butcher. . . . If Mr. Cleveland wants much gold, he must go to the big banker."

While making his fortune, Morgan brought rationality and organization to the national economy. He kept the system stable. He said: "We do not want financial convulsions and have one thing one day and another thing another day." He linked railroads to one another, all of them to banks, banks to insurance companies. By 1900, he controlled 100,000 miles of railroad, half the country's mileage.

Three insurance companies dominated by the Morgan group had a billion dollars in assets. They had $50 million a year to invest—money given by ordinary people for their insurance policies. Louis Brandeis, describing this in his book *Other People's Money* (before he became a Supreme Court justice), wrote: "They control the people through the people's own money."

Rockefeller and Carnegie

John D. Rockefeller started as a bookkeeper in Cleveland, became a merchant, accumulated money, and decided that, in the new industry of oil, who controlled the oil refineries controlled the industry. He bought his first oil refinery in 1862, and by 1870 set up Standard Oil Company of Ohio, made secret agreements with railroads to ship his oil with them if they gave him rebates—discounts—on their prices, and thus drove competitors out of business.

One independent refiner said: "If we did not sell out . . . we would be crushed out. . . . There was only one buyer on the market and we had to sell at their terms." Memos like this one passed among Standard Oil officials: "Wilkerson & Co. received car of oil

Monday 13th. . . . Please turn another screw." A rival refinery in Buffalo was rocked by a small explosion arranged by Standard Oil officials with the refinery's chief mechanic.

The Standard Oil Company, by 1899, was a holding company which controlled the stock of many other companies. The capital

---

The Meat Packing Trust

Journalist Matthew Josephson's influential 1934 book The Robber Barons *popularized the term "robber baron" and cemented the public image of rich industrialists as ruthless and unethical capitalists. The following excerpt focuses on the machinations of meat packers in Chicago.*

The most successful of the early industrial pools was formed toward 1880 by the slaughterhouses of Chicago. Here at the natural transshipment center where numerous great railroad trunk lines converged, the grain, produce, cattle and swine of the West seemed to flow toward the world markets as through a bottle-neck held in the hands of packing-houses, elevators and millers.

"I like to turn bristles, blood, and the inside and outside of pigs and bullocks into revenue . . ." said the astute Philip D. Armour. This puritanical and grasping dealer in pigs was among the first to note the enormous waste of labor and material in his trade. Both he and Nelson Morris had soon ceased to sell cattle "on the hoof," and had begun to systematize the work of despatching, dressing, smoking and canning steers in their stockyards by large-scale methods. . . .

Armour, Morris and the other packers who used to give each other "a wallop with a smile," at length arrived at a complete "gentlemen's agreement" which ended all competition between them. Thus unified, the Big Four of meat, as distributors, faced the consumers with their compact organization and fixed price system. On the other hand, as refiners (or "processors") of raw material, they confronted the disorganized producers, that is, the farmers, with the same concealed unanimity. . . .

The power of the kings of animal food was supreme, grandiose and feudal; and sad to relate, like many earlier dynasts they abused it. There was none to say nay if they used diseased swine, goats, or cows in making their famous sausages or hams or tinned beef. For thirty years, although millions of persons patronized them, the four or five overlords in Chicago alone decided what sanitary measures of inspection or approval should be taken. They themselves did not eat this dressed food which they disseminated so widely to an invisible public, toward whom their moral attitude was strictly detached and impersonal. Overwhelmingly bent on pecuniary gains to be derived from the handling of the animal carcasses, and also prone to utilize with ingenious technology a steadily inferior product, they were universally believed guilty of many lapses which did small honor to the American table.

was $110 million, the profit was $45 million a year, and John D. Rockefeller's fortune was estimated at $200 million. Before long he would move into iron, copper, coal, shipping, and banking (Chase Manhattan Bank). Profits would be $81 million a year, and the Rockefeller fortune would total two billion dollars.

Andrew Carnegie was a telegraph clerk at seventeen, then secretary to the head of the Pennsylvania Railroad, then broker in Wall Street selling railroad bonds for huge commissions, and was soon a millionaire. He went to London in 1872, saw the new Bessemer method of producing steel, and returned to the United States to build a million-dollar steel plant. Foreign competition was kept out by a high tariff conveniently set by Congress, and by 1880 Carnegie was producing 10,000 tons of steel a month, making $1½ million a year in profit. By 1900 he was making $40 million a year, and that year, at a dinner party, he agreed to sell his steel company to J.P. Morgan. He scribbled the price on a note: $492,000,000.

Morgan then formed the U.S. Steel Corporation, combining Carnegie's corporation with others. He sold stocks and bonds for $1,300,000,000 (about 400 million more than the combined worth of the companies) and took a fee of 150 million for arranging the consolidation. How could dividends be paid to all those stockholders and bondholders? By making sure Congress passed tariffs keeping out foreign steel; by closing off competition and maintaining the price at $28 a ton; and by working 200,000 men twelve hours a day for wages that barely kept their families alive.

And so it went, in industry after industry—shrewd, efficient businessmen building empires, choking out competition, maintaining high prices, keeping wages low, using government subsidies. These industries were the first beneficiaries of the "welfare state." By the turn of the century, American Telephone and Telegraph had a monopoly of the nation's telephone system, International Harvester made 85 percent of all farm machinery, and in every other industry resources became concentrated, controlled. The banks had interests in so many of these monopolies as to create an interlocking network of powerful corporation directors, each of whom sat on the boards of many other corporations. According to a Senate report of the early twentieth century, Morgan at his peak sat on the board of forty-eight corporations; Rockefeller, thirty-seven corporations.

The U.S. Government

Meanwhile, the government of the United States was behaving almost exactly as Karl Marx described a capitalist state: pretending neutrality to maintain order, but serving the interests of the rich. Not that the rich agreed among themselves; they had disputes over policies. But the purpose of the state was to settle upper-class disputes peacefully, control lower-class rebellion, and adopt policies that would further the long-range stability of the system. The arrangement between Democrats and Republicans to elect Rutherford Hayes in 1877 set the tone. Whether Democrats or Republicans won, national policy would not change in any important way.

When Grover Cleveland, a Democrat, ran for President in 1884, the general impression in the country was that he opposed the power of monopolies and corporations, and that the Republican party, whose candidate was James Blaine, stood for the wealthy. But when Cleveland defeated Blaine, Jay Gould wired him: "I feel . . . that the vast business interests of the country will be entirely safe in your hands." And he was right.

One of Cleveland's chief advisers was William Whitney, a millionaire and corporation lawyer, who married into the Standard Oil fortune and was appointed Secretary of the Navy by Cleveland. He immediately set about to create a "steel navy," buying the steel at artificially high prices from Carnegie's plants. Cleveland himself assured industrialists that his election should not frighten them: "No harm shall come to any business interest as the result of administrative policy so long as I am President . . . a transfer of executive control from one party to another does not mean any serious disturbance of existing conditions."

The presidential election itself had avoided real issues; there was no clear understanding of which interests would gain and which would lose if certain policies were adopted. It took the usual form of election campaigns, concealing the basic similarity of the parties by dwelling on personalities, gossip, trivialities. Henry Adams, an astute literary commentator on that era, wrote to a friend about the election:

> We are here plunged in politics funnier than words can express. Very great issues are involved. . . . But the amusing thing is that no one talks about rail interests. By common consent they agree to let these alone. We are afraid to discuss them. Instead of this the press is engaged in a most amusing dispute whether Mr. Cleveland had an illegitimate child and did or did not live with more than one mistress.

In 1887, with a huge surplus in the treasury, Cleveland vetoed a bill appropriating $100,000 to give relief to Texas farmers to help them buy seed grain during a drought. He said: "Federal aid in such cases . . . encourages the expectation of paternal care on the part of the government and weakens the sturdiness of our national character." But that same year, Cleveland used his gold surplus to pay off wealthy bondholders at $28 above the $100 value of each bond—a gift of $45 million.

The chief reform of the Cleveland administration gives away the secret of reform legislation in America. The Interstate Commerce Act of 1887 was supposed to regulate the railroads on behalf of the consumers. But Richard Olney, a lawyer for the Boston & Maine and other railroads, and soon to be Cleveland's Attorney General, told railroad officials who complained about the Interstate Commerce Commission that it would not be wise to abolish the Commission "from a railroad point of view." He explained:

> The Commission . . . is or can be made, of great use to the railroads. It satisfies the popular clamor for a government supervision of railroads, at the same time that that supervision is almost entirely nominal. . . . The part of wisdom is not to destroy the Commission, but to utilize it.

Cleveland himself, in his 1887 State of the Union message, had made a similar point, adding a warning: "Opportunity for safe, careful, and deliberate reform is now offered; and none of us should be unmindful of a time when an abused and irritated people . . . may insist upon a radical and sweeping rectification of their wrongs."

Republican Benjamin Harrison, who succeeded Cleveland as President from 1889 to 1893, was described by Matthew Josephson, in his colorful study of the post–Civil War years, *The Politicos:* "Benjamin Harrison had the exclusive distinction of having served the railway corporations in the dual capacity of lawyer and soldier. He prosecuted the [railroad] strikers [of 1877] in the federal courts . . . and he also organized and commanded a company of soldiers during the strike. . . ."

Harrison's term also saw a gesture toward reform. The Sherman Anti-Trust Act, passed in 1890, called itself "An Act to protect trade and commerce against unlawful restraints" and made it illegal to form a "combination or conspiracy" to restrain trade in interstate or foreign commerce. Senator John Sherman, author of the Act, explained the need to conciliate the critics of monopoly: "They had monopolies . . . of old, but never before such giants as in our day. You must heed their appeal or be ready for the socialist, the communist, the nihilist. Society is now disturbed by forces never felt before. . . ."

When Cleveland was elected President again in 1892, Andrew Carnegie, in Europe, received a letter from the manager of his steel plants, Henry Clay Frick: "I am very sorry for President Harrison, but I cannot see that our interests are going to be affected one way or the other by the change in administration." Cleveland, facing the agitation in the country caused by the panic and depression of 1893, used troops to break up "Coxey's Army," a demonstration of unemployed men who had come to Washington, and again to break up the national strike on the railroads the following year.

The Supreme Court

Meanwhile, the Supreme Court, despite its look of somber, black-robed fairness, was doing its bit for the ruling elite. How could it be independent, with its members chosen by the President and ratified by the Senate? How could it be neutral between rich and poor when its members were often former wealthy lawyers, and almost always came from the upper class? Early in the nineteenth century the Court laid the legal basis for a nationally regulated economy by establishing federal control over interstate commerce, and the legal basis for corporate capitalism by making the contract sacred.

In 1895 the Court interpreted the Sherman Act so as to make it harmless. It said a monopoly of sugar refining was a monopoly in manufacturing, not commerce, and so could not be regulated by Congress through the Sherman Act (*U.S.* v. *E.C. Knight Co.*). The Court also said the Sherman Act could be used against interstate strikes (the railway strike of 1894) because they were in restraint of trade. It also declared unconstitutional a small attempt by Congress to tax high incomes at a higher rate (*Pollock* v. *Farmers' Loan & Trust Company*). In later years it would refuse to break up the Standard Oil and American Tobacco monopolies, saying the Sherman Act barred only "unreasonable" combinations in restraint of trade.

A New York banker toasted the Supreme Court in 1895: "I give you, gentlemen, the Supreme Court of the United States—guardian of the dollar, defender of private property, enemy of spoliation, sheet anchor of the Republic."

Very soon after the Fourteenth Amendment became law, the Supreme Court began to demolish it as a protection for blacks, and to develop it as a protection for corporations. However, in 1877, a Supreme Court decision (*Munn* v. *Illinois*) approved state laws regulating the prices charged to farmers for the use of grain elevators. The grain elevator company argued it was a person being deprived of property, thus violating the Fourteenth Amendment's declaration "nor shall any State deprive any person of life, liberty, or property without due process of law." The Supreme Court disagreed, saying that grain elevators were not simply private property but were invested with "a public interest" and so could be regulated.

One year after that decision, the American Bar Association, organized by lawyers accustomed to serving the wealthy, began a national campaign of education to reverse the Court decision. Its presidents said, at different times: "If trusts are a defensive weapon of property interests against the communistic trend, they are desirable." And: "Monopoly is often a necessity and an advantage."

By 1886, they succeeded. State legislatures, under the pressure of aroused farmers, had passed laws to regulate the rates charged farmers by the railroads. The Supreme Court that year (*Wabash* v. *Illinois*) said states could not do this, that this was an intrusion on federal power. That year alone, the Court did away with 230 state laws that had been passed to regulate corporations.

By this time the Supreme Court had accepted the argument that corporations were "persons" and their money was properly protected by the due process clause of the Fourteenth Amendment. Supposedly, the Amendment had been passed to protect Negro rights, but of the Fourteenth Amendment cases brought before the Supreme Court between 1890 and 1910, nineteen dealt with the Negro, 288 dealt with corporations.

The justices of the Supreme Court were not simply interpreters of the Constitution. They were men of certain backgrounds, of certain interests. One of them (Justice Samuel Miller) had said in 1875: "It is vain to contend with Judges who have been at the bar the advocates for forty years of railroad companies, and all forms of associated capital. . . ." In 1893, Supreme Court Justice David J. Brewer, addressing the New York State Bar Association, said:

> It is the unvarying law that the wealth of the community will be in the hands of the few. . . . The great majority of men are unwilling to endure that long self-denial and saving which makes accumulations possible . . . and hence it always has been, and until human nature is remodeled always will be true, that the wealth of a nation is in the hands of a few, while the many subsist upon the proceeds of their daily toil.

This was not just a whim of the 1880s and 1890s—it went back to the Founding Fathers, who had learned their law in the era of *Blackstone's Commentaries*, which said: "So great is the regard of the law for private property, that it will not authorize the least violation of it; no, not even for the common good of the whole community."

Controlling the People

Control in modern times requires more than force, more than law. It requires that a population dangerously concentrated in cities and factories, whose lives are filled with cause for rebellion, be taught that all is right as it is. And so, the schools, the churches, the popular literature taught that to be rich was a sign of superiority, to be poor a sign of personal failure, and that the only way upward for a poor person was to climb into the ranks of the rich by extraordinary effort and extraordinary luck.

In those years after the Civil War, a man named Russell Conwell, a graduate of Yale Law School, a minister, and author of best-selling books, gave the same lecture, "Acres of Diamonds," more than five thousand times to audiences across the country, reaching several million people in all. His message was that anyone could get rich if he tried hard enough, that everywhere, if people looked closely enough, were "acres of diamonds." A sampling:

> I say that you ought to get rich, and it is your duty to get rich.
> . . . The men who get rich may be the most honest men you find in the community. Let me say here clearly . . . ninety-eight out of one hundred of the rich men of America are honest. That is why they are rich. That is why they are trusted with money. That is why they carry on great enterprises and find plenty of people to work with them. It is because they are honest men. . . .
>
> . . . I sympathize with the poor, but the number of poor who are to be sympathized with is very small. To sympathize with a man whom God has punished for his sins . . . is to do wrong. . . . let us remember there is not a poor person in the United States who was not made poor by his own shortcomings. . . .

Conwell was a founder of Temple University. Rockefeller was a donor to colleges all over the country and helped found the University of Chicago. [Henry Edwards] Huntington, of the Central Pacific, gave money to two Negro colleges, Hampton Institute and Tuskegee Institute. Carnegie gave money to colleges and to libraries. Johns Hopkins was founded by a millionaire merchant, and millionaires Cornelius Vanderbilt, Ezra Cornell, James Duke, and Leland Stanford created universities in their own names.

The rich, giving part of their enormous earnings in this way, became known as philanthropists. These educational institutions did not encourage dissent; they trained the middlemen in the American system—the teachers, doctors, lawyers, administrators, engineers, technicians, politicians—those who would be paid to keep the system going, to be loyal buffers against trouble.

In the meantime, the spread of public school education enabled the learning of writing, reading, and arithmetic for a whole generation of workers, skilled and semiskilled, who would be the literate labor force of the new industrial age. It was important that these people learn obedience to authority. A journalist observer of the schools in the 1890s wrote: "The unkindly spirit of the teacher is strikingly apparent; the pupils, being completely subjugated to her will, are silent and motionless, the spiritual atmosphere of the classroom is damp and chilly."

Back in 1859, the desire of mill owners in the town of Lowell that their workers be educated was explained by the secretary of the Massachusetts Board of Education:

> The owners of factories are more concerned than other classes and interests in the intelligence of their laborers. When the latter are well-educated and the former are disposed to deal justly,

controversies and strikes can never occur, nor can the minds of the masses be prejudiced by demagogues and controlled by temporary and factious considerations.

Joel Spring, in his book *Education and the Rise of the Corporate State,* says: "The development of a factory-like system in the nineteenth-century schoolroom was not accidental." This continued into the twentieth century, when William Bagley's *Classroom Management* became a standard teacher training text, reprinted thirty times. Bagley said: "One who studies educational theory aright can see in the mechanical routine of the classroom the educative forces that are slowly transforming the child from a little savage into a creature of law and order, fit for the life of civilized society."

It was in the middle and late nineteenth century that high schools developed as aids to the industrial system, that history was widely required in the curriculum to foster patriotism. Loyalty oaths, teacher certification, and the requirement of citizenship were introduced to control both the educational and the political quality of teachers. Also, in the latter part of the century, school officials—not teachers—were given control over textbooks. Laws passed by the states barred certain kinds of textbooks. Idaho and Montana, for instance, forbade textbooks propagating "political" doctrines, and the Dakota territory ruled that school libraries could not have "partisan political pamphlets or books."

Against this gigantic organization of knowledge and education for orthodoxy and obedience, there arose a literature of dissent and protest, which had to make its way from reader to reader against great obstacles. Henry George, a self-educated working-man from a poor Philadelphia family, who became a newspaperman and an economist, wrote a book that was published in 1879 and sold millions of copies, not only in the United States, but all over the world. His book *Progress and Poverty* argued that the basis of wealth was land, that this was becoming monopolized, and that a single tax on land, abolishing all others, would bring enough revenue to solve the problem of poverty and equalize wealth in the nation. Readers may not have been persuaded of his solutions, but they could see in their own lives the accuracy of his observations:

> It is true that wealth has been greatly increased, and that the average of comfort, leisure and refinement has been raised; but these gains are not general. In them the lowest class do not share. . . . This association of poverty with progress is the great enigma of our times. . . . There is a vague but general feeling of disappointment; an increased bitterness among the working classes; a widespread feeling of unrest and brooding revolution. . . . The civilized world is trembling on the verge of a great

movement. Either it must be a leap upward, which will open the way to advances yet undreamed of, or it must be a plunge downward which will carry us back toward barbarism. . . .

A different kind of challenge to the economic and social system was given by Edward Bellamy, a lawyer and writer from western Massachusetts, who wrote, in simple, intriguing language, a novel called *Looking Backward*, in which the author falls asleep and wakes up in the year 2000, to find a socialistic society in which people work and live cooperatively. *Looking Backward*, which described socialism vividly, lovingly, sold a million copies in a few years, and over a hundred groups were organized around the country to try to make the dream come true.

It seemed that despite the strenuous efforts of government, business, the church, the schools, to control their thinking, millions of Americans were ready to consider harsh criticism of the existing system, to contemplate other possible ways of living. They were helped in this by the great movements of workers and farmers that swept the country in the 1880s and 1890s. These movements went beyond the scattered strikes and tenants' struggles of the period 1830–1877. They were nationwide movements, more threatening than before to the ruling elite, more dangerously suggestive. It was a time when revolutionary organizations existed in major American cities, and revolutionary talk was in the air.

"If we seriously study entrepreneurs, the state, and the rise of big business in the United States we will have to sacrifice the textbook morality play of 'greedy businessmen' fleecing the public."

Robber Barons Have Been Unfairly Denigrated

Burton W. Folsom Jr. (b. 1947)

The term "robber baron" has been used to describe, often in a pejorative sense, the individuals who built and led large business enterprises in the second half of the nineteenth century. In the following viewpoint, Burton W. Folsom Jr. argues that many criticisms of these individuals have been misguided and that many of the so-called robber barons made significant contributions to American society. Folsom is a senior fellow for economic education at the Mackinac Center for Public Policy in Midland, Michigan, and adjunct professor of history at Northwood University in Michigan. He has taught history at the University of Pittsburgh and Murray State University in Kentucky. His books include *Urban Capitalists* and *The Myth of the Robber Barons;* portions of the concluding chapter of the latter work are reprinted here.

In his book, Folsom examines several key figures in American economic development between 1840 and 1920, including John D. Rockefeller, Andrew Carnegie, and others. He maintains that historians and writers of American history textbooks have unfairly characterized the actions of these "robber barons" as being corrupt, unethical, and greedy, and thus creating the need for government control and regulation of industry. According to Folsom, however, key individuals such as Rockefeller and Carnegie, far from being unscrupulous opportunists, were innovative entrepreneurs who helped make the United States the world's leading industrial power. He contends that government intervention in the form of regulations, tariffs, and federal subsidies for railroads and other industries were the source of, rather than the solution to, many of the problems of the era. According to Folsom, political corruption, stock market speculation and fraud, government waste, and state-enforced monopolies all resulted from such government intrusions.

Folsom concludes that a key distinction must be made between two types of industrialists of the era. Political entrepreneurs, who sought to make money with the aid of government deals and subsidies, harmed the economy. Market entrepreneurs (such as Rockefeller and Carnegie), who attained their competitive preeminence in various industries through business acumen and technological mastery, were a beneficial influence. Folsom also defends such entrepreneurs on the grounds that they contributed significantly to American society through their charitable giving.

One reason for studying history is to learn from it. If we can discover what worked and what didn't work, we can use this knowledge to create a better future. Studying the rise of big business, for example, is important because it is the story of how the United States prospered and became a world power. During the years in which this took place, roughly from 1840 to 1920, we had a variety of entrepreneurs who took risks and built very successful industries. We also had a state that created a stable marketplace in which these entrepreneurs could operate. However, this same state occasionally dabbled in economic development through subsidies, tariffs, regulating trade, and even running a steel plant to make armor. When the state played this kind of role, it often failed. This is the sort of information that is useful to know when we think about planning for the future.

The problem is that many historians have been teaching the opposite lesson for years. They have been saying that entrepreneurs, not the state, created the problem. Entrepreneurs, according to these historians, were often "robber barons" who corrupted politics and made fortunes bilking the public. In this view, government intervention in the economy was needed to save the public from greedy businessmen. This view, with some modifications, still dominates in college textbooks in American history.

American history textbooks always have at least one chapter on the rise of big business. Most of these works, however, portray the growth of industry in America as a grim experience, an "ordeal" as one text [*The National Experience*] calls it. Much of this alleged grimness is charged to entrepreneurs.

Thomas Bailey, in *The American Pageant*, is typical when he says of [Cornelius] Vanderbilt: "Though ill-educated, ungrammatical, coarse, and ruthless, he was clear-visioned. Offering superior railway service at lower rates, he amassed a fortune of $100 million." If this second sentence is true, to whom was Vanderbilt "ruthless"? Not to consumers, who received "superior service at lower rates," but to his opponents, such as Edward Collins, who were using the state to extort subsidies and impose high rates on consumers. This distinction is vital and must be stressed if we are to sort out the impact of different types of entrepreneurs.

I have systematically studied three of the best-selling college textbooks in American history: *The American Pageant*, by Thomas Bailey and David Kennedy of Stanford University; *The American Nation*, by John Garraty of Columbia University; and *The National Experience*, by John Blum of Yale University, Edmund Morgan of Yale University, William S. McFeely of the University of Georgia, Arthur Schlesinger, Jr., of the City University of New York, Kenneth Stampp of the University of California at Berkeley, and C. Vann Woodward of Yale University. These works have been written by some of the most distinguished men in the historical profession; all three books have sold hundreds of thousands of copies. In all three, John D. Rockefeller receives more attention than any other entrepreneur. This is probably as it should be. His story is a crucial part of the rise of big business: he dominated his industry, he drastically cut prices, he never lobbied for a government subsidy or a tariff, and he ended up as America's first near-billionaire.

The three textbooks do credit Rockefeller with cutting costs and improving the efficiency of the oil industry, but they all see his success as fraudulent. In *The National Experience*, Woodward says that:

> Rockefeller hated free competition and believed that monopoly was the way of the future. His early method of dealing with competitors was to gain unfair advantage over them through special rates and rebates arranged with the railroads. With the aid of these advantages, Standard became the largest refiner of oil in the country. . . . In 1881 [Standard Oil] controlled nearly 90 percent of the country's oil refining capacity and could crush any remaining competitors at will.

In *The American Nation*, John Garraty commends Rockefeller for his skill but adopts roughly the same line of reasoning as does Woodward:

> Rockefeller exploited every possible technical advance and employed fair means and foul to persuade competitors either to sell out or to join forces. . . . Rockefeller competed ruthlessly not

> primarily to crush other refiners but to persuade them to join
> with him, to share the business peaceably and rationally so that
> all could profit. . . . Competition almost disappeared; prices
> steadied; profits skyrocketed. By 1892 John D. Rockefeller was
> worth over $800 million.

In these views the cause and effect are clear: the rebates and "unfair competition" were the main causes of Rockefeller's success; this success gave him an alleged monopoly; and the alleged monopoly created his fortune. Yet as we have seen, Rockefeller's astonishing efficiency was the main reason for his success. He didn't get the largest rebates until he had the largest business. Even then, the Vanderbilts offered the same rebates to anyone who shipped as much oil on the New York Central as Rockefeller did. In any case, the rebates went largely to cutting the price of oil for consumers, not to Rockefeller himself.

Perhaps even more misleading than the faulty stress on the rebates is the omitting of the most important feature of Rockefeller's career: his thirty-year struggle with Russia to capture the world's oil markets. Not one of the three texts even mentions this oil war with Russia.

Three facts show the importance of Rockefeller's battle with the Russians. First, about two-thirds of the oil refined in America in the late 1800s was exported. Second, Russia was closer than the U.S. to all European and Asian markets. Third, Russian oil was more centralized, more plentiful, and more viscous than American oil. If Rockefeller had not overcome Russia's natural advantages, no one else could have. America would have lost millions of dollars in exports and might have even had to import oil from Russia. The spoils of victory—jobs, technology, cheap kerosene, cheap by-products, and cheap gas to spur the auto industry—all of this might have been lost had it not been for Rockefeller's ability to sell oil profitably at six cents a gallon. The omitting of the Russo-American oil war was so striking that I checked every college American history text that I could find (twenty total) to see if this is typical. It is. Only one of the twenty textbooks even mentions the Russian oil competition.

Obviously textbooks can't include everything. Nor can their authors be expected to know everything. Textbook writers have a lot to cover and we can't expect them to have read much on Rockefeller. Unfortunately, they also don't seem to be very familiar with the books on Vanderbilt, [James J.] Hill, [Charles] Schwab and other entrepreneurs. . . .

Some of the textbook authors do talk about Hill and his accomplishments. In fact, large sections of Bailey's, Garraty's, and Woodward's books tell us about the transcontinental railroads. But the problem of the government subsidies is often not well-reasoned. Bailey, for example, admits that Hill was "probably the greatest railroad builder of them all." Bailey even displays a picture of all four transcontinentals and says that Hill's Great Northern was "the only one constructed without lavish federal subsidies." But from this, he does not consider the possibility that federal subsidies may not have been needed. Instead, he says, "Transcontinental railroad building was so costly and risky as to require government subsidies." . . . However, when the federal aid to railroads came, so did political entrepreneurship and corruption. Bailey describes some of this boondoggling and blames not the government, for making federal aid available, but the "grasping railroads" and "greedy corporations," for receiving it.

Bailey later applauds the passing of the Sherman Anti-trust Act and the creation of the Interstate Commerce Commission.

> Not until 1914 were the paper jaws of the Sherman Act fitted with reasonably sharp teeth. Until then, there was some question whether the government would control the trusts or the trusts the government. But the iron grip of monopolistic corporations was being threatened. A revolutionary new principle had been written into the law books by the Sherman Anti-Trust Act of 1890, as well as by the Interstate Commerce Act of 1887. Private greed must henceforth be subordinated to public need.

. . . [H]owever, the efficient Hill was the one who got hurt by these laws: The Hepburn Act, which strengthened the Interstate Commerce Commission, throttled his international railroad and shipping business; the Sherman Act was used to break up his Northern Securities Company.

Organizational History

Not all historians accept the modified robber-baron view dominant in the textbooks. Specialists in business history have been moving away from this view since the 1960s. Instead, many of them have adopted an interpretation called the "organizational view" of the rise of big business. Where the authors of these textbooks say that entrepreneurs cheated us, organizational historians say that entrepreneurs were not very significant. Business institutions, and their evolution, were more important than the men who ran them. To organizational historians, the rise of the corporation is the central event of the industrial revolution. The corporation—its layers of specialized bureaucracy, its centralization of power, and its thrust to control knowledge—evolved to meet the new challenges in marketing, producing, and distributing goods. In this view, of course, moral questions are not so relevant. The entrepreneur's strategy was almost predetermined by the structure of the industry and the peculiarities of vertical integration. The corporation was bigger than the entrepreneur.

The organizational historians have contributed much to the writing of business history. Their amoral emphasis on the corporation is a refreshing change from the Robber Baron model. Yet, this points up a problem as well. Amoral organizational history has a deterministic quality to it. The structure of the corporation shapes the strategy of the business. In this setting, there is little room for entrepreneurship. Whatever happened had to happen. And if any entrepreneur had not done what he did, another would have come along and done roughly the same thing.

This point of view is perhaps most boldly stated by Robert Thomas:

> Individual entrepreneurs, whether alone or as archetypes, *don't matter*! (Thomas's emphasis) And if indeed they do not matter, the reason, I suggest, is that the supply of entrepreneurs throughout American history, combined with institutions that permitted—indeed fostered—intense competition, was sufficiently elastic to reduce the importance of any particular individual. . . . This is not to argue that innovations don't matter, only that they do not come about as the product of individual genius but rather as the result of more general forces acting in the economy.

Thomas illustrates his view in the following way:

> Let us examine an analogy from track and field; a close race in the 100-yard dash has resulted in a winner in 9.6 seconds, second place goes to a man whose time is 9.7, and the remaining six runners are clustered below that time. Had the winner instead not been entered in the race and everyone merely moved up a place in the standings, I would argue that it would only make a marginal difference to the spectators. To be sure they would be poorer because they would have had to wait one-tenth of a second longer to determine the winner, but how significant a cost is that? That is precisely the entrepreneurial historian's task, to place the contributions of the entrepreneur within a marginal framework.

It is only when we extend Thomas' logic that we see its flaws. For, in fact, small margins are frequently the crucial difference between success and failure, between genius and mediocrity. To continue the sports analogies, the difference between hitting the ball 311 feet and 312 feet to left field in Yankee stadium is probably the difference between a long out and a home run. The difference between a quarterback throwing a pass forty yards or forty-one yards may be the difference between a touchdown and an incompleted pass. When facing a ten-foot putt, any duffer can hit the ball nine or eleven feet; it takes a pro to consistently sink it.

The Importance of Small Margins

In the same way small margins can reveal the differences between an entrepreneur, with his creative mind and innovative spirit, and a run-of-the-mill businessman. John D. Rockefeller dominated oil refining primarily by making a series of small cuts in cost. For example, he cut the drops of solder used to seal oil cans from forty to thirty-nine. This small reduction improved his competitive edge: he gained dominance over the whole industry because he was able to sell kerosene at less than eight cents a gallon.

A better illustration would be the small gradual cost-cutting

---

Industrial Innovators

Alfred D. Chandler Jr., in a 1959 article for Business History Review, *writes that the industrialists called robber barons by some were in fact important business innovators who played a key role in America's industrial transformation after the Civil War.*

Between the depression of the 1870's and the beginning of the twentieth century, American industry underwent a significant transformation. . . .

By the beginning of the twentieth century, many more companies were making producers' goods, to be used in industry rather than on the farm or by the ultimate consumer. Most of the major industries had become dominated by a few large enterprises. These great industrial corporations no longer purchased and sold through agents, but had their own nation-wide buying and marketing organizations. Many, primarily those in the extractive industries, had come to control their own raw materials. In other words, the business economy had become industrial. Major industries were dominated by a few firms that had become great, vertically integrated, centralized enterprises. . . .

Why did the vertically integrated corporation come when it did, and in the way it did? The creation by nearly all the large firms of nation-wide selling and distributing organizations indicates the importance of the national market. It was necessary that the market be an increasingly urban one. . . .

What about the entrepreneurial talent? Certainly the best-known entrepreneurs of this period were those who helped to create the large industrial corporation. If, as [economist] Joseph A. Schumpeter suggests, "The defining characteristic [of the entrepreneur and his function] is simply the doing of new things, and doing things that are already done, in a new way (innovation)," Rockefeller, Carnegie, Frick, Swift, Duke, McCormick, the DuPonts, the Guggenheims, Coffin of General Electric, Preston of United Fruit, and Clark of Singer Sewing Machine were all major innovators of their time. And their innovations were not in technology, but rather in organization and in marketing "Doing a new thing" is, to Schumpeter, a "creative response" to a new situation, and the situation to which these innovators responded appears to have been the rise of the national urban market.

that allowed America to capture foreign steel markets. When Andrew Carnegie entered steel production in 1872, England dominated world production and the price of steel was $56 per ton. By 1900, Carnegie Steel, headed by Charles Schwab, was manufacturing steel for $11.50 per ton—and outstripping the entire production of England. That allowed railroad entrepreneur James J. Hill to buy cheap American rails, ship them across the continent and over the ocean to Japan, and still outprice England. The point here is that America did not claim these markets by natural advantages: they had to be won in international competition by entrepreneurs with vision for an industry and ability to improve products bit by bit.

It would be silly for someone to say that if Carnegie had not come along, someone else would have emerged to singlehandedly outproduce the country that had led the world in steel. Yet some organizational historians say exactly this. They are right in claiming that the rise of the corporation made some of Carnegie's success possible. But Carnegie was the only steel operator before Schwab to take full advantage of this rise. They are also right in saying that the environment (*e.g.* location and resources) plays some role in success. But Carnegie rose to the top *before* the opening of America's Mesabi iron range. American steel companies began outdistancing the British even when the Americans had to import some of their raw material from Cuba and Chile, manufacture it in Pennsylvania, and ship it across the country and over oceans to foreign markets.

This is not to denigrate the organizational view, but only to recognize its limitations. By focusing on the rise of the corporation, organizational historians have shown how corporate structure pervaded and helped to shape American economic and social life. However, the organizational view, like all other interpretations, can't explain everything. Specifically, it tends to ignore or downgrade the significant and unique contributions that entrepreneurs made to American economic development.

The "organizational" and "robber baron" views both have some merit. The rise of the corporation did shape economic development in important ways. Also, we did have industrialists, such as Jay Gould and Henry Villard, who mulcted government money, erected shoddy enterprises, and ran them into the ground. What is missing are the builders who took the risks, overcame strong foreign competition, and pushed American industries to places of world leadership. These entrepreneurs are a major part of the story of American business.

Many historians know this and teach it, but the issue is often muddled because textbooks tend to lump the predators and political adventurers with the creators and builders. Therefore, the teaching ends up like this: "Entrepreneurs cut costs and made many contributions to American economic growth, but they also marred political life by bribing politicians, forming pools, and misusing government funds. Therefore, we needed the federal government to come in and regulate business."

Social Mobility

Historians' misconceptions about entrepreneurs have led to problems in related areas as well. This is nowhere more apparent than in the studies of social mobility, which have become very popular among historians ever since the 1960s. Naturally, historians of social mobility have not operated in a vacuum. They have often been influenced by the prevailing historical theories denigrating the role of entrepreneurs and championing the role of government regulation. Put another way, if America's industrial entrepreneurs were a sordid group of replaceable people, then they could not have helped, and may have hindered, upward social mobility in cities throughout America. This is the implicit assumption in many social mobility studies conducted in the last generation.

Influenced by these prevailing views, many historians have argued two basic ideas about social mobility under American capitalism. First is the notion of low social mobility for manual laborers. In *Poverty and Progress: Social Mobility in a Nineteenth Century City*, Stephan Thernstrom finds that "the common workman who remained in Newburyport, [Massachusetts, from] 1850 to 1880 had only a slight chance of rising into a middle class occupation." As for the captains of industry at the opposite end of the spectrum, the second idea is that they usually got rich because they were born rich. This again suggests little mobility. For example, William Miller [in the *Journal of American Economic History*, November 1949] recorded the social origins of 190 corporation presidents between 1900–1910. He found that almost 80 percent of them had business or white collar professionals as fathers. More recently, Edward Pessen [in *American Historical Review*, October 1971] has argued that 90 percent of the antebellum elite in New York, Philadelphia, and Boston was silk-stocking in origin.

Fortunately, more careful research has discredited this negative view of social mobility. Newburyport, for example, was a stagnant town during the thirty years covered by Thernstrom's research. If new industries were rare and if opportunities were few, then, of course, we would expect social mobility to be low. Michael Weber sensed this and did a study of social mobility in Warren, Pennsylvania, an oil-producing boom town from 1880 to 1910 [*Social Change in an Industrial Town*]. In Warren, population multiplied every decade as market entrepreneurs created a climate for opportunity and growth. Growth and opportunity seem to have gone together: Warren residents were much more upwardly mobile than those living in Thernstrom's Newburyport.

Flaws are also apparent in William Miller's analysis of the social origins of America's corporate elite in 1910. Miller traced the background of 190 corporate presidents and board chairmen. But as diligent as his research was, he could not discover the social origins of 23 (12 percent) of these men. Miller draws no inference from this lack of evidence. If they left no record, however, the fathers were probably artisans at best, crooks at worst. Furthermore, 60 percent of Miller's industrialists came from farms or small towns (under 8,000 population). This almost certainly makes their fathers country merchants rather than urban capitalists. And the ascent from son of a country merchant to corporate president is indeed sensational. Miller's statistics do not "speak for themselves": they need careful thought and imaginative interpretation. . . .

The work of Edward Pessen has supported the idea that it was easy for rich men and their children to keep their wealth and influence over time. After studying New York City, Philadelphia, Brooklyn, and Boston, Pessen concluded [in *Riches, Class, and Power Before the Civil War*]:

> The rich with few exceptions had been born to wealth and comfort, owing their worldly success mostly to inheritance and family support. Instead of rising and falling at a mercurial rate, fortunes usually remained in the hands of their accumulators, whether in the long or the short. . . . Antebellum urban society [and, by implication, postbellum urban society] was very much a class society.

The Successful Are the Exception

In studying the continuity of wealth and talent in families over time, Pessen and others rarely look at all family members, only those who were successful. In fact, . . . the successful seem to be the exception, not the rule.

First glances can be deceptive. In Scranton [an industrial town in Pennsylvania], for example, James Blair and brothers Thomas and George Dickson held three of the five directorships of the First National Bank in 1880. In 1869, James Linen, a nephew of Thomas and George Dickson, married Blair's daughter, Anna; in 1891, Linen became president of the bank for a twenty-two-year stretch. To the casual observer, such an occurrence illustrates overpowering continuity of leadership. However, if one looks at all eight sons of Blair and the two Dicksons, a sharply etched picture of failure clearly emerges. Seven of their eight sons never darkened the door of a corporate boardroom; under the eighth, the Dickson Manufacturing Company disintegrated. Continuity from father to son may actually have been the undoing of the business. Furthermore, H. A. Coursen, like bank president James Linen, married a daughter of James Blair; yet Coursen remained a small retailer with no apparent economic influence. In the city of Scranton, at least, the scions of power were not the men their fathers were. Before historians can assert the continuity of economic leadership or family wealth, they must study all the children of the rich, not just the rare conspicuous successes. . . .

Naturally those born into wealth are, on the whole, more successful than those born into poverty. But to say this is merely to confirm what applies to all societies at all times. Yes, wealth counts; but so do talent, vision, initiative, and luck.

Errors and Misunderstandings

The classic question asked by those historians who study social stratification is this: "Who gets what and why?" We can see how many historians err when they assume that the rich got rich by being robber barons and stayed rich by keeping the corporation in the family and keeping newcomers out of their group as much as possible.

There is another realm of misunderstanding, too: some historians have implied that the economic pie was fixed. This is a weakness in many historical studies of social stratification. Edward Pessen, for example, tells how only one percent of the population held about forty percent of the wealth in many industrial cities in the 1840s. His research is careful, and he insists this share increased over time. Along similar lines, Gabriel Kolko [in *Wealth and Power in America*] has recorded the distribution of income from 1910 to 1959. He points out that the top one-tenth of Americans usually earned about thirty percent of the national income and that the lowest one-tenth consistently earned only about one percent. This may be true, but Pessen and Kolko also need to emphasize that the total amount of wealth in American society increased geometrically after 1820. This means that American workers improved their standard of living over time even though their percentage of the national income may not have increased. We must also remember that there was constant individual movement up and down the economic ladder. Therefore, the pattern of inequality may have persisted, but the categories of wealth-holding were still fluid in our open society. Finally, it needs to be stressed that one percent of the population often *created* not only their own wealth, but many of the opportunities that enabled others to acquire wealth.

To sum up, then, we need to divide industrialists into two groups. First were market entrepreneurs, such as Vanderbilt, Hill, the Scrantons, Schwab, Rockefeller, and Mellon, who usually innovated, cut costs, and competed effectively in an open economy. Second were political entrepreneurs, such as Edward Collins, Henry Villard Elbert Gary, and Union Pacific builders, all of whom tried to succeed primarily through federal aid, pools, vote-buying, or stock speculation. Market entrepreneurs made decisive and unique contributions to American economic development. The political entrepreneurs stifled productivity (through monopolies and pools), corrupted business and politics, and dulled America's competitive edge.

The second point is that, in the key industries we have studied, the state failed as an economic developer. It failed first as a subsidizer of industrial growth. Vanderbilt showed this in his triumph over the Edward Collins' fleet and the Pacific Mail Steamship Company in the 1850s. James J. Hill showed this forty years later when his privately built Great Northern outdistanced the subsidized Northern Pacific and Union Pacific. The state next failed in the role of an entrepreneur when it tried to build and operate an armor plant in competition with Charles Schwab and Bethlehem Steel. The state also seems to have failed as an active regulator of trade. The evidence . . . is far from conclusive; but we can see problems with the Interstate Commerce Commission and the Sherman Anti-trust Act, both of which were used against the efficient Hill and Rockefeller.

A third point is that the relative absence of state involvement—either through subsidies, tariffs, or income taxes—may have spurred entrepreneurship in the 1840–1920 period. One of the traditional arguments cited by some businessmen, especially the political entrepreneurs, is that a tariff or a subsidy given to a new industry will help that industry survive and eventually flourish against foreign competition. What really happened, though, is that, when Collins and [Samuel] Cunard got subsidies from their governments, they did not become efficient steamship operators; instead, they became lavish wastrels and soon came back asking for larger subsidies, which they then used to compete against more efficient rivals.

In the case of protective tariffs, neither George Scranton or John D. Rockefeller needed them in establishing their steel and oil companies. The Scranton group very profitably built America's first large quantity of rails in a time of a low tariff on British iron imports. Also Rockefeller never needed a tariff (though a small one did exist) on his way to becoming the largest oil producer in the world.

Taxes and Philanthropy

The American government also resisted the temptation to tax large incomes for most of the 1840–1920 period. Low taxes often spur entrepreneurs to invest and take risks. If the builders can keep most of what they build, they will have an incentive to build more. It is true that the state lost the revenue it could have raised if it had taxed large incomes. This was largely offset, however, by the philanthropy of the entrepreneurs. When the income tax became law in 1913, the most anyone had to pay was seven percent of that year's income. Most people paid no tax or only one percent of their earnings. In the years before and after 1913, however, John D. Rockefeller sometimes gave over 50 percent of his annual income to charitable causes. He almost always gave more than ten percent. Hill, Vanderbilt, the Scranton group, and Schwab were also active givers. Sometimes they gave direct gifts to specific people. Usually, though, they used their money to create opportunities that many could exploit. In academic jargon, they tried to improve the infrastructure of the nation by investing in human capital. A case in point consisted of the many gifts to high schools and universities, north and south, black and white, urban and rural. Cheap high-quality education meant opportunities for upwardly mobile Americans, and was also a guarantee that the United States would have quality leadership in its next generation. Vanderbilt University, the University of Chicago, Tuskegee Institute, and Lehigh University were just some of the dozens of schools that were supported by these five entrepreneurs.

Libraries were also sources of support. Not just Andrew Carnegie, but also Hill and Rockefeller were builders and suppliers of libraries. The free public library, which became an American institution in the 1800s, gave opportunities to rich and poor alike to improve their minds and their careers.

Finally, America has always been a farming nation: Rockefeller attacked and helped conquer the boll weevil in the South; Hill helped create dry farming and mixed agriculture in the North. America's cotton and wheat farmers took great advantage of these changes to lead the world in the producing of these two crops.

All of these men (except for Schwab) tried to promote self-help with their giving. They gave to those people or institutions who showed a desire to succeed and a willingness to work. Rockefeller and Hill both paid consultants to sort out the deadbeats and the gold diggers. They sympathized with the needy, but supported only those needy imbued with the work ethic.

Each entrepreneur, of course, had his own variations on the giving theme. Vanderbilt, for example, plowed a series of large gifts into Vanderbilt University and helped make it one of the finest schools in the nation. He almost never gave to individuals, though, and said if he ever did he would have people lined up for blocks to pick his pockets. Schwab, by contrast, was a frivolous giver and had dozens of friends and hangers-on who tapped him regularly for handouts. Rockefeller concentrated his giving in the South and the Midwest; the Scranton group and Schwab focused on the East; Hill gave mainly in the Northwest.

Even without an income or an inheritance tax, these entrepreneurs, and others, had trouble handing down their wealth to the next generation. This was true in part, of course, because they gave so much of it away. As we have seen with the Scranton group, though, most entrepreneurs did not have sons with the same talents the fathers had. Vanderbilt's son William was a worthy successor, but the rest of his children showed little aptitude for business. Hill's three sons did not come close to matching their father's accomplishments; one son, Louis, followed his father as president of the Great Northern, but Louis' career was lackluster. The *Oregonian* of Portland called him "impulsive"; not so much a railroad man, but "a painter of some ability." Charles Schwab and his wife were childless, which was probably fortunate because he squandered over $30 million and died a debtor. Rockefeller's only son, John D. Jr., became a full-time philanthropist. Granted, the senior Rockefeller's five grandsons were all multimillionaires, but their economic influence was much less than that of their grandfather. Sometimes the descendants of these original entrepreneurs parlayed their family names and what was left of their fortunes into political careers. During the 1960s, two of the grandchildren of John D. Rockefeller and one of the great-grandchildren of Joseph Scranton were governors of New York, Arkansas and Pennsylvania.

If we seriously study entrepreneurs, the state, and the rise of big business in the United States we will have to sacrifice the textbook morality play of "greedy businessmen" fleecing the public until at last they are stopped by the actions of the state. But, in return, we will have a better understanding of the past and a sounder basis for building our future.

For Discussion

Chapter One

1. Do both Thomas Jefferson and Alexander Hamilton make statements or contentions that are simply asserted as true rather than proved or reasoned out? If so, do such contentions strengthen or weaken their overall arguments? Explain.

2. At the time Alexander Hamilton's and Thomas Jefferson's viewpoints were written, the word "manufacturing" still retained most of its original meaning of "making by hand." One of the changes the industrial revolution brought was to transform the meaning of "manufacturing" to signify "making by machine." Does your understanding of Jefferson's and Hamilton's arguments regarding "manufactures" differ depending on which definition of the term you use? Are the authors' points strengthened or weakened depending on which definition is employed? Explain your answer.

Chapter Two

1. What similarities exist between working as a factory wage-worker and working as a slave, according to Orestes A. Brownson? What differences exist, according to Clementine Averill? On what basic points do the authors disagree? Which author makes a more convincing case? Explain.

2. Both Brownson and Charles Dickens write about factory workers from the perspective of outside observers, while Averill and "Amelia" write as workers themselves. Judging from the viewpoints, what are the advantages and disadvantages of each perspective in analyzing the conditions at factories? Defend your answer.

Chapter Three

1. What differences of opinion do Andrew Carnegie and Henry George express regarding the means by which great fortunes are made? What connection do both writers make between the means by which money is made and the legitimacy and social

utility of concentrations of wealth? What evidence or social theory does each introduce to support his argument? Which viewpoint do you find more convincing? Why?

2. What connection does Eugene V. Debs make between the invention of machinery and the development of capitalism? Does William Graham Sumner make a similar connection in his equation of the "capitalistic" and "industrial order of things"? Are these authors' disagreements a product of differing views of what society *is,* or of what it *should be?* Explain.

3. What two principles of democracy does William Graham Sumner define? Which one does he find objectionable? Does he present a convincing rebuttal to Eugene V. Debs's argument that America should create a new social order in which industrial resources would be shared equally? Why or why not?

4. Woodrow Wilson argues that "trusts" are harmful, but that he has nothing against "big business." Based on his and Walter Lippmann's arguments, do you think such a distinction is tenable? Explain why or why not.

Chapter Four

1. What does Henry Clews assert to be the fundamental goals of the labor movement? Does he agree with Samuel Gompers as to what the goals are, or do Clews and Gompers express different ideals? Explain.

2. Do George Ticknor Curtis and Terence V. Powderly dispute the facts of the Homestead strike of 1892, or merely what the facts mean. Explain your answer. Is there evidence in their viewpoints of preexisting opinion on the rights of labor that color their description of the events at Homestead? Defend your answer.

3. What analogy does Terence V. Powderly make between labor unions and corporations? In your opinion, does this argument constitute a convincing response to George Ticknor Curtis's arguments about the individual rights of workers? Why or why not?

Chapter Five

1. David Wells acknowledges that industrialization has caused disruptions in the lives of some, even as he argues that it is generally beneficial. Do his concessions strengthen or weaken his arguments? Explain.

2. Of the problems of industrialism described by Wells and W.D. Dabney, which, if any, do they believe are amenable to political reforms? Which are not? Explain.

3. What fundamental assumptions does Washington Gladden make about the "natural order" as it pertains to women, men, and labor. Are such assumptions necessary in order to accept the argument that industrialization harms women? Why or why not?

4. At the time, were the arguments of Ida Husted Harper relevant for all working women, including the class of women who worked in sweatshops and factories? Explain your answer.

5. What parts of Edwin Markham's arguments on child labor are appeals to his audience's emotions? What parts are appeals to reason? Which sort of argument predominates? Which do you find most effective? Explain.

6. If child labor had been prohibited by law, would it have made economic sense for the South Carolina farmer to give up his farm and go to work in the cotton mill by himself without his children? Would such laws, in your opinion, unfairly penalize families such as this one? Why or why not?

Chapter Six

1. What same individuals are described in the viewpoints by both Howard Zinn and Burton W. Folsom Jr.? How does each writer use expressive words, phrases, and ideas to describe these people and their activities in positive or negative ways? Explain.

2. Compare the viewpoints of Zinn and Folsom with those of Andrew Carnegie, Henry George, Eugene V. Debs, and William Graham Sumner. Are the two historians' viewpoints essentially restatements of these earlier arguments on wealthy industrialists, or do they add much in the way of historical perspective? Defend your answer.

General

1. Based on the materials presented in this book, how would you rate the predictions of Alexander Hamilton and Thomas Jefferson concerning the impact of industry on American life? Which viewpoints would tend to support Hamilton's views on

the positive impact of industry? Which lend support to Jefferson's fears of industrialization?

2. Judging from the viewpoints presented in this volume, how did the industrial revolution affect the lives of Americans? Can the industrial revolution be judged on what it did for American society as a whole, or did it have qualitatively different effects on America's upper and lower economic classes? Explain.

Chronology

1750–1850	The world's first industrial revolution takes place in Great Britain. Key inventions and developments include the invention of the modern steam engine by James Watt in 1769, the invention of the spinning jenny by James Hargreaves in 1764 and other new devices that mechanize the making of cloth, and the development and improvement of coal-powered blast furnaces to make iron out of iron ore.
1790	America's first national census reveals that only 3 percent of its population of 4 million live in cities of more than eight thousand people. The United States is primarily an agrarian nation that imports most of its manufactured goods.
	Samuel Slater, a British immigrant mechanic, designs and constructs a water-powered cotton mill in Rhode Island.
1791	Treasury Secretary Alexander Hamilton issues his Report on Manufactures, urging Congress to support the development of American "infant industries" through subsidies, protective tariffs, and the building of roads and canals.
	Congress charters the Bank of the United States.
1793	Eli Whitney invents the cotton gin.
1794	The first major "turnpike" or toll road in America, from Philadelphia to Lancaster, Pennsylvania, begins operation.
1798	Eli Whitney wins a government contract for manufacturing guns and begins development of manufacture with interchangeable parts.
1807	Robert Fulton's steamboat, the *Clermont*, travels up the Hudson River from New York City to Albany, inaugurating the era of commercial steamboat navigation.
1807–1815	American manufacturing flourishes as British imports are cut off by worsening U.S.-British relations, the 1807 Embargo Act, and the War of 1812. When relations improve in 1815, a flood of

goods from Great Britain causes many American enterprises to close.

1813	The Boston Manufacturing Company is incorporated; the next year it builds America's first fully mechanized textile mill, complete with power loom, in Waltham, Massachusetts.
1815	Construction begins on the National Road, a government-funded road that will eventually run from Baltimore, Maryland, to Ohio and Illinois.
1816	Congress moves to protect American industries by raising tariffs on imports, signaling a shift in federal policy towards protectionism that will endure for three decades. Congress establishes the Second Bank of the United States, five years after the charter of the first national bank was allowed to expire.
1820	Urban residents make up 7 percent of the total U.S. population.
1824	In *Gibbons v. Ogden*, the Supreme Court strengthens the power of Congress to regulate interstate commerce.
1825	The Erie Canal is officially opened, providing a water route between the Atlantic Ocean and the Great Lakes. Its success prompts a boom in canal construction that peaks in 1828.
1826	The town of Lowell, Massachusetts, is founded; six textile firms are established there.
1827	The Baltimore and Ohio Railroad is chartered by the state of Maryland. Within a few years it begins to replace horses with steam locomotives.
	Child mill workers in Paterson, New Jersey, go on the first recorded strike of factory workers in American history.
1830	The Tom Thumb, the first locomotive built in America, begins service out of Baltimore, Maryland.
1832	President Andrew Jackson vetoes rechartering the Second Bank of the United States.
1833–1837	More than 170 strikes are called as many workers, including seamstresses, bookbinders, and shoemakers form unions. Membership in labor organizations grows from 26,000 to 400,000.
1834	Cyrus McCormick patents his mechanical reaper.

1837	Economic collapse throws many laborers out of work and sets back the burgeoning labor movement.
	Connecticut passes the country's first general incorporation law.
	In *Charles River Bridge v. Warren Bridge*, the Supreme Court expands commerce and industry by striking down a state-granted monopoly.
1839	Charles Goodyear pioneers the vulcanization of rubber.
1840	Total railroad mileage in the country reaches that of total canal mileage.
1842	The Massachusetts Supreme Court rules in *Commonwealth v. Hunt* that trade unions are lawful organizations rather than illegal conspiracies.
1844	Samuel F.B. Morse demonstrates the telegraph; within ten years, the United States is linked by twenty-three thousand miles of telegraph cable.
1848	Cyrus McCormick moves his mechanical harvester plant to Chicago, signaling the rising industrial importance of this midwestern city.
1850	The proportion of Americans working on farms has fallen from more than three-quarters to little more than half.
1850–1860	American production of iron products and machinery doubles, while numerous new railroad lines link the eastern seaboard with midwestern cities including Chicago and St. Louis.
1859	The first oil well is drilled by Edwin L. Drake near Titusville, Pennsylvania. Within four years three hundred firms are competing to drill, refine, and sell petroleum.
1860	Total railroad trackage in the country reaches thirty thousand miles.
	The U.S. census reports that nearly twenty thousand sawmills and fourteen thousand flour mills are in operation in the United States.
1861	The telegraph spans the country.
1861–1865	In the Civil War, the industrializing North defeats the agrarian South.
1862	Congress authorizes the Central Pacific and the Union Pacific to build the nation's first transcontinental railroad.

1865	The first steel rails are manufactured in Chicago.
1866	The National Labor Union, the country's first such national organization, is established. It falls apart in 1872, three years after the death of its founder, William H. Sylvis.
1868	George Westinghouse patents the railroad air brake.
	Abram Hewitt introduces the main features of the open-hearth steelmaking process to the United States.
	Congress mandates the eight-hour day for public works projects.
1869	The nation's first transcontinental railroad is completed.
	The Knights of Labor, a labor organization, is founded.
	Urban residents make up 15 percent of the total U.S. population.
1870	John D. Rockefeller organizes the Standard Oil Company; by 1879 the corporation owns or controls over 90 percent of the nation's oil-refining capacity.
1871–1874	Several midwestern states pass legislation regulating railroads.
1873	The Panic of 1873 triggers a four-year economic downturn.
	Andrew Carnegie opens his steelworks in Pittsburgh.
1876	Alexander Graham Bell invents the telephone.
1877	Strikes spread throughout the nation's railways as workers protest wage reductions; two-thirds of the nation's railroads are paralyzed. The strike is broken by federal troops at a cost of one hundred lives.
	Thomas Edison invents the phonograph.
	In *Munn v. Illinois*, the Supreme Court upholds state regulation of railroads.
1879	Edison perfects the electric light.
	Henry George publishes *Progress and Poverty*.
1880–1900	Textile mills and other factories are built in the South, including 120 in North Carolina alone.
1880–1914	A wave of immigration brings more than 20 mil-

lion immigrants to the United States, mostly from southern and eastern Europe. Many settle in cities and provide the labor force for America's industries.

1882   Thomas Edison's central electrical power plant is in operation in New York City.

John D. Rockefeller reorganizes Standard Oil into the first industrial "trust."

1883   At the urging of the railroad industry the country is divided into four time zones.

1884   The construction of the world's first skyscraper begins in Chicago.

1886   In *Wabash, St. Louis and Pacific Railway Company v. Illinois*, the Supreme Court strikes down a state law regulating a railroad or other business involved in interstate commerce.

Between forty and sixty thousand workers participate in nationwide strikes and demonstrations on May 1.

On May 4, seven police officers are killed when a bomb explodes at a political gathering in Chicago's Haymarket Square. Eight anarchists are later arrested, tried, and convicted.

The American Federation of Labor is founded.

1887   Congress passes the Interstate Commerce Act establishing the nation's first independent government regulatory body, which is empowered to regulate railroad rates.

1888   Edward Bellamy publishes his critique of the modern industrial world, *Looking Backward*.

1889   New Jersey changes its laws of incorporation to permit companies to buy up other companies; its effect is to blunt efforts by states to regulate or abolish trusts.

1890   The U.S. census reports that for the first time in American history manufacturing output is greater in dollar value than agricultural production.

Responding to growing public outcry against trusts, Congress passes the Sherman Antitrust Act, making arrangements "in restraint of trade" illegal.

1892   The Homestead strike hits the Carnegie Steel Company.

	The Supreme Court orders the dissolution of the Standard Oil trust; the corporation is reorganized in New Jersey as a holding company.
1893	An economic collapse sets in motion four years of hard times across the country.
	James J. Hill's Great Northern is the fourth transcontinental railroad to be completed, the first without benefit of government subsidies.
	Charles E. and J. Frank Duryea build America's first gasoline-powered automobile.
1894	President Grover Cleveland calls out federal troops to put down a strike against the Pullman Palace Car Company.
	Henry Demarest Lloyd publishes *Wealth Against Commonwealth*, an attack on the Standard Oil trust.
1895	In *U.S. v. E.C. Knight*, the Supreme Court rules that the Sherman Antitrust Act does not apply to manufacturing.
1897	The Dingley Tariff Act sets the highest protective tariff rates in U.S. history, averaging 57 percent of the value of imported goods.
1898–1905	More than three thousand significant corporate mergers take place, leaving 40 percent of American industry in the hands of three hundred industrial combinations. The largest is United States Steel; created by financier J.P. Morgan in 1901 to buy out Andrew Carnegie's company, it becomes the first billion-dollar corporation.
1900	According to the U.S. census, the value of manufacturing output is double that of agriculture.
	The International Ladies Garment Workers Union is founded.
	America's railroad network of 200,000 miles of track is virtually completed at a total cost of approximately $11 billion; six railroad groups control all but 38,000 miles.
1902	President Theodore Roosevelt directs his attorney general to file suit against the Northern Securities Company, a railroad trust. The Supreme Court's 1904 decision to dissolve the company solidifies Roosevelt's reputation as a "trust-buster."
1903	Wilbur and Orville Wright make the first successful manned aircraft flight.

1903–1910	The journalism of "muckrakers" who expose and document abuses of industries and other social problems peaks in popularity.
1904	In *Lochner v. New York*, the Supreme Court finds unconstitutional a state law regulating working hours.
	A strike involving twenty-five thousand workers brings to national attention conditions in Massachusetts textile mills.
	The National Child Labor Committee is formed to promote child labor restrictions and reforms.
1905	The Industrial Workers of the World (IWW), a radical labor organization, is founded.
1907	In *Muller v. Oregon*, the Supreme Court rules that the state may regulate hours and working conditions for women.
1907–1908	An economic downturn leads to severe declines in industrial production.
1908	The Ford Motor Company introduces the Model T, an inexpensive, mass-produced automobile.
1910	American factory output is double that of Germany, its nearest rival.
1911	The Supreme Court orders the dissolution of the American Tobacco Company and of Standard Oil.
	Frederick Taylor publishes *The Principles of Scientific Management*, an influential work detailing his theories about managing industrial workers and increasing output.
	The Triangle Shirtwaist fire kills 146 workers trapped in a New York City sweatshop; the tragedy leads to a public investigation of factory conditions.
1913	The Ford Motor Company fully incorporates the moving assembly line in its manufacture of cars.
1914	Congress passes the Clayton Antitrust Act exempting labor unions from prosecution as illegal "combinations" in restraint of trade.
	The Federal Trade Commission is established to ensure free competition among America's industries.
1915	The first transcontinental telephone line opens.
1917	The nation's railroad system is nationalized for the war effort.

1919	A series of postwar strikes cripple a number of American industries.
1920	The Transportation Act returns the railroads to private control.
	The 1920 U.S. census reveals for the first time that more Americans live in urban areas than in rural areas.

Annotated Bibliography

Richard M. Abrams, ed. *The Issues of the Populist and Progressive Eras, 1892–1912*. Columbia: University of South Carolina Press, 1969. A document collection that includes articles about labor, urbanization, and other issues related to America's industrial revolution.

Graham Adams Jr. *Age of Industrial Violence, 1910–1915*. New York: Columbia University Press, 1966. A history of labor-management strife in the early twentieth century.

Walter Adams, ed. *The Structure of American Industry: Some Case Studies*. 3rd ed. New York: Macmillan, 1961. A series of essays on the development of key American industries, including the petroleum, steel, chemical, coal, and automobile industries.

Joyce Appleby. *Capitalism and a New Social Order: The Republican Vision of the 1790s*. New York: New York University Press, 1984. A series of essays on the impact of capitalism and the market on American politics at the onset of the industrial revolution.

Paul Avrich. *The Haymarket Tragedy*. Princeton, NJ: Princeton University Press, 1984. The most recent and most compelling account of the background to the riot, the riot itself, and the trials and executions of the major participants.

Lance Banning. *The Jeffersonian Persuasion: Evolution of a Party Ideology*. Ithaca, NY: Cornell University Press, 1978. A study of the thought of Thomas Jefferson and the reasons for his opposition to provide federal aid to American industry.

Rosalyn Baxandall, Linda Gordon, and Susan Reverby, eds. *America's Working Women*. New York: Vintage Books, 1976. An extensive source collection that includes many documents pertaining to women workers in American industries.

Mary H. Blewett. *Men, Women, and Work: Class, Gender, and Protest in the New England Shoe Industry, 1780–1910*. Urbana: University of Illinois Press, 1988. An examination of the sexual division of labor in an important regional industry that also examines the "distinctly female pattern of protest" that developed among its workers.

David Brody. *In Labor's Cause: Main Themes on the History of the American Worker.* New York: Oxford University Press, 1993. A series of essays on American labor, including labor politics, the marketing of unions in the coal industry, and the impact of the New Deal on the labor movement.

Stuart Weems Bruchey. *The Roots of American Economic Growth, 1607–1861: An Essay in Social Causation.* New York: Harper & Row, 1965. A general history of American economic development from the colonial period to the Civil War that stresses the impact of national values and technology on economic growth.

Monte A. Calvert. *The Mechanical Engineer in America, 1830–1910: Professional Cultures in Conflict.* Baltimore: Johns Hopkins University Press, 1967. A study of the conflict between an older "shop culture" and a newer "school culture" in early American factories.

Alfred D. Chandler Jr. *The Visible Hand: The Managerial Revolution in American Business.* Cambridge, MA: Belknap Press, 1977. An impressive work of historical synthesis that stresses the increasing power of the "visible hand" of management, as opposed to the "invisible hand" of the market in governing American economic life.

Alfred D. Chandler Jr., ed. *The Railroads, the Nation's First Big Business, Sources and Readings.* New York: Harcourt, Brace & World, 1965. A useful collection of primary sources concerning the railroad industry, including such topics as the financing of the railroads, corporate management, labor relations, government regulation, and competition within the industry.

Dan Clawson. *Bureaucracy and the Labor Process: The Transformation of U.S. Industry, 1860–1920.* New York: Monthly Review Press, 1980. A highly critical study of the changes wrought by the bureaucratization of major industries in the United States.

Thomas C. Cochran. *Business in American Life: A History.* New York: McGraw-Hill, 1972. A unique effort to examine the impact of American business on such matters as the family, education, religion, law, and politics.

Thomas C. Cochran. *Frontiers of Change: Early Industrialization in America.* New York: Oxford University Press, 1981. An analysis of American industrialization between 1790 and 1850 that argues that the American willingness to accept innovation played a critical role in boosting economic activity.

Thomas C. Cochran and William Miller. *The Age of Enterprise: A Social History of Industrial America.* Rev. ed. New York: Harper, 1961. An interesting history of the United States tracing the development of its commerce, industry, and labor from 1800 to approximately 1930.

Paul K. Conkin. *Prophets of Prosperity: America's First Political Economists.* Bloomington: Indiana University Press, 1980. A collective intellectual biography of some twenty nineteenth-century thinkers and their efforts to understand, celebrate, and at times criticize American economic development.

Robert F. Dalzell Jr. *Enterprising Elite: The Boston Associates and the World They Made.* Cambridge, MA: Harvard University Press, 1987. A study of the pioneering efforts of Boston merchant Francis Cabot Lowell and his partners to begin textile manufacturing in the United States.

Edward J. Davies II. *Anthracite Aristocracy: Leadership and Social Change in the Hard Coal Regions of Northeastern Pennsylvania, 1800–1930.* Dekalb: Northern Illinois University Press, 1985. An economic and social history of the coal industry.

Margery W. Davies. *Woman's Place Is at the Typewriter: Office Work and Office Workers, 1870–1930.* Philadelphia: Temple University Press, 1982. A lively history of office work with an emphasis on the dual rise of scientific management and the private secretary in the workplace.

Alan Dawley. *Class and Community: The Industrial Revolution in Lynn.* Cambridge, MA: Harvard University Press, 1976. A history of the pre–Civil War shoe industry in this small Massachusetts town, focusing on the everyday lives of its residents.

Carl N. Degler. *The Age of the Economic Revolution, 1876–1900.* Glenview, IL: Scott, Foresman, 1977. A brief survey of American economic history during the heart of the transformation of America from an agricultural to an industrial society.

Douglas F. Dowd. *The Twisted Dream: Capitalist Development in the United States Since 1776.* Cambridge, MA: Winthrop Publishers, 1974. A highly critical account of the development of American capitalism and a call for its abolition.

Thomas Dublin. *Women at Work: The Transformation of Work and Community in Lowell, Massachusetts, 1826–1860.* New York: Columbia University Press, 1979. A history of the women labor force in the New England textile industry as its composition evolved from rural New England girls to immigrants from Ireland.

Stanley Elkins and Eric McKitrick. *The Age of Federalism.* New York: Oxford University Press, 1993. This monumental study of the early national period of American history includes an examination of Alexander Hamilton's efforts to encourage American industrialization.

Harold U. Faulkner. *The Decline of Laissez Faire, 1897–1917*. New York: Holt, Rinehart and Winston, 1951. A narrative history of industrialization and the responses it generated among social reformers.

Robert Fogel. *Railroads and American Economic Growth: Essays in Econometric History*. Baltimore: Johns Hopkins University Press, 1964. A history that questions whether railroads were in fact indispensable to American economic growth in the nineteenth century.

Burton W. Folsom Jr. *The Myth of the Robber Barons*. 3rd ed. Herndon, VA: Young America's Foundation, 1996. A spirited defense of leading nineteenth-century industrialists and their contributions to American economic development.

Michael Brewster Folsom and Steven D. Lubar, eds. *The Philosophy of Manufactures: Early Debates over Industrialization in the United States*. Cambridge, MA: MIT Press, 1982. A collection of documents from the late 1700s and early 1800s focusing on the question of whether the United States should pursue industrialization.

Ray Ginger. *Age of Excess: The United States from 1877 to 1914*. New York: Macmillan, 1965. An iconoclastic, muckraking history of this era of rambunctious expansion and one that stresses the primacy of economic factors in explaining social and cultural developments.

Josephine Goldmark. *Impatient Crusader: Florence Kelley's Life Story*. Urbana: University of Illinois Press, 1953. A highly readable account of the work of this Progressive-era reformer and her efforts to mitigate the evils that accompanied American industrialization.

Constance M. Green. *Eli Whitney and the Birth of American Technology*. Boston: Little, Brown, 1956. A brief biography of Whitney that argues that his most significant contribution was not the invention of the cotton gin, but his work in developing interchangeable parts in industry.

Julius Grodinsky. *Transcontinental Railway Strategy, 1869–1893: A Study of Businessmen*. Philadelphia: University of Pennsylvania Press, 1962. An account of efforts of entrepreneurs to garner subsidies and build railroads across the country in the second half of the nineteenth century.

Samuel Haber. *Efficiency and Uplift: Scientific Management in the Progressive Era, 1890–1920*. Chicago: University of Chicago Press, 1964. An important history of the impact of Frederick Taylor and scientific management on the American industrial process during the late nineteenth and early twentieth centuries.

Louis M. Hacker. *Major Documents in American Economic History*. Princeton, NJ: Van Nostrand, 1961. A useful collection of primary source material relating to American economic history.

270

David Freeman Hawke. *John D.: The Founding Father of the Rocke-fellers.* New York: Harper & Row, 1980. An accessible biography of John D. Rockefeller and his efforts to monopolize the oil-refining industry in the United States.

Samuel P. Hays. *The Response to Industrialism, 1885–1914.* Chicago: University of Chicago Press, 1957. A general history of American industrialization and American reform and the interrelations between these two important phenomena.

Robert L. Heilbroner and Aaron Singer. *The Economic Transformation of America: 1600 to the Present.* 2nd ed. San Diego: Harcourt Brace Jovanovich, 1984. A general survey of American economic history from colonial times to the Reagan era.

Robert Hessen. *Steel Titan: The Life of Charles M. Schwab.* New York: Oxford University Press, 1975. A thorough biography of this controversial leader of the steel industry.

Robert Higgs. *The Transformation of the American Economy, 1865–1914.* New York: Wiley, 1971. An attempt to place American economic growth in a social context, as well as a history of the economics of property rights in late-nineteenth-century America.

Brooke Hindle and Steven Lubar. *Engines of Change: The American Industrial Revolution, 1790–1860.* Washington, DC: Smithsonian Institution Press, 1986. An informative pictorial history of American technological and industrial development prior to the Civil War.

Ari and Olive Hoogenboom. *A History of the ICC: From Panacea to Palliative.* New York: Norton, 1976. A history of the impact of the Interstate Commerce Commission on American economic life.

David A. Hounshell. *From the American System to Mass Production, 1800–1932: The Development of Manufacturing Technology in the United States.* Baltimore: Johns Hopkins University Press, 1984. A history of the American factory system featuring case histories of the Singer Sewing Machine Company, the woodworking industry, the McCormick Reaper Works, the bicycle industry, and the Ford Motor Company.

Thomas P. Hughes. *American Genesis: A Century of Invention and Technological Enthusiasm, 1870–1970.* New York: Viking, 1989. A history of American inventions and an argument that American inventors, engineers, and designers have been the real makers of modern America.

Frederic C. Jaher. *The Age of Industrialism in America: Essays in Social Structure and Cultural Values.* New York: Free Press, 1968. A series of scholarly essays that examine the social ramifications of industrialization.

271

Matthew Josephson. *The Robber Barons: The Great American Capitalists, 1861–1901.* New York: Harcourt, Brace and Company, 1934. The classic critical account of this generation of industrialists of the late nineteenth century.

Robert Kanigel. *The One Best Way: Frederick Winslow Taylor and the Enigma of Efficiency.* New York: Viking, 1997. A thorough biography of the founder of scientific management and a history of the labor-management movement he helped create.

John F. Kasson. *Civilizing the Machine: Technology and Republican Values in America, 1776–1900.* New York: Grossman Publishers, 1976. A compelling account of how nineteenth-century Americans viewed the arrival of machine technology and its effect on the pastoral idea of American life.

Alice Kessler-Harris. *Out to Work: A History of Wage-Earning Women in the United States.* New York: Oxford University Press, 1982. The best single-volume history of a long-overlooked aspect of industrialization.

Edward C. Kirkland. *American Economic History Since 1860.* New York: Appleton-Century-Crofts, 1971. A still most useful general economic history of the United States.

Edward C. Kirkland. *Industry Comes of Age: Business, Labor, and Public Policy, 1860–1897.* New York: Holt, Rinehart, and Winston, 1961. A general history of economic policy, public and private, and its relation to economic performance.

Gabriel Kolko. *The Triumph of Conservatism: A Re-Interpretation of American History, 1900–1916.* New York: Free Press of Glencoe, 1963. A revisionist history of the Progressive era that contends that businessmen and industrialists played key roles in advancing regulatory reform in an effort to stave off more radical changes.

Gary Kulik et al., eds. *The New England Mill Village, 1790–1860.* Cambridge, MA: MIT Press, 1982. A collection of primary source documents on what may be considered the birthplace of industry in the United States.

Harold C. Livesay. *Andrew Carnegie and the Rise of Big Business.* Boston: Little, Brown, 1975. A brief but very useful biography of this giant of the steel industry.

Harold C. Livesay. *Samuel Gompers and Organized Labor in America.* Boston: Little, Brown, 1978. A brief biography of the founder of the American Federation of Labor.

Albro Martin. *James J. Hill and the Opening of the Northwest.* New York: Oxford University Press, 1976. A sympathetic portrait of this railroad magnate and his successful efforts to build the Great Northern Railroad.

Otto Mayr and Robert C. Post, eds. *Yankee Enterprise: The Rise of the American System of Manufactures: A Symposium.* Washington, DC: Smithsonian Institution Press, 1981. A wide-ranging series of essays on subjects from military entrepreneurship to manufacturing practices.

Martin V. Melosi. *Thomas A. Edison and the Modernization of America.* New York: HarperCollins, 1990. A brief introduction to the life, ideas, and inspirations of this genius of American invention.

Thomas J. Misa. *A Nation of Steel: The Making of Modern America, 1865–1925.* Baltimore: Johns Hopkins University Press, 1995. A comprehensive account of all facets of this critical industry from the making of steel to the breaking of worker efforts at unionization.

David Montgomery. *The Fall of the House of Labor: The Workplace, the State, and American Labor Activism, 1865–1925.* New York: Cambridge University Press, 1987. A general history of the union movement from the onset of national unions to the 1920s.

David Montgomery. *Workers' Control in America: Studies in the History of Work, Technology, and Labor Struggles.* New York: Cambridge University Press, 1979. A series of essays on workers' efforts to obtain greater control over their lives.

Elting E. Morison. *Men, Machines, and Modern Times.* Cambridge, MA: MIT Press, 1966. A series of essays on the nature and impact of technological change in nineteenth-century America.

Daniel Nelson. *Managers and Workers: Origins of the New Factory System in the United States, 1880–1920.* Madison: University of Wisconsin Press, 1975. A study that focuses on the ever-changing relationship between factory managers and workers during this critical period of industrial expansion.

R. Kent Newmyer. *The Supreme Court Under Marshall and Taney.* New York: Crowell, 1968. A brief survey of the Supreme Court at a time when critical decisions were being made that would affect American industrial development.

David F. Noble. *America by Design: Science, Technology, and the Rise of Corporate Capitalism.* New York: Knopf, 1977. An ambitious study of the history of two forces that have shaped modern America: technology and corporate capitalism.

David F. Noble. *Forces of Production: A Social History of Industrial Automation.* New York: Knopf, 1984. An account of the economic and social impact of machine tools on American industry.

Douglass C. North. *Growth and Welfare in the American Past: A New Economic History*. Englewood Cliffs, NJ: Prentice-Hall, 1966. A reappraisal of American economic history based on quantitative data.

Albert Rees. *Real Wages in Manufacturing, 1890–1914*. Princeton, NJ: Princeton University Press, 1961. A detailed analysis that contends that real wages rose steadily and significantly during this critical period of industrial expansion.

Daniel T. Rodgers. *The Work Ethic in Industrial America, 1850–1920*. Chicago: University of Chicago Press, 1978. An inventive history of various attempts to make work more compelling to those caught in the routine of factory labor.

W.J. Rorabaugh. *The Craft Apprentice: From Franklin to the Machine Age in America*. New York: Oxford University Press, 1986. A history of the apprentice in the first half of the nineteenth century, based largely on autobiographies, diaries, and letters.

Nathan Rosenberg and David C. Mowery. *Technology and the Pursuit of Economic Growth*. New York: Cambridge University Press, 1989. A comparative history of research and development systems in industrial countries, but one that focuses most on the United States.

Nick Salvatore. *Eugene V. Debs: Citizen and Socialist*. Urbana: University of Illinois Press, 1982. A biography of the leader of the American Railway Union and perennial Socialist Party presidential candidate.

Thomas J. Schlereth. *Victorian America: Transformations in Everyday Life, 1876–1915*. New York: HarperCollins, 1991. A social history of domestic life that documents the impact of industrialization on American society.

Charles G. Sellers. *The Market Revolution: Jacksonian America, 1815–1846*. New York: Oxford University Press, 1991. An interpretive, class-based history of this era, which saw the transformation of the U.S. economy from subsistence agriculture to industrial capitalism.

Ronald E. Shaw. *Canals for a Nation: The Canal Era in the United States, 1790–1860*. Lexington: University Press of Kentucky, 1990. An account of canal construction and canal promotion.

Kathryn Kish Sklar. *Florence Kelley and the Nation's Work: The Rise of Women's Political Culture, 1830–1900*. New Haven, CT: Yale University Press, 1995. A solid study of the increasingly important role of women in dealing with problems created by industrialization.

John F. Stover. *The Life and Decline of the American Railroad*. New York: Oxford University Press, 1970. A general history of the American railroad industry.

W. Paul Strassmann. *Risk and Technological Innovation: American Manufacturing Methods During the Nineteenth Century.* Ithaca, NY: Cornell University Press, 1959. A sweeping examination of the interaction between business enterprise and technological change.

Ida M. Tarbell. *All in the Day's Work: An Autobiography.* New York: Macmillan, 1939. The autobiography of the muckraking journalist who exposed the activities of the Standard Oil Company.

Peter Temin. *Iron and Steel in Nineteenth Century America: An Economic Inquiry.* Cambridge, MA: MIT Press, 1964. An explanation of the growth of these two industries concentrating on the 1830s and 1840s.

Cecelia Tichi. *Shifting Gears: Technology, Literature, Culture in Modernist America.* Chapel Hill: University of North Carolina Press, 1987. A history of how the technological revolution captured the popular culture, both high and low, and the American literary mind.

Alan Trachtenberg. *The Incorporation of America: Culture and Society in the Gilded Age.* New York: Hill & Wang, 1982. An analysis of just how corporate organization came to describe and redefine American life.

Barbara M. Tucker. *Samuel Slater and the Origins of the American Textile Industry, 1790–1860.* Ithaca, NY: Cornell University Press, 1984. This case study of the development of the first American cotton spinning mill to use water power successfully includes information on how it affected sex roles, family life, and religion.

Joseph F. Wall. *Andrew Carnegie.* New York: Oxford University Press, 1970. A monumental biography of this important figure in American industry.

Anthony F.C. Wallace. *Rockdale: The Growth of an American Village in the Early Industrial Revolution.* New York: Knopf, 1978. A detailed study by an anthropologist on the development of an early textile community near Philadelphia, Pennsylvania, that examines the lives and ideas of factory workers and owners.

Michael P. Weber. *Social Change in an Industrial Town: Patterns of Progress in Warren, Pennsylvania, from Civil War to World War I.* University Park: Pennsylvania State University Press, 1976. A social history of an industrial town that emphasizes the positive impact of entrepreneurship on the community.

Arthur and Lila Weinberg, eds. *The Muckrakers: The Era in Journalism That Moved America to Reform, the Most Significant Magazine Articles of 1902–1912.* New York: Simon and Schuster, 1961. An edited collection of articles published between 1902 and 1912, many of which deal with American industries and their abuses.

Robert H. Wiebe. *Businessmen and Reform: A Study of the Progressive Movement.* Cambridge, MA: Harvard University Press, 1962. An imaginative study of the role of businessmen and industrialists in promoting and refining reform legislation during the Progressive era.

Robert H. Wiebe. *The Search for Order, 1877–1920.* New York: Hill & Wang, 1967. A pioneering history of the development of national institutions and organizations at a time when the country was being knit together by nationwide industries and businesses.

Sean Wilentz. *Chants Democratic: New York City & the Rise of the American Working Class, 1788–1850.* New York: Oxford University Press, 1984. A provocative social, political, and economic history of the development of a working-class consciousness in the early years of American industrialization.

Harold F. Williamson and Arnold R. Daum. *The American Petroleum Industry: The Age of Illumination, 1859–1899.* Evanston, IL: Northwestern University Press, 1959. This study remains the standard history of the early years of the oil industry.

David A. Zonderman. *Aspirations and Anxieties: New England Workers and the Mechanized Factory System, 1815–1850.* New York: Oxford University Press, 1992. A study of New England workers' responses to their working conditions in factories.

Olivier Zunz. *Making America Corporate, 1870–1920.* Chicago: University of Chicago Press, 1990. A study of corporate culture as revealed by the history of selected large industrial companies, including Ford and Du Pont.

Index